Natural Approaches to Optimal Wellness

Natural Approaches to Optimal Wellness: Integrating EcoWellness into Counseling offers a groundbreaking perspective on holistic human wellness by introducing the EcoWellness framework to counselors and psychotherapists.

The book integrates discussion of nature's therapeutic benefits with an understanding of clients' broader ecological and sociocultural contexts. It addresses foundational professional issues, such as the clinician's scope of practice, ethics, and nature worldview, and explores the empirical and conceptual bases of the EcoWellness model through a comprehensive review of the multidisciplinary literature and supporting theories. Interspersed with the author's own clinical experience, the book offers practical examples for applying the EcoWellness perspective in counseling and psychotherapy. With a roadmap for ethical EcoWellness counseling practice, including assessment, treatment planning, specialized strategies, and advocacy, this book equips professionals with tools to enhance client wellness, advocate for environmental and climate justice, and foster a deep, respectful connection to the more-than-human world.

This essential guide equips counselors and psychotherapists with innovative, inclusive, and effective practices to enhance client wellness and foster restorative connections with the natural world.

Ryan F. Reese, PhD, is a counseling scholar and licensed professional counselor, pioneering the integration of EcoWellness into traditional counseling and psychotherapy settings.

"Socially conscious therapists offer a powerful gift in therapy by meeting people where they are or guiding them to discover themselves within their surroundings. Dr. Ryan Reese's motivation for developing the EcoWellness counseling framework is truly compelling. It highlights the importance of going beyond traditional counseling methods and genuinely exploring the unknown. The client and personal narratives interwoven throughout the book are intriguing, adding depth, brilliance, and charm to this socially just approach to holistic counseling. Nature treats everyone equitably and serves as the great equalizer, in a profound way, nature is an essential part of who we are. Reese places the elements center stage, elevating his vision of counseling and therapy to a new level of optimal wellness."

S. Kent Butler, *PhD, NCC, NCSC, American Counseling Association past president and fellow*

"Through his innovative work, Dr. Reese illustrates what a cisgender heterosexual male counselor educator can accomplish when harnessing his privilege for the betterment of humankind. This book belongs in the bookshelves of *every counselor* wishing to embrace nature-based, holistic, and emancipatory mental health counseling practices. Filled with poignant vignettes and practical assessment and trauma-informed, ethical individual and group intervention strategies, this book is *an invaluable resource for clinicians!*"

Ana Puig, *PhD, clinical professor of counselor education and research director at the University of Florida, American Counseling Association and Association for Specialists in Group Work fellow*

"*Natural Approaches to Optimal Wellness* sets a new standard for professional counseling practice. Ryan Reese's model of EcoWellness is based in good science. It's accessible, flexible, and actionable, with attention to diversity, equity, and inclusion throughout. This book will be useful for practitioners, researchers, educators, and students. At a time when nature and wellbeing can seem under threat, EcoWellness provides a blueprint for hope and action."

Thomas Doherty, *PsyD, fellow of the American Psychological Association and past president of the Society for Environmental, Population, and Conservation Psychology*

"While the healing potential of nature is apparent to most, how counselors intentionally integrate the setting and experience of nature into practice can be enigmatic. Ryan Reese is the thought leader in EcoWellness counseling, and this book could be his magnum opus. Each chapter is a perfect blend of philosophy and practice. This book is an invaluable text for new and longtime adherents to ecological approaches who are considering ways to their deepen practice."

Matthew Lemberger-Truelove, *PhD, professor of counseling at the University of North Texas, editor of the* Journal of Counseling *and* Development *and an American Counseling Association fellow*

"This book is a valuable addition to the literature on the human-nature relationship and its essential role in the therapeutic process. Well researched and enriched by illustrative examples, Ryan Reese offers a comprehensive understanding of EcoWellness, from conceptualization to applications in client care and community advocacy."

Patricia H. Hasbach, *PhD, author of* Grounded: A Guided Journal to Help You Connect with the Power of Nature and Yourself

"*Natural Approaches to Optimal Wellness* addresses the critical need of conceptualizing wellness by addressing our connection (or disconnection) with the natural world. Dr. Reese provides an accessible guide to understanding his evidenced-based model of EcoWellness, a comprehensive, evaluative approach to counseling that incorporates the growing, multidisciplinary research linking the natural world with human holistic wellness. With touching vignettes, practical suggestions, multicultural considerations and reflection questions, Dr. Reese's book is a must have for all counseling professionals."

Megan Delaney, *PhD, LPC, associate professor of psychology at Monmouth University and author of* Nature is Nurture: Counseling and the Natural World

"By drawing on scientific research and anecdotal case study material, this book provides a comprehensive guide to *EcoWellness Counseling*. The approach incorporates a broad understanding of social justice in ecotherapy via, for example, client and community advocacy for greater access and protection of greenspaces. The book provides an opportunity for practitioner self-development via reflection and is a timely examination of the dual issues of environmental and human health."

Joe Hinds, *DPhil, psychotherapist in private practice and senior lecturer in therapeutic counselling, University of Greenwich, London*

"Natural Approaches to Optimal Wellness is one of a kind and long overdue. As one of the authors of the empirically validated wellness models in professional counseling (i.e., IS-Wel), I am delighted to endorse this book's substantive, groundbreaking work. Dr. Reese's mentor, Dr. Jane E. Myers, would be very pleased."

Thomas J. Sweeney, *PhD, professor emeritus of counselor education, Ohio University*

"Embrace nature as co-therapist with this insightful guide on EcoWellness counseling practices. Authored by a seasoned practitioner, this book comfortably blends therapeutic techniques with the restorative benefits of connecting with nature, offering a refreshing approach to mental health and well-being. Packed with practical examples and informed by current research, this is a valuable resource for therapists and wellness enthusiasts seeking to take their practice outdoors."

Nevin J. Harper, *PhD, professor, outdoor therapist, co-author of* Nature-based Therapy *and co-editor of* Outdoor Therapies

"Dr. Reese integrates his passion, clinical experience, and extensive research to offer a compelling text about an important aspect of wellness. Rich with case examples and practical applications for counseling, this book is an essential read for clinicians seeking to embrace a holistic approach to wellness."

Jacqueline M. Swank, *PhD, LMHC, LCSW, RPT-STM, associate teaching professor of mental health practices in schools at the University of Missouri*

"Dr. Reese provides readers with an important and multidimensional approach to the foundations of EcoWellness. Perhaps the thing that most clinicians crave is what he offers in Part II: the practical applications, assessment, trauma-informed considerations, and advocacy. The case vignettes and examples help the reader connect immediately to the potential of EcoWellness within their work. A lovely and important contribution!"

Debbie C. Sturm, *PhD, LPC, professor, James Madison University*

"Ryan Reese is one of the leading counselor educators integrating nature into both his research and practice in the counseling profession. This book thoroughly showcases his scholarly and clinical work, offering a rich exploration of EcoWellness and its practical applications in the field."

Sang Min Shin, *PhD, LPC, NCC, RPT, associate professor, University of Texas at El Paso*

Natural Approaches to Optimal Wellness

Integrating EcoWellness into Counseling

Ryan F. Reese

Routledge
Taylor & Francis Group

NEW YORK AND LONDON

Designed cover image: Getty Images

First published 2025
by Routledge
605 Third Avenue, New York, NY 10158

and by Routledge
4 Park Square, Milton Park, Abingdon, Oxon, OX14 4RN

Routledge is an imprint of the Taylor & Francis Group, an informa business

© 2025 Ryan F. Reese

ISBN: 978-1-138-90244-2 (hbk)
ISBN: 978-1-138-90245-9 (pbk)
ISBN: 978-1-315-69743-7 (ebk)

DOI: 10.4324/9781315697437

Typeset in Adobe Caslon Pro
by Apex CoVantage, LLC

For my children, clients, and students

CONTENTS

ILLUSTRATIONS

Figures

Tables

ACKNOWLEDGMENTS

To my parents: you shaped who I am as a human, including my wonderment of the natural world and my heart for people. I drafted the final chapter of this book on the Oregon Coast. Our special vacations there laid the foundation for the mysticism of nature that remains wholly present within my consciousness and spirit. Thank you. And to my brothers, Kip and Shawn, you put me through a lot in our younger years, but I've always looked to you as my guiding stars. Thanks for teaching me creativity, critical thinking, and passion, all of which I embrace as a scholar and clinician.

Thanks to my many teachers: Doug Barram, my dear friend and confidant, who has consistently modeled what it is to walk with the sacred; Sharon Kaufman-Osborn and Tobin Kaufman-Osborn, who both imparted principles of social justice during my critical adolescent years; Drs. Mary Ann Clark and Harry Daniels, who both instilled a commitment to counselor professional identity; Dr. Ana Puig, who demonstrated and inspired a spirit of social advocacy; the late Dr. Jane Myers, my mentor, inspiration, and fellow nature lover.

With gratitude to my doctoral cohort mates who have inspired, encouraged, and contributed to my growth over the years as a human, scholar, and clinician: Dr. Janeé Avent Harris, Dr. Laura Jones, Dr. Myra

Jordan, Dr. Lucy Purgason, Dr. Edward Wahesh, Dr. Ben Willis, and Dr. Melissa Wheeler.

I am appreciative of my colleagues in the Counseling Academic Unit at Oregon State University-Cascades for enabling me to take sabbatical during the 2023–2024 academic year to write this book. I am also humbled by the support of the leadership at OSU, who, from the moment I inquired about sabbatical, supported me every step of the way. I am deeply grateful to have had the opportunity to travel a different path while writing this manuscript during a year that included numerous unexpected peaks, valleys, and transformative growth.

I'm indebted to the many counseling graduate students I've taught and supervised over the years. I wrote this book with you in mind. Teaching has truly been the most humbling professional endeavor I've navigated to this point, which has pushed me to question more rigorously the values, biases, and assumptions that I bring to this work.

This book would not have been possible without the many clients I've served over my years as a clinician. You are the inspiration for the EcoWellness philosophy and approach outlined in these pages.

Thank you to my children—Riley, Oakley, and Ava—for encouraging me to write this book as I coalesced a significant part of my life's work. Thank you for enabling me to make this contribution to the world of professional counseling and psychotherapy. I'm grateful for the kindness and patience each of you extended to me for all the times my mind was preoccupied with this book's contents. You inspired creativity and awe as I wrote. I admire your developing connections with the more than human world.

Lastly, to Lindsey, my life partner and best friend: you've made immense sacrifices for me to write this manuscript. You enabled me to start sabbatical with a two-week journey to northern British Columbia, a much-needed respite following what felt like 11 nonstop years at the university and following five nonstop years of graduate work. You encouraged me to write at any and all times and challenged me to take time away from writing the book to get out of town and to get out of my head—including our most memorable trip to Kauai. You are our family's hero. I am forever grateful for your patience, selflessness, and kindness. I love you.

PREFACE

Positionality, Development, and Nature: My Journey to EcoWellness

Our relationship with the more than human world is touched by our individual and collective life experiences, identities, and sociocultural contexts. Undoubtedly, my human development has impacted the EcoWellness philosophy and framework outlined in this book. Thus, I believe that it is imperative for you to know about my lived context and broader development with the natural world so you can better understand some of the assumptions and biases underlying the EcoWellness counseling approach.

My Identities

My immediate maternal ancestors immigrated to the United States from the Czech Republic. My great grandmother and great grandfather came to Chicago, Illinois after World War I. They were bakers and had a shared love for fishing. On my paternal side, the primary lineage is of German descent. My first ancestor to arrive in America served in the American Revolutionary War, settling in Pennsylvania afterward. I additionally have English, Irish, and Scottish blood running through my veins, though I most closely identify with my Czech heritage by tradition.

I was born with white skin and assigned male at birth with full eyesight, auditory functioning, and with all my limbs and organs intact. Over the course of my life, I have identified as a cisgender man and heterosexual. While my ancestors were immigrants to the lands that we now call the United States, to date, I have yet to meet criteria for immigrant or refugee status in the places I've lived. My entire life I have been a US citizen. My childhood home comprised a cohesive family structure that included my white heterosexual cisgender mother and my white heterosexual cisgender father. I grew up with two older brothers who identified (and still do) as heterosexual cisgender men. One brother is five years older, and the other three years my senior. I received care, nurturance, and unconditional love throughout all my development from these primary caregivers. Prior to and upon birth I had immediate and continued access to sustenance and healthcare. My mother received some college education, and my father completed his bachelor's degree in engineering. I grew up solid middle class.

Raised within a fundamentalist Christian worldview, I attended a private Christian school between kindergarten and the eighth grade. Religiously, I departed evangelical Christianity at age 17, and I am agnostic relative to the existence of our universe. Spiritually, I am influenced by several western and eastern traditions focused on community, wholeness, unconditional love, mindfulness, and connection with the more than human world.

Identities Summary

These intersecting visible and invisible identities, lived contexts, worldview, familial ties, community resources, and affordances impact my sociopolitical power and status. My life has been one of undisputable privilege. I can't recall a time when I felt physically unsafe based on my gender, sexuality, or nationality. At no point have I experienced discrimination based on the color of my skin, my worldview, my cognition, my body, or my body's abilities. My privilege and life history have affected my view on the natural world and my opportunities for experiencing the earth as a restorative and healing entity across my development.

My Development With the More Than Human World

Parents' Background

Both of my parents were born in the mid-1950s and raised in rural southern Idaho where the economy was predominantly agriculturally based. Flat land, dry hot summers, and cold and sometimes snowy winters. Mom and dad grew up within 30 miles or so from one another, though they did not meet until their late teens. My dad's family, after farming for many years on their own, leased their land to other farmers and became partners in a company that processed and sold agricultural products such as potatoes and beans. My mom grew up on farm acreage with and near farm animals. She raised cattle and rode horses; she developed an affinity for nonhuman animals, contributing to her creative, kind, and nurturing spirit.

My parents' families possessed both functional and appreciative outlooks toward nature. My mother can recall milking cows and butchering cattle for sustenance and sale. Both my mom and dad grew up with the perspective that the land and our natural resources were created by God to both sustain us and for us to enjoy, with humans having the responsibility of being good stewards of what God created.

When my parents married in their early 20s, they possessed similar values around religiosity and spirituality. They unified with evangelical Christianity, which further impacted their practical outlook toward nature and how they would raise their children. While nature was something to be ruled over, it was also deemed miraculous within my family of origin. My parents observed and respected nature with a deep sense of awe and wonderment, and they would pass on to their children a similar fascination with and attachment to animals, natural living systems, and landscapes. They would relive the same outdoor adventures with their own children that they themselves experienced in their youth.

Childhood

I was born and raised in eastern Oregon and eastern Washington. My parents, my two older brothers, and I lived in a small double-wide home on beautiful acreage the first four years of my life. I recall spending expansive amounts of time outdoors. We had a horse and various farm animals. My parents leased much of our land to a farmer growing alfalfa. From our property, or at least from our driveway, we could see the beautiful foot-hills of the Blue Mountains, of which the colors changed depending on the season and the harvest—green in spring, gold in summer, yellow and orange during the fall, and blue and snow-covered white in the winter.

I was free to explore the world around me. I learned that nature was beautiful and something to appreciate, but it was also something to dominate for humankind's purposes. I recall thinking that my care for nature had limits. Ultimately, the world would fall away, and I would experience eternity in heaven. This literal interpretation of my right to control nature contributed to the snuffing of butterflies, grasshoppers, bees, wasps, and other insects during my early years, and a lack of understanding that my actions on this planet had direct and lasting impacts on this earth and all the creatures inhabiting it.

At age five, my family moved to the outskirts of Walla Walla, Washington, a big city in comparison to our prior residence just across the state line in Umapine, Oregon. We downgraded to five acres of land, which included alfalfa and corn fields, but the tradeoff was a home with more advanced technologies. Plus, each of us boys had our own room. My father converted several of the open fields into grass, where we enjoyed playing sports for much of our childhood.

We planted Douglas fir trees, many of which still stand today. We roamed wherever we pleased on the property, and I again felt safe to let my imagination and creativity run wild. During my elementary years we had a horse, two to three goats and a pot belly pig at any given time, and anywhere between 15 to 40 rabbits, depending on if we were breeding them to sell. We had six cats and several dogs. I learned the ins and outs of interacting with and caring for these nonhumans. We personified these critters, observing their unique personalities and family contributions. They were all part of the family.

Each summer we journeyed on camping trips in our tent trailer. We traveled to the Oregon Coast once per year and combed the beach for sand dollars at low tide. A magical set of tide pools lay two miles south of our campground, accessible only at low tide and rarely visited by others. Sea creatures animated the small, clear pools of water, and one time we even found a stranded octopus. My family also travelled to Montana, where my maternal grandfather lived. A small creek meandered through his ranch, and he had acres upon acres to explore. On these same trips, we adventured through the jagged Sawtooth Mountains of Idaho and swam the cool waters of Redfish Lake. I learned to effectively navigate these natural settings, and over time, developed confidence in how to maintain safety and cultivate competence within nature-based activities.

One such activity included fishing, inspired by my brother, Shawn, who, like my great maternal grandparents, possessed an infectious obsession with angling. I vividly remember the late summer day I became hooked to the pursuit. I was 11 years old and going into the sixth grade that coming fall. My dad dropped us off at the nearby Walla Walla River for the afternoon. We used worms as bait, and the fishing was stellar. I landed a large rainbow trout and saw a buck whitetail deer with huge antlers. The cool, rushing water soothed my bare skin, the smells of autumn approaching excited my spirit, and the river's reverberations calmed my nervous system. Satisfied, I stopped fishing and sat in the shade while my brother hiked downriver to fish one last pool. Several minutes passed, and I suddenly heard Shawn shouting in the distance. Concerned, I dropped my fishing pole and sprinted and tumbled over the river rocks littering the streambed. As I rounded the bend I could see my brother, rod in hand, fighting the largest fish I'd ever seen. "It's a steelhead!" he exclaimed. He pulled the massive fish out of the water; I stared in utter disbelief. I could not believe the sheer size and beauty[1] of this fish.

That fall and winter I fell in love with steelhead. Given their unlikely survivability, coupled with the fact that steelhead were so hard to catch, they attained mythical status in my mental and spiritual frameworks: steelhead were God's chosen fish. During the months between October and April, I began spending most of my afternoons and weekends on the river, where I would spend countless hours attempting to catch steelhead. Very rarely did I catch one, but indeed, sometimes I would.

Little did I know at that time that steelhead, both the species and their surrounding ecosystems, would inspire my growth and provide endless healing for decades to come. Their existence and the associated piscatorial pursuit would propel my quest for deeper meaning and purpose in my life. The literal and metaphorical rivers that steelhead led me to are the rivers where I grew, where I struggled, and where I transformed.

Adolescence

Depression and anxiety plagued the entirety of my adolescence. I used to blame my older brothers and fundamentalism, but the reality is that the seeds of depression existed far outside my control or anyone else's. Like a dark and ominous cloud, depression arrived sometime between my seventh and eighth grade years when I was 13 years old. Depression hit me the hardest in high school. I existentially crumbled, particularly as I transitioned away from a private and religious education and into a public one. The question of my life's meaning and purpose troubled my spirit but also contributed to a deep love affair with the land, the rivers, and the steelhead inhabiting these places. Any chance I could escape, I was on the river. When I received my driver's license, my access to previously unexplored rivers expanded. So much new territory to discover. As my affinity for steelhead grew, I developed greater awareness and desire for protecting them and their surrounding environments. I became a board member of a local steelhead conservation group. I joined community efforts to plant trees and worked booths at local kids' fishing derbies. I went from keeping most fish I caught to letting them go.

In my senior year of high school, I developed enough gumption to apply to become a summertime guide at fly-fishing lodges in southwest Alaska, a region known for its large runs of sockeye salmon, behemoth brown bears, extraordinary king salmon fishing, and world-class fly-fishing for rainbow trout and arctic char. It's a remote wilderness, accessible only by float plane or boat. In my 17-year-old mind, I just had to experience it, and amazingly, a reputable company hired me, known for its off-kilter and erratic ownership. Many of the guides and staff reflected the owner's style, and I felt intimidated and frightened as a depressed and newly minted adult. But I had a knack for salmon fishing and skillfully navigating a powered jet boat through skinny and, at times, treacherous waters. These proficiencies earned me the opportunity to work with clients right out of the gate, with very little training. My first clients included one high-profile guest who returned to the lodge year after year. He took one look at me and went to the head guide, demanding a different and more experienced chaperon. But the answer was "no," and he had to tolerate me for the week. I helped him and his friends hook a boatload of fish, which bolstered my shaky confidence. Nonetheless, my depression got so bad that summer that I ended up departing a month early on account of developing suicidal thoughts. But even amidst such crippling emotional pain, my self-confidence in nature rose to new levels, inspiring me to return the next summer, and the summers that followed, six in total.

Early Adulthood to the Present

My depression continued throughout my college years. Natural environments, particularly rivers, continued to play a critical role in helping me cope with the ups and downs in my life. While nature didn't take away the depression, it shifted how I experienced and related to it. My expanded "self" was not just my *self*; my being was part of a bigger picture, part of a broader ecosystem and larger meaning-making entity. This perspective contributed to a view toward depression that became less black and white over time. While depressive symptoms manifested within my individual being, they were not me. The more I spent time with the natural world, the more capable I felt in managing my wellness.

Following college, I attended the University of Florida to pursue my master's degree in counseling. Right around this time, Richard Louv sparked the No Child Left Inside movement with the publishing of his 2005 book titled, *Last Child in the Woods: Saving Our Children from Nature-Deficit Disorder*. Louv contended that children everywhere were increasingly losing the opportunity to spend time in nature on account of urbanization, the degradation of natural environments, exponential technological advancement, and parental fears surrounding letting their children outdoors. He argued that the natural world was pertinent to childhood development, citing a host of research suggesting that natural living systems positively impact mental and physical health, critical thinking, and decision-making.

As a young graduate student, I exuberantly rode the No Child Left Inside bandwagon. Louv's work empowered my urgency and passion to connect clients with the outdoors. As I contemplated my future as a clinician, I fantasized taking clients into pristine, wilderness settings. I projected images from my youth and envisioned the remote natural settings I explored in my late teens and early 20s. This naiveté was quickly dismantled as I began working with youths who possessed life experiences and identities far different from my own. Seldom did they share my same interest and passion for the natural world, at least in the ways I conceived it. I came into greater recognition of how privileged my access to and relationship with nature had been. Many clients with whom I worked had minimal access to wilderness settings, and some clients faced environmental hazards affecting their day-to-day access to and perceptions of nature.

I extended my eventual return to the Pacific Northwest to complete my doctorate in counseling in North Carolina. There I was clear in my focus: I aimed to develop a culturally responsive EcoWellness counseling framework that would address the more than human nature connection in licensed counseling and psychotherapy settings. As an approach to assessment and intervention planning, I envisioned incorporating EcoWellness into any treatment modality, regardless of whether therapy occurred indoors or outdoors. In the past decade, I've continued to research EcoWellness as a counseling scholar and incorporate it into my clinical practice with clients. My passion drives me to help others cultivate culturally sustaining EcoWellness for themselves and their communities. This book stems from my desire to share my knowledge and experiences with current and future mental health professionals.

Conclusion

Reflecting on my ancestral history, childhood, adolescent years, and early adult development, I recognize how these formative and privileged experiences shaped my outlook toward the natural world and its potential role in cultivating human development and fostering holistic wellness. As you proceed in reading this text, I invite you to reflect on your own developing relationship with the more than human world and consider how your identities and lived experiences have come to shape your outlook on nature's potential place within counseling and psychotherapy.

Note

1 Steelhead are a seagoing rainbow trout. Depending on the population and drainage, steelhead, like salmon, hatch in freshwater and spend just shy of a year in their native headwaters. They then begin their nascent migration to the ocean, sometimes

traversing hundreds of miles of creeks and rivers before arriving to saltwater. Steelhead spend between one to three years in the Pacific and can travel thousands of miles into or around the Bering Sea, but where they specifically go mostly remains a mystery to fish biologists. After the fish grow and sexually mature, they return to their original home waters to spawn in the same gravel where they hatched. Depending on the population and body of water, the odds of a steelhead surviving to become a spawning adult is somewhere between 1 to 10%.

Reference

Louv, R. (2005). *Last child in the woods: Saving our children from nature-deficits disorder.* Algonquin Books.

EcoWellness

An Introduction

"Come on, let's go!"

I trailed closely behind Jayden, my nine-year-old client, as he darted towards his favorite park nook. A small dry creek, waterless throughout much of the year, meandered through the lightly forested park. We visited this same spot now for nearly ten sessions. Here, Jayden constructed makeshift dams and began discovering who he was alongside the critters we encountered.

"Ryan, come help me get these sticks, we need to create a dam for the fish!" Jayden was in the third grade. He primarily lived with his mom. They were poor. She held down a part-time job while Jayden's father was unemployed. Jayden visited his father every other weekend. On this day, I noticed Jayden's mom sitting off in the distance, watching us gather the woody debris. I awkwardly handled an armful of limbs as I tottered towards Jayden.

Within 15 minutes we had fashioned the small dam, plugging any visible holes we saw with rocks. The water sluggishly accumulated behind the temporary barrier, producing a small pool. Each week Jayden had built a more effective structure in holding back the water. I couldn't believe how solid the structure was this week. We sat and admired the scene.

"Jayden, tell me about the dam," I prompted.

DOI: 10.4324/9781315697437-1

Jayden explained the different intricacies of the structure. He shared certain decisions he made in its construction and forgave me for some of my miscalculations. He noted what he learned from the previous weeks. Pride emerged as the central feeling Jayden experienced in that moment. When asked if that pride extended to other places in his life, he excitedly shared about his grades in school—they were getting better.

"Can we show my mom?" Jayden asked as he pointed to the dam. I nodded, and Jayden sprinted across the park to find her.

Together, Jayden and his mother leisurely approached. As they neared, Jayden enthusiastically shared how the dam was improved over previous iterations. His mom wore a look of astonishment. "Wow, Jayden. You are really getting good at this," she commended. Jayden beamed with delight when he saw the look on his mother's face. She recounted the specific growth she observed in Jayden's disposition the past several weeks at home. She emphasized the shifts in confidence she witnessed and noted that Jayden seemed less reactive both at home and at school. It was readily apparent to all three of us that Jayden was in the midst of developing a newfound, positive identity.

EcoWellness

Jayden's story is not just about a child playing in the woods; it illustrates the profound impact of reconnecting with the natural world in the purview of counseling and psychotherapy. My journey into EcoWellness began with a deep interest in ecotherapy. Inspired by Linda Buzzell's and Craig Chalquist's (2009) *Ecotherapy: Healing with Nature in Mind*, I explored and integrated various nature-based therapies into my work with clients and students. However, I encountered significant ethical and scope of practice challenges, motivating me to develop the EcoWellness counseling framework. Unlike ecotherapy, which broadly encompasses a variety of nature-based therapeutic practices across multiple disciplines, EcoWellness specifically focuses on the holistic integration of the natural world within traditional professional counseling and psychotherapy settings (e.g., outpatient agency, private practice, and K–12 schools). This distinction is critical, as EcoWellness emphasizes a client-centered, culturally responsive approach that aligns with professional ethical standards in the licensed helping professions.

In an era of technological advancement, urbanization, environmental degradation, and climate change, EcoWellness opens an avenue for clients to connect with the more than human world as part of their developmental and healing journeys. Within its conceptual foundation, EcoWellness unites the expansive multidisciplinary research pointing toward the natural world's profound effects on human holistic wellness. In its application, an EcoWellness philosophy acknowledges that nature is defined through the unique lens of each client and community. Clinicians thoughtfully phase EcoWellness into traditional therapeutic processes based in a client's worldview, positionality, and lived context. The approach requires clinicians to have an in-depth understanding of their own ways of perceiving and experiencing the natural world, thereby limiting the degree to which they project their own nature worldviews onto clients.

My work with Jayden illustrates the EcoWellness ethos. Jayden and his mother lived in an apartment in the middle of Greensboro, North Carolina, with an urban park right down the street, but they hadn't been there before. Jayden's mother grew up in the city with minimal access to what she considered nature. She endured several traumatic experiences in outdoor settings and suspected that the park near their home might be unsafe. Consequently, both lacked a schema for what it would be like to connect with the outdoors for wellness purposes. Jayden, nevertheless, had an interest in fish and snakes, and when I mentioned the idea of going to the park during our first meeting, he literally jumped out of his seat with excitement.

Jayden's mother was understandably skeptical at first, and thus, we exclusively met indoors for the first month of therapy. I assessed Jayden's EcoWellness as part of his broader well-being and came to better understand how his family's belief structures and adverse experiences manifested into avoidance of the natural world. I spent time outside session learning more about the park near their apartment. It was a lovely green space that included a playground and pond. The park was well-maintained, and from what I learned in my research, essentially free of documented legal misconduct. I explored the idea of going on a picnic during session and what each of us might bring. Jayden wanted to bring a soccer ball while his mom wanted to know the particulars of what to include—she had never been on a picnic before.

The picnic was a success, and both Jayden and his mother walked away wanting to return. Gradually, we increased our visits to the park over the course of the year we worked together. Jayden became familiar with and confident in exploring the park's terrain. His mother began bringing a book to read, and she enjoyed watching Jayden play during session. They gained enough confidence to visit the park and other nearby green spaces on their own. Life changed for Jayden and his mom, in part, through the awakening of their quiescent connection with the natural world.

Book Overview

This book provides a comprehensive guide to EcoWellness counseling. Part I explores foundational professional issues for addressing the human–nature connection in licensed counseling and psychotherapy settings. In Chapter 1, various ecotherapeutic approaches are reviewed, highlighting their historical context and therapeutic potential, while also examining their scope of practice limitations and the challenges they face in clinical application. Chapter 2 identifies the ethical challenges clinicians must navigate when incorporating the more than human world into mental health settings. Guiding ethical principles for EcoWellness counseling are reviewed and grounded in the American Counseling Association *Code of Ethics* (2014). Chapter 3 delves into the concept of nature worldview, exploring how it is shaped by client positionality and external factors, with a critical examination of the pervasive colonial influences that prioritize economic gain over environmental and human wellness in modern society.

Part II introduces the empirical and conceptual bases of the EcoWellness model. In Chapter 4, the multidisciplinary literature and supporting theories highlighting nature's effects on human holistic wellness are reviewed. The development of the EcoWellness model and its three iterations to date are reviewed in Chapter 5, contextualized within the wellness models of professional counseling.

Part III provides a roadmap for engaging in EcoWellness counseling practice. Chapter 6 introduces a tiered approach to EcoWellness assessment based in client positionality, life context, and client interest. In Chapter 7, a trauma-informed and phased approach to incorporating the outdoors into EcoWellness counseling is discussed. Chapter 8 surveys a variety of EcoWellness-based strategies, conceptualized as adjunctive, complementary, or core interventions. Special considerations for merging the EcoWellness approach within group counseling settings are reviewed in Chapter 9. To conclude, EcoWellness issues pertaining to client, institutional, and professional advocacy are examined in Chapter 10.

Through case vignettes and practical examples, this book emphasizes clinical practice while maintaining scholarly rigor.[1] Each chapter concludes with reflection questions to enhance self-awareness, knowledge acquisition, and application of EcoWellness in your practice setting(s). As you proceed, I invite you to actively engage with the material, dialogue with others, reflect on your nature worldview, and find practical ways of integrating EcoWellness into your clinical practice.

Onward, with peace.

Note

1 To honor and protect client identities, I changed demographic information and aspects of the clients' stories. Additionally, in some instances, I combined multiple client presentations to illustrate concepts more fully. While the factual details of clients have been adjusted in some instances, the applied lessons within all narratives are genuine.

References

American Counseling Association. (2014). *ACA code of ethics*. ACA.
Buzzell, L., & Chalquist, C. (2009). *Ecotherapy: Healing with nature in mind*. Sierra Club Books.

PART I
NATURE IN COUNSELING AND PSYCHOTHERAPY
PROFESSIONAL CONSIDERATIONS

1

ECOTHERAPY AND THE LICENSED HELPING PROFESSIONS

As a master's student at the University of Florida, one of my final internship experiences included a three-month rotation at an outdoor-based school for adjudicated secondary-aged youth, comprised mostly of portable and dated outbuildings. Located on the outskirts of Gainesville, Florida, the school was remote and surrounded by a swamp. The youth, predominantly African American cisgender boys, arrived and departed on a bus Monday through Friday. The adolescents often described themselves as physically trapped. To run away from the school meant traversing the two-mile dirt road to get back to the highway or braving the alligator-ridden swamp.

Nature abounded. Trees towered above the small, makeshift campus, and my clinical supervisor approved my attempts at bringing the youth outdoors for counseling sessions. Franklin was one such client. We initially attempted meeting indoors on several occasions, but we mostly sat, staring at one another. He didn't want to be there.

One session I asked him, "Would you be open to taking our conversation outside?"

I recall him glancing up and responding, "Whatever."

With this dubious green light, we headed out to walk the perimeter of campus. We wandered in silence for the first few minutes, but it wasn't

DOI: 10.4324/9781315697437-3

long before the client broached his fear of snakes. After some time discussing his near phobia of slithering reptiles, we found an area to sit with a deathly looking tree glaring toward us.

"What else are you afraid of?" I inquired.

"My dad," Franklin responded. "He's like that tree over there, ugly and dead on the inside."

Stunned by the sudden depth of the client's disclosure, I had no idea how to respond. The client continued, talking about his upbringing, his girlfriend, and a recent pregnancy scare. For sessions, this seemingly resistant teen had barely uttered a word, and now he was opening his soul. I felt that there was nothing I could say or express in that moment that could adequately reflect his internal experience. So, the tree and the space held us both in shared silence.

Applied Ecopsychology: Ecotherapy

In 1992, Theodore Roszak introduced ecopsychology as "awaken[ing] the inherent sense of environmental reciprocity that lies within the ecological unconscious . . . to heal the more fundamental alienation between the person and the natural environment" (p. 320). Roszak suggested that the ecological unconscious encompasses the innate connection humans have with nature. Nonhuman life is simply an extension of the self; when the world hurts, humans hurt. Roszak and others sharply criticized reductionist western science for contributing to a false sense of separation between humans and nonhumans, and suggested dominant western culture should look to societies emphasizing spirituality, holism, and connection with the natural world to save our species from our expanding materialistic culture.

Right around the same time that Roszak and others introduced the ecopsychological paradigm, Edward O. Wilson (1984) forwarded the biophilia hypothesis, which he defined as the "innate tendency to focus on life and lifelike processes" (p. 1). Like the ecological unconscious, he emphasized the "innately emotional affiliation of human beings to other living organisms" (Wilson, 1996, p. 165). Wilson argued that humans engaged with and relied upon other nonhuman species to aid in humanity's survival across our evolutionary history. He cited evidence for biophilia residing within our attraction to certain species and landscapes (e.g., an affinity for open and unthreatening shaded spaces near water sources) and the aversion (i.e., bio-phobia) from other species and land-scapes (e.g., avoidance of snakes and enclosed landscapes). He believed that human's kinship with other nature evolved through "gene-culture coevolution" where "a certain genotype makes a behavioral response more likely, the response enhances survival and reproductive fitness, the gen-otype consequently spreads through the population, and the behavioral response grows more frequent" (Wilson, 1996, p. 167).

Howard Clinebell (1996) was one of the first scholars to conceptu-alize ecotherapy as an application of ecopsychology, suggesting that the natural world should play a role within therapeutic processes. Thomas Doherty (2016), a leading ecopsychologist in the United States, broadly defined ecotherapy as including a variety of therapeutic activities encompassing psychotherapy, counseling, social work, self-care activi-ties, and public health interventions. Similarly, Linda Buzzell and Craig Chalquist (2009) suggested that ecotherapy serves as "an umbrella term for nature-based methods of physical and psychological healing" (p. 18). They described the ecological unconscious as a major theoretical driv-ing force of the ecotherapies and distinguished two potential areas of focus. The first approach centers on the utilization of nature to unilat-erally address human health and wellness. For example, an ecotherapist may have a practice where they incorporate ecotherapuetic principles in treating mental health symptomology. The second approach to ecother-apy includes a focus on mutual healing. Interventions might focus on addressing human mental health within the context of healing nature and our fractured relationship with the natural world.

Applied ecopsychology, or ecotherapy, is a multifaceted field. While several scholars have written texts describing applications of ecotherapy in the helping professions (e.g., Delaney, 2019; Jordan, 2014; Jordan & Hinds, 2017), ecotherapy is not limited to counseling and psychotherapy, which clouds its potential place in professional practice. In this chapter I overview some of the ecotherapies and their supporting research. As we'll discuss, each approach has possible merit, though the application of ecotherapy within traditional psychotherapeutic settings can pose both pragmatic and ethical considerations that licensed clinicians must navigate.

Wilderness Therapy

Wilderness therapy (also referred to as outdoor behavioral healthcare) is one of the more well-known applications of ecotherapy. Kurt Hahn, a German educator, is considered the creator of the outward bound movement, which focused on providing youth with adventurous challenges and experiences. Outward bound made its way to the United States, and wilderness therapy gained traction in the 1970s. Scholars such as Michael Gass, Anita Tucker, and Nevin Harper have engaged in scholarship pointing toward the approach's utility and effectiveness. Wilderness therapy has predominantly been described as an application of adventure-based therapy, which utilizes challenging activities to address teamwork, personal development, and problem-solving skills. Wilderness therapy additionally appropriates interventions rooted within indigenous traditions, such as rites of passage rituals (e.g., solo vision quests) and ceremonial story-telling circles.

Clients in wilderness therapy programs reside anywhere between a couple of weeks to multiple months living in the wilderness environment. Most of their time is spent with unlicensed field instructors, therapeutic guides who ensure the safety and well-being of residents. In addition, field instructors lead therapeutic groups, provide individual mentoring and interpersonal de-escalation, and work closely with therapists by providing key insights and observations that support an individual's treatment plan. Licensed therapists typically visit the field one to two times per week and provide a combination of individual and group therapy services during their visit. Additionally, family therapy and parent coaching are often part of wilderness programs, wherein the therapist, the resident and the parents or guardians meet via phone or telehealth to address issues pertinent to the family system as part of a client's treatment plan.

Residents learn a variety of practical skills that aid in survival and success in the wilderness. Often, responsibilities such as prepping and making meals, setting up and breaking down camp, and building a fire rotate across residents. Clients nearing their departure teach and model wilderness skills to newcomers, and in some instances, may help to facilitate conflict resolution and peer mediation. The primary therapeutic elements of wilderness therapy include experiential learning, group treks (i.e., hiking), social interaction, family systems work, overcoming challenges, learning from natural consequences, and connection with nature, though relatively few conceptual models explicitly include nature connection in wilderness therapy. Russell and Gillis (2017) created the 20-item Adventure Therapy Experience Scale. Through exploratory and confirmatory factor analysis, the researchers identified four factors including Group Adventure, Reflection, Challenge, and Nature. Items assessing the Nature factor include a sense of getting away, attention restoration, valuing time in nature, and appreciating nature's beauty. However, minimal conceptual and empirical direction in the literature to date informs the intentional application of nature within wilderness therapy settings (Reese et al., 2018).

Given the complexity of wilderness settings and interventions, rigorous research supporting wilderness therapy is generally lacking. Natalie Beck and Jennifer Wong (2022) conducted a meta-analysis wherein they analyzed the effect sizes of 11 studies relative to self-reported and caregiver-reported delinquency. They identified large effect sizes (.83 and 1.02), suggesting that wilderness therapy might serve as one possible tool in reducing delinquent behaviors within youth. However, they cited a lack of overall quality research in the field, with studies plagued by small sample sizes and the presence of extraneous confounding variables. Annerstedt and Währborg (2011) reported the effect sizes of three meta-analyses conducted on wilderness therapy. The average effect sizes were reported as .34, .31, and .18, suggesting marginal evidence for the effectiveness of WT on measures of self-concept, self-confidence, and locus of control.

It is difficult for researchers to employ rigorous research designs in assessing the effectiveness of wilderness therapy. Very few, if any, outcome studies have explored its efficacy on clients presenting with specific diagnoses such as depression or anxiety. As mentioned, the research is often limited by small convenience samples, inattention to confounding factors, and poor methodology. Additionally, parsing out nature's effects is also quite difficult. Imagine a study where participants are randomly assigned to a wilderness setting and a non-wilderness setting. This would be immensely expensive, cumbersome, and obvious to research participants. The financial costs also bring up an additional critique of wilderness therapy where the predominant populations served include economically advantaged clients.

Moreover, the psychotherapy component in wilderness therapy is opaque. Clinical contact with a licensed therapist in most wilderness therapy programs is limited to one or several meetings each week and the therapeutic modalities employed by therapists are diverse. Participants interact most frequently with non-licensed practitioners, which further clouds our ability to apply this approach and the supporting research within traditional counseling and psychotherapy settings. With few exceptions, outpatient clinicians are unlikely to spend days or weeks at a time with clients in a wilderness setting, and this form of therapy would likely be inaccessible to many client populations on account of its need for a wilderness setting and economic costs. Nevertheless, when I initially share with fellow professionals and counselors in training about EcoWellness they often equate it with therapy occurring in a wilderness setting. "Ah, you're like a wilderness therapist," they'll muse.

Horticultural Therapy

While wilderness therapy is an ecotherapy predominantly focused on remediation and symptom reduction with minimal focus on positively affecting the natural world, horticultural therapy (HT) emphasizes tending to human wellness through contributing to the lives of plants. HT spans the disciplines of nursing, hospice care, psychotherapy, and education. Rebecca Haller et al. (2019) published an edited volume where they described horticultural therapy as a distinct profession, though such practices are primarily described within rehabilitative, vocational, and community settings. HT is client-centered and can include indoor and outdoor gardens as well as ponds, sculptures, quiet, and open spaces. HT includes scheduled and programmed activities with trained helpers occurring within well-defined and safe spaces bearing a unified design dominated by the presence of plants (Horowitz, 2012). As a broad profession, horticultural therapy has been applied as an ancillary approach when treating conditions such as Alzheimer's, dementia, cancer, stress-related illnesses, and mental health disorders.

Horticultural therapy can encompass one-off sessions, or it can span multiple sessions. The approach is delivered in both outpatient individual and group formats and often incorporates psychoeducation where participants learn about the health benefits of the approach. Moreover, horticultural programs include active and passive elements. Active components include interaction with the live plant or crop, whether it be planting seeds, tending to a plant's growth (e.g., watering and pruning), or harvesting vegetables and fruit. Passive elements encompass observing or exercising in nature, self-reflection in a garden, watching wildlife, and preparing flower bouquets.

Jang and colleagues (2010) conducted a meta-analysis of 108 research studies on the general health effects of HT and calculated an effect size of .71, concluding that HT is an effective form of therapy for a variety of illnesses and conditions. Positive physical health outcomes were the most consistent finding across HT studies, although researchers reported some cognitive, emotional, and social benefits. Hung-Ming Tu (2022) conducted a meta-analysis of 19 randomized control trials exploring the effects of horticultural therapy on mental health assessments (e.g., depression, anxiety, and stress). Tu calculated an effect size of .55, suggesting that horticultural therapy had a moderate and positive effect on mental health indicators such as depression, stress, and anxiety. Tu concluded that at least four sessions are likely needed for the therapy to be effective to gain familiarity with gardening and establishing rapport with the therapist. While impressive, the studies included in the meta-analysis mostly comprised older adults. Additionally, uniformity in the horticultural conditions across studies was lacking and the natural elements included in studies were diverse, consisting of farms, urban gardens, or hospital gardens.

As with wilderness therapy, horticultural therapy is not consistently employed within traditional professional counseling or psychotherapy settings. It has also been viewed as an auxiliary approach and not the primary treatment modality employed. Thus, our ability to generalize HT research findings within traditional counseling settings is somewhat limited.

Shinrin-yoku

Shinrin-yoku, or forest bathing, was developed in Japan for the purposes of mindfully paying attention to the five senses while immersed in forest settings. With roots in both Shinto and Buddhist traditions, its overarching goal includes full sensory and spiritual integration in the natural environment and coming into harmony with nature, often a forest environment. This integration includes guided or unguided nature-based experiences wherein participants sit, walk, or exercise in nature. Additional intervention elements might include yoga, meditation, or cooking. Shinrin-yoku is not limited to healthcare settings and can occur within individual, group, or community-based contexts. Licensed therapists, forest therapy guides, health educators, and ecotourist guides all lay claim to this approach. Some scholars believe forest bathing may contribute to the possible alleviation of mood disorder symptomology and stress via enacting relaxation processes, though much of the research to date has focused on the physical health benefits of shinrin-yoku (Park et al., 2012).

The study of forest bathing has presented numerous logistical and practical challenges, leading to a prevalence of observational and qualitative research designs. Margaret Hansen and colleagues (2017) conducted a literature review exploring the effects of forest bathing across 64 studies that occurred between 2007 and 2017. Studies spanned both structured and unstructured forest bathing activities within community contexts in Japan and China, including at least one study that merged cognitive behavioral therapy psychoeducational practices (e.g., goal setting, self-reflection, and meditation). The researchers concluded that the studies of shinrin-yoku, while methodologically diverse and often limited by confounding factors, identified potential positive effects on indicators of stress reduction and overall wellness. Yasuhiro Kotera et al. (2022) conducted a systematic review and meta-analysis of 20 studies exploring the potential effects of forest bathing on mental health. The duration of forest bathing interventions occurred anywhere between 15 minutes to 9 days and transpired in a variety of settings. The study authors concluded that forest bathing may be useful in the short-term reduction of anxiety symptoms and mental health symptoms overall (i.e., reducing stress), but that additional study is needed to clarify treatment protocols and the approach's longer-term effects.

As with many of the ecotherapies, most shinrin-yoku research has fallen outside the licensed helping professions. While some professional counselors and therapists might use the forest bathing literature to justify taking clients outdoors, it is once again difficult to translate the research findings of the forest bathing literature directly to traditional counseling and psychotherapy settings.

Animal-assisted Therapy

Animal-assisted therapy (AAT) is considered another form of ecotherapy, and again, this approach spans multiple fields. AAT incorporates animals such as dogs, horses, and dolphins. It is goal directed, and the therapy animal is a central component of therapy aimed at increasing human physical, social, emotional, and cognitive health. While it may not be an uncommon practice for counselors and therapists to have a furry pal accompanying them with clients in traditional settings, AAT includes a credentialed treatment provider guiding the relationship between the person and animal to address goals as outlined within a treatment plan. Additionally, the therapy animal often undergoes a registration or certification process whereby both the animal and the handler go through testing to demonstrate the animal's ability to remain calm and safe in potentially stressful situations.

Licensed therapists have written about the different ways therapy animals, particularly dogs and horses, might be incorporated into counseling (Fine, 2015). The American Counseling Association published *Animal-Assisted Therapy in Counseling Competencies* (Stewart et al., 2016). The competencies focus on proficiencies pertaining to knowledge of evidence-based practices in AAT, skills (e.g., matching AAT interventions appropriately and intentionally), and attitudes (e.g., recognizing animal rights relative to their participation in AAT).

The presence of therapy animals can be profound for many clients. In equine-facilitated work, participants engage in activities that include grooming, leading, and haltering. Concepts of trust, relationship skills, and nonverbal communication are critical components in facilitating connection between the client and the horse. While the therapist guides the intervention, the horse serves as a vital co-facilitator in the process. Interactions with horses and the ways in which the horse responds to the client serve as rich metaphors for how a client relationally operates in the world. In the group context, equine therapy can be utilized to enhance both communication and group cohesion (e.g., working together as a group to move the horse from one location to the other).

One meta-analysis demonstrated that AAT, such as equine-facilitated therapy, might serve as an effective intervention for persons presenting with autistic symptomology, medical challenges, behavioral problems, and emotional disorders (Nimer & Lundahl, 2007). In a systematic analysis, researchers (Hediger et al., 2021) analyzed the effectiveness of 41 studies on reducing depressive and PTSD symptomology. In many studies, interventions were facilitated by a licensed mental health professional, and of the studies, most included equine-facilitated therapy. Intervention duration occurred between 4 days to 15 months and the average intervention was ten weeks in length and ten sessions. The study authors concluded that AAT can be effective in reducing symptoms of depression and PTSD.

AAT has received considerable empirical support, including several studies employing rigorous research designs. Specifically, treatment protocols and training programs exist for licensed professionals interested in pursuing AAT. Nonetheless, considerations exist for licensed helping professionals practicing in traditional counseling and psychotherapy settings. Some clients may possess specific animal phobias or allergic reactions to animals. In addition, the time and monetary costs associated with AAT might keep this approach out of reach for some clients, and many licensed professionals may face barriers to integrating AAT into traditional therapy spaces, whether those include training limitations or the pragmatic challenges of bringing a horse to the office. Thus, while AAT has some of the most robust research evidence amongst the ecotherapies, these limitations may make the approach challenging to access for many clinicians in traditional counseling settings.

Nature-based Counseling

Several additional ecotherapeutic approaches have been introduced specifically within the helping professions of clinical psychology, counseling psychology, and professional counseling. Berger and McLeod (2006) defined nature therapy as "a postmodern experiential approach based on the integration of elements from art and drama therapy, Gestalt, narrative, ecopsychology, transpersonal psychology, adventure therapy, shamanism, and body-mind practices" (p. 82). Nature is viewed as a co-facilitator in the therapeutic process, and clinicians use interventions focusing on the interdependence amongst people and nature and through nature as a metaphor of one's life journey and the counseling process. Physical touch with nature is used to reconnect clients to the earth, suggesting "nature contains resources that can support emotional, spiritual, mental, and physical personal well-being, which in turn can be used for psychotherapeutic purposes" (p. 91). Nature therapy is thus broadly defined as the integration of nonhuman nature as a primary change agent in counseling experiences.

George Burns wrote *Nature-Guided Therapy* in 1998 and advanced notions of connecting with nature to facilitate expedient change. Burns recommended assigning tasks in nature to facilitate awareness into client sensory and emotional experience and suggested that solution-focused and client-centered behavioral strategies may help clients find greater motivation to address mental health challenges. He believed clients positively benefit from nature on account of its biodiversity and ever-changing processes, and additionally, through nature's potential to activate pleasurable sensations. By incorporating nature into counseling and psychotherapy, helping professionals may open a host of sensory experiences and emotions that may further catalyze a client's or patient's progress toward their treatment goals.

While both nature therapy and nature-guided therapy provided initial models for employing the more than human world into traditional counseling and psychotherapy settings, neither has received substantive research support or protocols for incorporating nature into traditional settings. Jacqueline Swank and Sang Min Shin (2015) developed nature-based, child-centered play therapy (NBCCPT), which has received modest empirical support. As an adaption of child-centered play therapy, the approach emphasizes both the client's relationship with nature as well as their relationship with the counselor. In lieu of human-created toys, the NBCCPT approach uses natural elements in an outdoor context. Swank and colleagues (2015) used a single-case research design in evaluating the effectiveness of 14 30-minute sessions. The researchers identified reductions in problem behaviors in two of the four elementary-aged students included in the study. They (Swank et al., 2017) found similar effects when incorporating NBCCPT in group counseling in a school setting when comparing to a wait-list group.

Applying Ecotherapy in Licensed Counseling and Psychotherapy

Maria Rueff and Gerhard Reese (2023) conducted a systemic literature review comparing ecotherapy with cognitive behavioral therapy (CBT). They reviewed studies wherein researchers analyzed outcomes relative to depression and anxiety. Example ecotherapeutic interventions included forest healing programs, exercise in nature, mindful walking through the forest, and animal-based interventions (e.g., caring for farm animals). The timing of interventions ranged from 15 minutes to multi-day immersive forest experiences. Most interventions occurred outside psychotherapy and counseling contexts. CBT interventions primarily included one-to-two-hour sessions within traditional, indoor psychotherapeutic environments.

The researchers' findings suggested that ecotherapy evidenced improvements within depression, though CBT demonstrated stronger effects when compared to ecotherapy. Relative to anxiety, all but one ecotherapy study indicated reduction in anxiety symptoms, though the ecotherapies demonstrated modest improvements by comparison with traditional psychotherapy. The study authors highlighted several limiting factors within the current state of the ecotherapy literature. As highlighted when reviewing the aforementioned ecotherapeutic modalities, differing conceptions of nature across studies make it difficult to draw too many conclusions about it as a viable option for clinicians in applied practice. Additionally, no long-term follow-up was conducted across most studies, which indicates that the distal effectiveness of ecotherapy remains unknown.

As a standalone approach, ecotherapy has considerable limitations when applied within licensed psychotherapeutic environments. Proponents of the ecotherapies and nature-based counseling have broadly suggested that the biophilia hypothesis and the ecological unconscious help explain the positive therapeutic outcomes cited in studies. However, neither construct is falsifiable; that is, they cannot be proven wrong, which is a cornerstone of the western scientific method. Nevin Harper and colleagues (2021) conducted a review of systematic and meta-analytic reviews on 14 studies on the ecotherapies. They concluded that comprehensive theoretical frameworks inclusive of intervention elements with causal links to outcomes were missing in most studies.

Moreover, with exception to animal-assisted therapy, and to some degree, wilderness therapy, much of the research on ecotherapy has occurred outside of counseling and psychotherapy contexts. For example, while horticultural therapy has evidenced some effectiveness, evidence-based protocols for counseling are absent from the literature. Sam Cooley and colleagues (2020) conducted a meta-synthesis of 38 publications focused on talk therapy taking place in natural outdoor spaces published between 1994 to 2019. The outdoor therapy contexts cited in the meta-synthesis varied, spanning walking in an urban park to wilderness expeditions. Indeed, the nature-based interventions and the therapeutic modalities varied significantly across studies. Most articles were professional practice or case studies, 14 articles included qualitative methods, and just two of the articles used quantitative methods. Clearly, additional research with replicable designs is needed to further substantiate the ecotherapies as standalone approaches when applied within counseling and psychotherapy.

Conclusion

While we have a long way to go in building more robust research evidence for the ecotherapies in the counseling and psychotherapy professions, there may be considerable therapeutic potential in applying nature-based interventions when working with clients. Meeting in the outdoors with Franklin transformed his openness to counseling and deepened our therapeutic relationship. He developed an appreciation for and relationship with nature that ultimately contributed to an expanded view of self and greater clarity into who he was and what he wanted in life. However, since many of the ecotherapies are common across various disciplines, their integration into licensed professional counseling and psychotherapy can present scope of practice challenges. At times, licensed clinicians may find themselves having to navigate roles or practices outside their areas of competence. Chapter 2 addresses these and other ethical considerations for incorporating the natural world into clinical practice.

Chapter 1 Reflection Questions

Self-awareness:

1. What aspects of this chapter stood out to you or were particularly surprising? Are there any points or discussions that challenged your previous understanding of ecotherapy?
2. How do you define ecotherapy based on your current understanding, and the insights provided in this chapter? Consider how this definition aligns or contrasts with the traditional therapeutic approaches for which you may align.
3. How does ecotherapy align with your personal values and professional goals as a clinician or clinician in training? How might it challenge your current practice paradigms?

Knowledge:

4. Were there any specific ecotherapies discussed in this chapter that piqued your interest? Are there any other ecotherapies or nature-based approaches not covered that you might like to explore further?
5. Reflect on the scope of practice limitations addressed in this chapter. How might these limitations affect your ability to integrate ecotherapy effectively and ethically into your professional practice?
6. Based on the discussion in the chapter, what evidence supports the application of ecotherapy in counseling and psychotherapy? What additional research would you like to see to strengthen the case for ecotherapy?

Application:

7. Identify and discuss the major challenges you might face when trying to integrate ecotherapy into your practice. How might you overcome them?
8. How would you explain the benefits and possible limitations of ecotherapy to a client who is new to this approach? What strategies might you use to incorporate their preferences and beliefs into ecotherapy-based interventions?

References

Annerstedt, M., & Währborg, P. (2011). Nature-assisted therapy: Systematic review of controlled and observational studies. *Scandinavian Journal of Public Health, 39,* 371–388. https://doi.org/10.1177/1403494810396400

Beck, N., & Wong, J. S. (2022). A meta-analysis of the effects of wilderness therapy on delinquent behaviors among youth. *Criminal Justice and Behavior, 49*(5), 700–729. https://doi.org/10.1177/00938548221078002

Berger, R., & McLeod, J. (2006). Incorporating nature into therapy: A framework for practice. *Journal of Systemic Therapies, 25*(2), 80–94. https://doi.org/10.1521/jsyt.2006.25.2.80

Burns, G. (1998). *Nature guided therapy: Brief integrative strategies for health and wellbeing.* Taylor & Francis.

Buzzell, L., & Chalquist, C. (2009). *Ecotherapy: Healing with nature in mind.* Sierra Club Books.

Clinebell, H. (1996). *Ecotherapy: Healing ourselves, healing the earth.* Augsburg Fortress Press.

Cooley, S. J., Jones, C. R., Kurtz, A., & Robertson, N. (2020). 'Into the wild': A meta-synthesis of talking therapy in natural outdoor spaces. *Clinical Psychology Review, 77,* 101841. https://doi.org/10.1016/j.cpr.2020.101841

Delaney, M. E. (2019). *Nature is nurture: Counseling and the natural world.* Oxford University Press.

Doherty, T. J. (2016). Theoretical and empirical foundations for ecotherapy. In *Ecotherapy: Theory, research & practice* (pp. 12–31). Palgrave Macmillan.

Fine, A. H. (2015). Incorporating animal-assisted therapy into psychotherapy: Guidelines and suggestions for therapists. In A. H. Fine (Ed.), *Handbook on animal-assisted therapy: Theoretical foundations and guidelines for practice* (4th ed., pp. 91–101). Academic Press.

Haller, R. L., Kennedy, K. L., & Capra, C. L. (2019). *The profession and practice of horticultural therapy.* CRC Press.

Hansen, M. M., Jones, R., & Tocchini, K. (2017). Shinrin-Yoku (forest bathing) and nature therapy: A state-of-the-art review. *International Journal of Environmental Research and Public Health, 14*(8), 851. https://doi.org/10.3390/ijerph14080851

Harper, N. J., Fernee, C. R., & Gabrielsen, L. E. (2021). Nature's role in outdoor therapies: An umbrella review. *International Journal of Environmental Research and Public Health, 18*(10), 5117. https://doi.org/10.3390/ijerph18105117

Hediger, K., Wagner, J., Künzi, P., Haefeli, A., Theis, F., Grob, C., Pauli, E., & Gerger, H. (2021). Effectiveness of animal-assisted interventions for children and adults with post-traumatic stress disorder symptoms: A systematic review and meta-analysis. *European Journal of Psychotraumatology, 12*(1), 1879713. https://doi.org/10.1080/20008198.2021.1879713

Horowitz, S. (2012). Therapeutic gardens and horticultural therapy. *Alternative and Complementary Therapies, 18*(2), 78–83. https://doi.org/10.1089/act.2012.18205

Jang, E. J., Han, G. W., Hong, J. W., Yoon, S. E., & Pak, C. H. (2010). Meta-analysis of research papers on horticultural therapy program effect. *Korean Journal of Horticultural Science & Technology, 28*(4), 701–707.

Jordan, M. (2014). *Nature and therapy: Understanding counselling and psychotherapy in outdoor spaces.* Routledge.

Jordan, M., & Hinds, J. (2017). *Ecotherapy: Theory, research and practice.* Bloomsbury Publishing.

Kotera, Y., Richardson, M., & Sheffield, D. (2022) Effects of shinrin-yoku (forest bathing) and nature therapy on mental health: A systematic review and ,eta-analysis. *Int J Ment Health Addiction, 20,* 337–361 (2022). https://doi.org/10.1007/s11469-020-00363-4

Nimer, J., & Lundahl, B. (2007). Animal-assisted therapy: A meta-analysis. *Anthrozoos*, *20*(3), 225–238. https://doi.org/10.2752/08927930uX224773

Park, B.-J., Tsunetsugu, Y., Lee, J., Kagawa, T., & Miyazaki, Y. (2012). Effect of the forest environment on physiological relaxation—the results of field tests at 35 sites throughout Japan. In Q. Li (Ed.), *Forest medicine* (pp. 55–65). Nova Science Publishers.

Reese, R. F., Hadeed, S., Gosling, M., Beyer, A., & Craig, H. (2018). EcoWellness: Integrating the natural world into wilderness therapy settings with intentionality. *Journal of Adventure Education & Outdoor Learning*, *19*(3), 202–215. https://doi.org/10.108 0/14729679.2018.1508357

Roszak, T. (1992). *The voice of the earth: An exploration of ecopsychology*. Phanes Press, Inc.

Rueff, M., & Reese, G. (2023). Depression and anxiety: A systematic review on comparing ecotherapy with cognitive behavioral therapy. *Journal of Environmental Psychology*, 102097. https://doi.org/10.1016/j.jenvp.2023.102097

Russell, K., & Gillis, H. L. (2017). The adventure therapy experience scale: The psychometric properties of a scale to measure the unique factors moderating an adventure therapy experience. *Journal of Experiential Education*, *40*(2), 135–152. https://doi.org/10.1177/1053825917690541

Stewart, L. A., Chang, C. Y., Parker, L. K., & Grubbs, N. (2016). *Animal-assisted therapy in counseling competencies*. American Counseling Association, Animal-Assisted Therapy in Mental Health Interest Network.

Swank, J. M., Cheung, C., Prikhidko, A., & Su, Y. W. (2017). Nature-based child-centered group play therapy and behavioral concerns: A single-case design. *International Journal of Play Therapy*, *26*, 47–57. https://doi.org/10.1037/0pla0000031

Swank, J. M., & Shin, S. M. (2015). Nature-based child-centered play therapy: An innovative counseling approach. *International Journal of Play Therapy*, *24*, 151–161. https://doi.org/10.1037/a0039127

Swank, J. M., Shin, S. M., Cabrita, C., Cheung, C., & Rivers, B. (2015). Initial investigation of nature-based, child-centered play therapy: A single-case design. *Journal of Counseling & Development*, *93*, 440–450. https://doi.org/10.1002/jcad.12042

Tu, H. M. (2022). Effect of horticultural therapy on mental health: A meta-analysis of randomized controlled trials. *Journal of Psychiatric and Mental Health Nursing*, *29*(4), 603–615. https://doi.org/10.1111/jpm.12818

Wilson, E. O. (1984). *Biophilia*. Harvard University Press.

Wilson, E. O. (1996). *In search of nature*. Island Press.

2

ETHICAL FOUNDATIONS OF ECOWELLNESS COUNSELING

"Can we find an area that's a bit more private today?" Benny inquired at the beginning of our outdoor therapy session.

"No problem," I assured him as we walked away from the parking lot and into the forested park.

I had been seeing Benny, a 19-year-old cisgender man for about three months. During that time, we visited this park for many of our counseling sessions. Benny preferred a combination of walking the trails and sitting by the creek for our meetings. He didn't typically mind encountering bystanders on the trail. But today was different.

It was October, and the leaves were turning gold, orange, red, and purple. The crisp air beckoned an additional outer layer. We sported fleeces and walked with our chilled hands in our pockets. I knew this forested park well, like the back of my hand. It included multiple trail systems and a small, clear stream that tumbled through the forest canopy. I had been coming here with clients for about four years, and I took pride in selecting which trail was most appropriate for which client, depending on the day.

We hiked for about ten minutes, making good distance from the primary trail. "How does this area feel to you?" I asked, gesturing with my hand toward the space, which was enclosed by manzanita bushes, towering ponderosa pines, and the rushing creek immediately behind us.

DOI: 10.4324/9781315697437-4

"It's really good, thanks."

Tears flooded Benny's eyes. He just got dumped by his partner without explanation. "I don't know what I did wrong, I just didn't see this coming," Benny lamented.

I listened intently as he shared about his loss and how he was currently coping. Benny previously reported that he liked meeting outdoors because it "opened things up" for him. Just a week earlier he commented about the freedom he felt by coming to therapy and being able to experience nature while sharing. Outdoor therapy felt much more effective to him than meeting indoors.

Soon there was a natural break in our conversation. We sat in silence for about a minute, listening to the creek and absorbing the fall colors. Suddenly, a cluster of bushes shook with intermittent movement, and soon, a woman with sunglasses and a sunhat appeared. "Why, hello there, gentlemen! Beautiful day, isn't it? I'm just out exploring, as you can see. How are you both today?"

The client averted his gaze down and away from the woman, and I could sense his discomfort. The well-intentioned interloper was determined to engage us in dialogue. I did all the responding, deflecting the flood of comments and curiosities as the client continued to remain silent. Finally, she asked, "Well, how do you both know one another?"

"Colleagues," I responded. "We are both colleagues, and we are unfortunately in the middle of a meeting. So, we must let you go about your exploring as we are wrapping things up."

"Righty-o! Well, don't mind me interrupting," the exuberant passerby hailed. "You both have a wonderous day!"

Dumbfounded, I looked over at Benny, who had witnessed and endured the awkward two-minute grilling from our fellow traveler. He looked at me, a smile gradually pursing his lips. He burst into laughter. "Where the hell did she come from?" Benny quipped. "Seriously, she must have crawled her way down the creek or something!"

In shared disbelief, we reflected on the practicalities of the woman's probable route. We agreed that she must have bushwhacked for hundreds of yards to find her way to us. While Benny seemed rather amused by the unsolicited interruption, I was concerned about the invasion of his privacy. "I know solitude was imperative today, Benny. What was that like for you?" I asked.

"It was definitely a surprise, but it actually kind of made my day," Benny reflected. "I mean, we've talked about the possibility of someone interrupting our meetings before, but I didn't think it would happen like that, especially when we found such a secluded spot," Benny said with a chuckle.

Our session continued, revisiting Benny's heartache and addressing areas he would like to lean into that week to address and work through his feelings of loss. At our session the following week, I checked in with Benny again about the intrusion, highlighting our prior conversations during informed consent about confidentiality. Benny assured me that he understood the limits of his privacy when meeting in nature, and insisted he preferred continuing meeting outdoors.

As I reflect on this experience years later, Benny's reaction to the unexpected invasion of privacy likely would have been far different had we not thoroughly prepared for the unexpected. Before we set foot outdoors, and as part of the holistic assessment process, we explored Benny's connection with the natural world and his motivations for wanting to engage in a nature-based paradigm. We reviewed the physical and psychological risks, and any number of social encounters we might realistically face when meeting outdoors. We developed a client-centered plan for navigating interactions with fellow community members. Only after developing a clear and intentional roadmap did we mutually agree to moving counseling outdoors.

Considerable clinical intent must be applied when addressing the human–nature connection in counseling. As this case highlighted, meeting outside the office environment introduces potential legal and ethical ramifications licensed professionals must navigate to prevent harm to their clients and protect themselves from legal quandaries and ethical violations (Reese, 2016). In this chapter, we consider guiding principles for ethically addressing a client's connection with the natural world as part of licensed counseling and psychotherapy. Through application of the American Counseling Association (2014) *Code of Ethics*, we examine ethical standards pertaining to competence, informed consent, confidentiality, professional boundaries, environmental justice and advocacy, and nature worldview (see Table 2.1).

Table 2.1 EcoWellness Ethical Principles and Applicable ACA Ethical Codes

ETHICAL PRINCIPLE	DESCRIPTION	APPLICABLE ACA ETHICAL CODES
1. ECOWELLNESS COMPETENCE	Clinicians understand and stay attuned to EcoWellness related research, theory, and ethics. They possess prior training and skills for applying EcoWellness within their applied setting(s).	C.2.a. C.7.a. C.2.b. C.7.b. C.2.f. C.7.c.
2. INFORMED CONSENT	Clinicians inform clients of the possible benefits, risks (psychological and physical), and limitations prior to and during the application of EcoWellness-based intervention in counseling and psychotherapy.	A.2.a. A.2.c A.2.b. C.7.b.
3. HONORING CLIENT NATURE WORLDVIEW	Clinicians prevent imposing their own nature worldview onto clients. Clinicians become familiar with and base EcoWellness interventions in the client's nature worldview, sociopolitical context, and goals for therapy.	A.4.b.
4. CONFIDENTIALITY	Confidentiality cannot be guaranteed in public outdoor settings. Clinicians work with clients to minimize risks and address breaches of privacy if they occur. Outdoor locations are appropriate to the client's treatment plan.	B.1.c. B.1.d
5. PROFESSIONAL BOUNDARIES	Clinicians clarify their clinical intent when meeting in outdoor contexts, explain boundary extensions, and explore client comfort. They proactively reduce the risk of boundary violations.	A.6.b. A.6.d. A.6.c.
6. ENVIRONMENTAL JUSTICE & ADVOCACY	Clinicians assist clients in acquiring safe and sustaining access to nature in ways that promote wellness for the individual, their community, and more than human world.	A.7.a.

Note: Copyright Ryan F. Reese, 2016

Competence

My colleague, Jacqueline Swank, and I (2021) surveyed a United States sample of 406 helping professionals (e.g., licensed psychologists, clinical social workers, and professional counselors) regarding their attitudes toward and current practices for addressing the human–nature connection in counseling. The clinicians practiced in agency, school, private practice, inpatient, and residential settings. Sixty-four percent of the sample reported incorporating nature-based counseling in their therapy practices. Of those, 12% engaged in wilderness therapy, 10% used adventure-based counseling, 27% reported engaging in horticultural therapy, and 34% reported using animal-assisted therapy. Forty-three percent of the sample engaged clients in outdoor activities during session, and 51% sat outside during counseling sessions. However, just 18% of the sample indicated that they had completed prior training in ecotherapy.

The ethical codes within the licensed helping professions mandate competence. This includes acquiring the knowledge, skills, dispositions, awareness, and supervised clinical experiences necessary to deliver therapeutic interventions with effectiveness while minimizing the potential for causing harm. Utilizing any therapeutic modality without prior training and supervised practice would be considered ethically problematic. Thus, applying ecotherapeutic strategies and meeting outdoors with clients without training could place clinicians in some sticky situations.

Section C.2. of the ACA (2014) *Code of Ethics* centers on professional competence. Professional counselors only practice within their boundaries of proficiency (C.2.a.). When developing a specialty area, clinicians seek the appropriate training and supervised experiences prior to incorporating novel practices into their approach (C.2.b.). While an increasing number of ecotherapeutic and nature-based counseling certificate programs and trainings are being developed in the United States and elsewhere (e.g., forest therapy, ecotherapy), no training standards exist in the licensed professions, and many of these approaches are shared across disciplines, making it difficult to decipher their ethical application in traditional therapy settings. Thus, counselors and therapists assume an unknown and inherent level of professional risk when it comes to employing eco-based strategies in their practice.

Because no training standards exist, clinicians must also be transparent regarding the legitimacy of their credentials and not overstate or misrepresent their actual expertise in a particular area (C.4.a.). Similarly, clinicians must be candid about the theoretical and empirical foundations that underlie their approach. As discussed in Chapter 1, while the ecotherapies have garnered some empirical support, these approaches generally lack the same level of research as other evidence-based approaches to treatment. Clinicians must effectively communicate with clients any modalities or interventions that may be considered innovative, experimental, or lacking empirical basis (C.7.b.). Often, non-applied research (which we'll further explore in Chapter 4) is utilized to support the inclusion of nature into therapy or medical settings. When doing so, it's important to clarify with clients that most of the research pointing toward the wellness effects of nature falls outside licensed counseling and psychotherapy settings.

Competence also pertains to specific nature-based interventions, wherein clients might be engaged in activities falling outside a clinician's scope of practice. In such cases, clinicians must do all they can to acquire sufficient skills. For example, I'm familiar with clinicians who integrate rock climbing and hiking experiences into therapy. Whatever the activity may be, it's pertinent that the clinician has the sufficient expertise and knowledge for incorporating that approach into therapy.

Ethical issues surrounding nature-based competence aren't always as obvious. For example, being prepared for shifting weather or trail conditions when meeting outdoors, carrying a first aid kit, and being intimately familiar with the outdoor setting where you meet with clients. There are also population-specific competencies. Over the years, I've worked quite a lot with elementary-aged children in outdoor settings. When in open, parklike spaces kids love to run. Thus, I learned early on the importance of creating structural boundaries and setting limits. Without them, I had to do a lot of running to ensure children stayed away from natural features that may have resulted in harm. Counselors must be able to anticipate such issues with their respective client populations and fully consider whether they feel capable and competent to address concerns as they emerge.

In my view, competence also means getting to know your clients holistically before taking them outdoors. As we'll explore in Part III, the EcoWellness counseling approach is centered on thorough assessment practices. My preference is to meet with clients a minimum of two sessions indoors prior to ever taking a client outdoors, even if they request meeting outdoors from the outset. Following the initial assessment, licensed counselors and therapists collaboratively work with clients to determine the treatment plan and which outdoor-based interventions will be administered throughout the treatment process, if any. It is paramount that clinicians assess the potential factors that contribute to the appropriateness of integrating nature into counseling, such as medical concerns, allergies, and prior trauma that may be activated in the outdoor setting. Standard C.7.c. in the ACA *Code of Ethics* states that counselors do not apply techniques or modalities into counseling "when substantial evidence suggests harm, even if such services are requested" (p. 10). In this way, clinicians should apply a trauma-informed lens on clients, which we'll further discuss in Chapter 7.

Informed Consent

An extension of competence includes the ongoing act and art of informed consent (A.2a.-A.2.c.). The informed consent process is sacred, ongoing, and based in the developing therapeutic alliance. It has a clear beginning wherein the client completes the intake paperwork, signs your disclosure forms, and any practice or agency documents. Within the informed consent process resides our virtue ethics: veracity, fidelity, nonmaleficence, beneficence, autonomy, and justice. At the outset, we transparently disclose our approaches and don't overpromise results or outcomes. We develop a clear contract with our clients outlining our scope of practice and articulating any potential benefits or harm that may come to the client as part of engaging with us in treatment. Clients (and their guarantors) have a clear right to collaboratively engage in treatment decisions. We treat our clients with fairness and view them through contextual and sociocultural lenses and take into consideration our own values and biases and how these may come to impact the client through issues of transference and countertransference. In my experience, the inclusion of the human–nature connection into counseling processes necessitates above and beyond informed consent processes, particularly if the therapeutic team collaboratively decides to venture outdoors.

As I will advocate throughout this text, the integration of outdoor sessions into EcoWellness counseling is never an all-or-nothing pursuit. It is based on an ongoing informed consent process wherein the client and counselor monitor the effectiveness of including nature in counseling, whether nature is incorporated indoors or outdoors. At the outset, it is essential to fully inform the client of what they might expect around the inclusion of EcoWellness into counseling, including the potential risks and benefits. Clinicians should explain the complexity of the indoor or outdoor environment and its potential for unpredictability and uncertainty that may contribute to psychological or physical distress.

The park I mentioned in the case of Benny is one of my favorite outdoor meeting spaces. It includes a web of trails with varying privacy and complexity. Some of the areas at the park include panoramic views where one can see all around themselves. Other areas have steeper inclines and sharp, blind turns. The flat trails offer greater accessibility and predictability. The client can see all around them, what is behind, and what is before them. Conversely, the trails with the steeper inclines tend to meander in and out of trees and brush, making the path less accessible and more unpredictable. Hence, during the informed consent process, the client collaboratively works with me to identify what trails seem most conducive to their preferred meeting environment. And again, these preferences might shift across the counseling relationship, thus extending the informed consent process as the client progresses toward their goals. From both a client safety and liability perspective, it is imperative that the clinician document ongoing conversations around informed consent within their clinical progress notes.

Clinicians must also clearly articulate the above and beyond risks that are part of meeting outdoors. Depending on the outdoor setting and the nature-based activities clients might engage during sessions, clients may be more likely to experience physical risks to their health when meeting outdoors in the form of bumps, scratches, broken limbs, or death. Clients might also encounter shifting weather conditions and anticipated or unanticipated interactions with community members. These risks must be clearly articulated within your paperwork and clients must clearly sign or initial the sections outlining these risks. I strongly encourage you to seek legal consultation when developing or modifying your informed consent paperwork to address these concerns. As we'll discuss in the coming sections, clients must also clearly understand limits to auditory confidentiality when meeting in outdoor, public spaces and the potential boundary crossings that can occur when meeting outdoors.

Confidentiality

One of the more obvious ethical issues surrounding a nature-based or EcoWellness counseling approach is client confidentiality. Ethically, clinicians are to respect the confidentiality of clients, and the disclosure of information should only occur with the appropriate consent and with ethical and legal justification (B.1.c.). As we'll discuss in the coming chapters, just because you are addressing EcoWellness as part of counseling, it doesn't mean you will be meeting with clients outdoors. Thus, confidentiality may not be an issue. However, if your client agrees to move counseling beyond the four walls, confidentiality cannot be guaranteed. This includes both the confidentiality of the counseling relationship and client auditory confidentiality.

While you cannot guarantee confidentiality when meeting in a public setting, you can proactively protect client privacy. In the case of Benny, we collaboratively put effort into identifying an outdoor private space.

Without a doubt, Benny's privacy was breached, but his auditory confidentiality was protected on account of our location. When the passerby approached, we stopped talking, and neither I nor the client disclosed the counseling relationship.

Regardless, we as clinicians must explain the limitations of confidentiality and plan for situations wherein confidentiality may be compromised (B.1.d.; B.2.e.). This is not dissimilar from instances in which clinicians take clients into public settings for approaches such as exposure therapy. During the informed consent process, clients should learn about the limits of confidentiality when meeting outdoors. It should be clearly stated both verbally and within the paperwork that auditory confidentiality cannot be guaranteed and that it is possible for the therapeutic relationship to be exposed. For example, if a community member sees me and knows I'm a licensed therapist, they might assume I'm walking with a client. It goes without saying that if a client and/or their guardian has concerns about meeting outdoors for confidentiality reasons, you should refrain from doing so.

Professional Boundaries

Within the initial and ongoing informed consent process, it's also critical to communicate and evaluate the different ways that meeting outdoors can impact the counseling relationship. Until you meet outdoors with a client, neither you nor that client can fully predict how meeting outside the office will affect progress toward the treatment plan. As such, this ethical consideration is one of the most difficult to navigate and requires considerable clinician self-awareness and discretion. Managing boundaries in the outdoor setting also points toward the importance of developing competence through supervised practice in further developing judgment for when it may be prudent to take counseling outdoors.

The meeting context can contribute to subtle differences in how the personality of the clinician or client "shows up" in session. The mental framework for talk therapy in western culture typically includes a client meeting with the clinician in the indoor context. We conjure an image of a couch and the therapist's chair. Child therapists might envision a modifiable play space including toys, games, and a sand tray. The office environment contributes to perceived and experienced power differences within the therapeutic relationship. The clinician is expected to provide expertise and facilitate a process wherein the client acquires knowledge, skills, and self-awareness. Merging the traditional therapy schema with our differing life experiences relative to the outdoors can result in differing expectations for counseling that occurs outside the office setting. For some of us, meeting in a park setting represents recreation, adventure, and relaxation. For others, the outdoors might trigger adverse trauma responses.

Early in my time as a therapist, I found it easy to become absorbed in the immediate environment or activity when meeting with clients outdoors. I would, at times, lose focus of my intentionality, becoming distracted by my own individual interests and curiosities. I find this true with many novice clinicians, which again points toward the importance of prior training and supervised practice when incorporating the outdoors into counseling or psychotherapy. Depending on the client's background, they might also experience a shift in the counseling relationship, where they view you or the counseling relationship differently. The client's expectations for counseling and their ways of communicating within the counseling relationship might also differ.

There can be certain advantages to the shifting of boundaries when meeting outdoors. There often tends to be greater openness and space; the conversation flows more naturally, and it can feel less forced. Similarly, dialogue can feel more informal, with both the clinician and the client observing and absorbing their shared surroundings. Meeting outside the clinician's office can feel more like neutral ground, evening out the power differential. These factors can help to catalyze the working relationship and contribute to feelings of safety and security early in the relationship. The improvisation of the outdoor counseling session also can help to bring the treatment plan into the here and now, wherein both the client and clinician become witness to or participants within the natural world.

But just as there are advantages, there can also be downsides in extending our professional boundaries to meeting outdoors. Meeting outside of the office setting contributes to amplified feelings of vulnerability. While some clients can go deeper and faster as a result, other clients might feel less emotionally or physically safe with the clinician. Depending on the circumstances, the therapist might also feel less safe with the client.

Similarly, unpredictable triggering events can happen when meeting in nature. As such, we don't always know how we will individually and collectively react to meeting in an outdoor context. Without ongoing communication and frequently checking in with the client, the counseling relationship can experience an emotional distancing that might not otherwise occur within the indoor context. In this way, the natural stimuli encountered outdoors can serve as a deterrent within the treatment plan. Moreover, a client's view toward the clinician or therapy may shift in such a way that the therapeutic quality of the interaction diminishes (i.e., the client might come to view the clinician as a friend). When this occurs, the therapist, the client, or the relationship can begin to lose sight of the therapeutic intent for meeting outdoors.

Furthermore, counselors may, at times, take on an additional role to their clinician scope of practice, which might also be considered as a boundary crossing. For example, if a clinician took a client rock climbing or hiking as part of therapy, the lines could be blurred between the therapist's scope of practice and their complementary role as guide or teacher (A.6.d.). A boundary crossing can also occur if a clinician agrees to transport a client. The clinician should clearly articulate and document their rationale for such boundary crossings. Additionally, they should communicate with clients the foreseeable structure of these counseling sessions and the clinician's anticipated roles. Before and during the experience, the client should always have a clear and autonomous pathway for declining the proposed boundary crossing. When boundary crossings do occur, the therapist must be able to always maintain their clinical intent. Should the clinician's complementary role become paramount, and the clinician loses sight of clinical intent, they may be at risk of committing a boundary violation wherein there is potential for client harm. I can't reiterate enough that clients should be fully informed of any possible risks or benefits to boundary crossings within the counseling relationship.

In summary, clinicians need to discuss with clients the differing ways that meeting outdoors can impact the counseling relationship. As part of this process, clinicians must communicate and document boundary crossings (A.6.c.) and have a clinical justification for extending counseling boundaries past "conventional parameters" (A.6.b.). Thus, meeting outdoors should serve a mutually agreed upon function within the client's treatment plan, whether that be addressing EcoWellness or meeting in an environment that is more conducive to the client's preferences for treatment setting. Lastly, I encourage us as clinicians to find ways to reduce instances where we may be serving in a role that is in addition to our clinician scope of practice. When possible, we should consider partnering with professionals who are adept and responsible for the activity (and associated liability) so the therapist can maintain their clinical focus and intentionality.

Environmental Justice and Advocacy

The ethical codes in the licensed helping professions direct clinicians to honor diversity and engage in a multicultural approach to therapy. Clinicians are also called to promote social justice and advocacy (e.g., A.7.a.). As we'll discuss in the coming chapters, natural resources that humans rely upon for survival (e.g., clean air to breathe, safe drinking water, and nutritious foods) often favor economically affluent communities. For example, environmental hazards such as oil refineries, toxic waste plants, and industrial pollution are more prevalent in communities of color (Intergovernmental Panel on Climate Change [IPCC], 2023). Similarly, safe access to the natural environment for wellness-related purposes favors privileged identities (The Trust for Public Land, 2021). Safe access to parks or trail systems is often limited or nonexistent within many urban areas. Weather-related events exacerbated by the climate crisis can further amplify environmental hazards, which disproportionally impact vulnerable populations, including people of color, women, and children (IPCC). When climate events strike, they serve to amplify the health-related consequences of environmental hazards that contribute to greater incidences of respiratory illnesses, cancer, and a reduced lifespan. In Chapter 10, we'll discuss the application of the ACA *Advocacy Competencies* (Toporek & Daniels, 2018) when addressing issues pertinent to environmental and climate justice. Clinicians can work with clients, and in some instances, their communities, to identify tangible individual or collective actions that can be taken to address environmental and climate inequities within the communities served.

Another aspect of environmental justice includes caring for the natural world. When clinicians engage in outdoor-based approaches, for instance, they must prioritize doing no harm within the spaces where sessions occur. Clinicians can ensure that meeting in the outdoors has minimal impact on the natural landscapes explored and the organisms inhabiting those spaces. This might include setting boundaries and shared expectations for behaviors. For example, facilitating a mutual understanding of leave-no-trace principles, which is a framework for having a minimal impact for visiting the outdoors (Leave No Trace, 2024). Examples of leave no trace include having familiarity with the regulations of a particular outdoor area, properly disposing waste, staying on trails, respecting wildlife, leaving what is found, and respecting the rights of others accessing the outdoors. Importantly, when it comes to discussing environmental values with clients, clinicians must work to understand the beliefs of their clients and not impose their own nature worldview.

Honoring Client Nature Worldview

Every client we work with will define nature differently. Despite this diversity, the discussion of nature worldview has not always been at the forefront of the ecotherapeutic literature reviewed in Chapter 1. Like many of the psychotherapeutic approaches broadly applied in the helping professions, the ecotherapies and their underlying theories have predominantly been developed by white cisgender men. Additionally, much of the ecotherapy research, to date, has been conducted with participants and clients of European descent, and thus, generalizability of those approaches to clients of color may be limited. These details are critical to consider as we entertain the broader application of addressing the human–nature connection in counseling and psychotherapy.

In Chapter 3, we'll discuss at length varying conceptions of nature, or nature worldview. Underlying nature worldview includes positionality and the ways in which our clients come to define nature through their intersecting identities. It is our ethical imperative to clarify our own nature worldview (i.e., values) as the clinician, our motivations for addressing nature in counseling, and ensuring that we are engaging in culturally sustaining practices. We must consider how our identities, relationships, lived contexts, and resources impact the way(s) we view and perceive the natural world around us. Without genuine self-analysis, we risk projecting our own nature worldview onto our clients and thus alienating them from their unique beliefs and value systems. Moreover, licensed professionals must be vigilant to prevent culturally appropriating nature-based interventions. The utilization of vision quests, for example, teeters the line of ethical practice, given their sacred roots within many indigenous traditions. It is imperative that counselors gain permission, acknowledge, and bring honor to client cultural traditions when such interventions are incorporated into therapeutic processes.

Conclusion

The EcoWellness approach delineated in this book is grounded in professional counseling scope of practice and ethics. With prior training and an ongoing commitment to continuing education, licensed helping professionals can reduce the potential for harm and increase their competence and intentionality. Through initial and ongoing informed consent processes, the clinician and client can collaboratively consider the potential benefits and risks for engaging the outdoors during sessions. These ethical considerations include possible impacts on the client and counseling relationship, such as maintaining confidentiality and boundary crossings. The EcoWellness framework further honors our professional commitments to social justice and advocacy, which includes addressing issues pertinent to environmental and climate justice. In the forthcoming chapter, we focus on issues pertinent to nature worldview, wherein clinicians are called to honor and prioritize the clients' values and preferences for addressing the human–nature connection within the treatment plan.

Chapter 2 Reflection Questions

Self-awareness:

1. Consider the ethical principles discussed in this chapter. Which concern you the most, and how would you address these concerns in your specific setting(s)?
2. Reflect on the ethical implications of boundary crossings in EcoWellness therapy. What strategies can help you maintain professional boundaries?

Knowledge:

3. Discuss the importance of informed consent in EcoWellness counseling. How does it differ from traditional approaches to counseling and psychotherapy?
4. What are some potential risks of conducting therapy in outdoor settings and how can these be mitigated?
5. How can therapists ensure they remain within their competence when incorporating EcoWellness practices?

Application:

6. In what ways can the physical setting of therapy (indoors vs. outdoors) influence the therapeutic relationship?
7. How can counselors maintain client confidentiality and privacy when sessions are held in public or semipublic outdoor areas?
8. Consider the role of environmental justice in counseling practice. How can therapists incorporate advocacy into their work with clients?

References

American Counseling Association. (2014). *ACA code of ethics*. ACA.

IPCC. (2023). Sections. In Core Writing Team, H. Lee, & J. Romero (Eds.), *Climate change 2023: Synthesis report. Contribution of working groups I, II and III to the sixth assessment report of the intergovernmental panel on climate change* (pp. 35–115). IPCC. https://doi.org/10.59327/IPCC/AR6-9789291691647

Leave No Trace. (2024). *The 7 principles*. https://lnt.org/why/7-principles/

Reese, R. F. (2016). EcoWellness and guiding principles for the ethical integration of nature into counseling. *International Journal for the Advancement of Counselling, 38*(4), 345–357. https://doi.org/10.1007/s10447-016-9276-5

Swank, J. M., & Reese, R. F. (2022). Do counselors and other helping professionals use nature-based counseling? *Journal of Creativity in Mental Health, 17*(4), 443–455. https://doi.org/10.1080/15401383.2021.1911725

Toporek, R. L., & Daniels, J. (2018). *American counseling association advocacy competencies*. American Counseling Association. https://www.counseling.org/docs/default-source/competencies/aca-advocacy-competencies-updated-may-2020.pdf

The Trust for Public Land. (2021). *Parks and an equitable recovery*. https://www.tpl.org/parks-and-an-equitable-recovery-parkscore-report

3

POSITIONALITY, COLONIZATION, AND THE DEVELOPMENT OF NATURE WORLDVIEW

Gwyneth presented to counseling with social anxiety. Her grandfather passed away a year prior and she described significant difficulty moving forward in her life. For months after his death, Gwyneth lacked motivation to engage socially, and she withdrew from her primary friend group. She recently attempted reengaging, but in doing so, experienced debilitating and unexpected anxiety. As a second-year doctoral intern, I emboldened myself to ask clients questions about nature and wellness during the initial intake appointment, and I was approved by my doctoral internship supervisor to walk with clients to the nearby park in Greensboro, North Carolina. As we neared the end of our initial meeting, I inquired about the possible role nature might play in Gwyneth's life relative to managing her presenting anxiety.

"Excuse me, what did you ask me?" she retorted.

"Nature, like trees or animals, hiking in the woods, or going to the park," I replied.

She cracked a smile and laughed: "I don't do nature. Do you see me? I'm black."

As Gwyneth expanded upon her experiences with the more than human world, I learned about her family of origin and the explicit forms of racism her parents endured in their own youth. Gwyneth inherited an internalized fear of spending time outdoors, rooted in her sociocultural

DOI: 10.4324/9781315697437-5

context and positionality. The message she received was clear: be cautious where you go, mindful of who you are with, and always have an alibi. The experience of nature, from her perspective, was based in white privilege. Black people could not freely go about exploring the outdoors in the ways that white people could. People of color, she experienced, needed to watch themselves at nearby parks or remote wilderness areas for fear of being targeted or falsely accused of crimes. Besides, she argued, most black folks were too poor to access nature, anyway.

The Multicultural and Social Justice Counseling Competencies (Ratts et al., 2016) emphasize counselor self-awareness and call clinicians to prioritize client worldview in the process of therapy. Nature worldview, the subject of this chapter, offers a vital lens for comprehending how client positionality actively shapes their attitudes and encounters with natural environments. A pervading and dominant nature narrative exists in western society, based in colonial ideology and white supremacy. If clinicians aren't vigilant, they can easily and unintentionally reinforce these oppressive forces onto their clients. Thus, how we address a client's view on the natural world in counseling and psychotherapy deserves considerable care and attention.

Nature Worldview and Positionality

I've worked with clients across various walks of life espousing a variety of attitudes, values, and experiences surrounding nature. Some people possess a general fearfulness of nature, based on their lived experience or from a lack of historical contact with nature. Some people are generally fond of nature. For others, affinity for the more than human world depends on context.

Nature worldview embodies one's vantage point toward the natural world, based on the accumulation of their life experiences, positionality, and ultimately, the immediate context and situational demands. Positionality characterizes an individual's sociocultural location within the broader context of society and how this position impacts life opportunities, life experiences, and worldviews. It is a useful construct in conceptualizing how power and privilege come to impact individual lived experiences. Some individual factors of identity impacting positionality include race and ethnicity, nationality status, language proficiency, gender, physical traits, sexual orientation, physical ability and disability, education, economic and employment status, religion and spirituality, and lived experience (e.g., adverse childhood experiences). Sociocultural factors impacting positionality can include family structure, familial wealth, intergenerational experiences and beliefs, and cultural norms. All such elements are viewed within an individual's lived context, including their geographic location, governmental policy, and historical context.

The development of our unique individual nature worldview is ever evolving as we progress through life, and as we grow older, we possess some level of agency to direct our actions. According to Life Course Development Theory (Elder et al., 2003), our development is impacted by the interplay between cultural, historical, economic, social, physical, and biological contexts. Our lives are linked with all other living and nonliving objects, and we cannot escape the inseparable reality that our immediate and extended relationships shape our lives—including our connectedness with the more than human world.

The degree of connectedness to or separation from nature varies across cultures and individuals. Wesley Shultz (2002) developed the *Inclusion of Nature in Self* construct, defined as the degree to which an individual incorporates nature into their "cognitive representation of self" (p. 67). Schultz developed a single-item measure to assess this construct that included seven different variations of two circles (see Figure 3.1). The more area the two circles share, the greater the perception that one's identity is interdependent with nature. The instructions state, "Please circle the picture below which best describes your relationship with the natural environment. How connected are you with nature?" On one end of the continuum, the "self" is conceptualized as being separate and distinct from nature. On the other, just one circle represents the unified "self" with "nature," signifying full interdependence.

Across the self-nature continuum, our clients possess varying and often conflicting beliefs, values, and interpretations about the natural world. By no means an exhaustive set of values, possible nature worldviews include anthropocentrism, utilitarianism, biocentrism, ecocentrism, nihilism, science, aesthetic appreciation, transcendentalism, and bio-phobia.

Anthropocentrism centers humans as the most important organisms in the world, if not the universe. Within this worldview, human wellness is

PLEASE CIRCLE THE PICTURE BELOW WHICH BEST DESCRIBES
YOUR RELATIONSHIP WITH THE NATURAL ENVIRONMENT.
HOW INTERCONNECTED ARE YOU WITH NATURE?

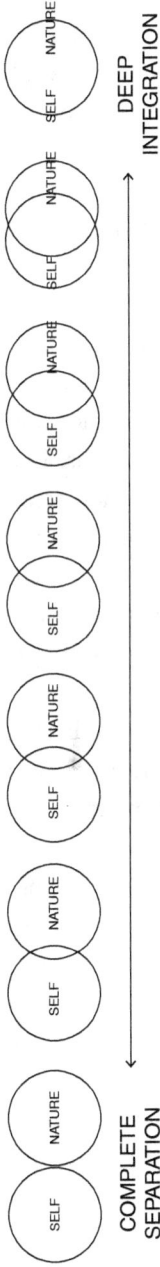

COMPLETE
SEPARATION

DEEP
INTEGRATION

Figure 3.1 The Inclusion of Nature in Self Scale

Note. Adapted from Schultz, 2002

prioritized over other species or living systems. As we'll soon discuss, the anthropocentric worldview is rampant in western, colonized culture, and lies at the foundation of the exploitation of natural resources and non-human species for human benefit and pleasure. Instead of being viewed as living entities with soul or spirit, nonhuman entities are viewed as commodities that can be possessed, purchased, and sold. This includes ownership of land, animals, and the devaluation of indigenous cultures possessing interdependent relationships with nature.

Utilitarianism prioritizes human interests above other entities, but this position also acknowledges the inherent value that nonhuman nature possesses. Nature is utilized as a resource for the benefit of and advancing human wellness, but in doing so, moral consideration is extended to consider how human actions impact the well-being of the natural environment and nonhuman organisms. Utilitarianism is closely related to environmental conservation, which refers to the protection and preservation of natural resources. For example, the Environmental Protection Agency (EPA) theoretically exists to manage or mitigate human impacts on ecosystems to ensure their sustainability.

Biocentric views on nature suggest that all living organisms possess intrinsic value and are worthy of protection, independent of their value or utility to the human species. Each individual living organism has worth and dignity, regardless of its sentience. An *ecocentric* perspective views all living beings and nonliving beings as part of an interconnected whole. It differs from biocentrism in that the moral consideration moves beyond an individual organism and extends to interconnected ecosystems and the earth as a whole. If one aspect of an ecosystem is impacted, all other aspects will also be impacted. Some indigenous perspectives, for example, suggest that all of nature is a living entity and that humans possess a reciprocal relationship with all beings.

A *scientific* lens on nature includes an analytical stance, one that seeks to deeply understand, objectify, and explain nature's patterns and phenomena in ways that can be studied and replicated. On one hand, the scientific method breaks nature down into component and isolated parts, but on the other, scientists examine the interconnections between different species within their ecosystems. A scientific lens can incorporate anthropocentric, utilitarian, biocentric, or ecocentric views, often depending on academic discipline and funding sources. For example, in counseling and psychotherapy, we most often prioritize human wellness within our counseling approaches on account of our ethical codes, with less emphasis on the broader wellness of the ecosystems that humans inhabit.

Nihilism is an increasingly important value for helping professionals to consider in the context of EcoWellness counseling. While a scientific lens might acknowledge the importance of and interconnectedness of humans with their surrounding environments, a nihilistic view would suggest that life, and nature more broadly, lacks inherent meaning or value. Instead, any values surrounding nature are subjective and humans lack moral responsibility to protect or conserve nature. By extension, EcoWellness is simply a subjective experience and lacks any fundamental or global value. A nihilistic view is critical to consider when addressing the environmental and climate crises with clients. The dissonance resulting from climate-manifested threats, disasters, and resulting solostalgia (i.e., distress resulting from climate change) may contribute to apathy or denial in clients. Additionally, some communities may question the value of protecting the broader natural environment if they perceive nature as lacking inherent or immediate personal value.

Aesthetic appreciation includes noticing nature's beauty with the assumption that nature possesses inherent value. This appreciation may contribute to a greater commitment to protecting or conserving the environment. Imagine the most beautiful, serene place you've ever witnessed, whether that be in person, in a mural, or on a screen. Spend a moment recalling this image or experience, and let your recollection fill your senses. What are you hearing? Seeing? Smelling? Touching? Tasting? Regardless of your background and positionality, or whether you possess predominantly utilitarian or eco-centric views of nature, I am guessing that something has come to mind for you, even if it took you a moment to access this place or experience.

One layer deeper than aesthetic appreciation includes *transcendentalism*. Abraham Maslow (1964) characterized nature's ability to provide humans with peak experiences wherein one can see with greater clarity their place in the broader world. Carl Jung (1968) believed nature was a key component in helping individuals find inner connection and purpose in life. Nature houses archetypes, universal symbols, and metaphors that transcend culture and reside within an ecological unconscious. Both scholars recognized the ability that natural environments might have to facilitate a greater sense of interconnectedness with all living things and the universe and help people reach their highest potential.

The last view on nature that we'll name here includes *bio-phobia*, which is having a fear or aversion to the natural world. Bio-phobia can be general, or it can be specific to nonhuman species or experiences in nature. For example, some people may have an aversion to snakes, spiders, or heights. Scholars have suggested that some bio-phobic experiences might be rooted in our species' evolution (Wilson, 1993), but bio-phobia can also be attributed to life experiences and intergenerational traumas.

These ethical attitudes toward nature point toward key differences in how diverse individuals or communities might discuss or experience EcoWellness, depending on one's worldview. A *hedonic* perspective on wellness prioritizes pleasure and seeks to minimize egocentric pain and suffering. Hedonic experiences provide us with instant pleasure or satisfaction with a focus on individual well-being. In this way, the dominant nature worldview discussed in the following section tends to encompass more anthropocentric or utilitarian values and might include outdoor recreation or time spent relaxing in nature. In contrast, *eudaimonia* emphasizes meaning, purpose, and growth. Wellness extends beyond the individual's need for gratification and spreads to the surrounding environment or ecosystem. Wellness is viewed across time, putting one on a journey of greater connectedness to self and others within their environmental context. Environmental stewardship is one example of eudemonic well-being.

The EcoWellness counseling framework we explore in Part III incorporates shades of nearly each of these different nature worldviews, as well as hedonic and eudemonic wellness. When we serve clients, we gather a holistic background on their identities, lived contexts, and life experiences to inform diagnosis (when relevant) and subsequent treatment planning. Similarly, each aspect of client positionality impacts the development of their nature worldview. Broader systems of power and privilege also have a tremendous impact on how our client communities view and experience the natural world relative to their wellness.

The Colonial Nature Worldview

The word *nature* means many things to many people, though in my experience, client populations and helping professionals in the United

States often conceptualize nature as being "out there" and distinct from our species and the built environment. By contrast, our human ancestors (and many indigenous groups across the world to this day) inhabited and lived in immediate proximity with all of nature. Within this ecocentric worldview, humans are part of an interdependent web with all the land, sea, and other-than-human entities; humanity shares a profound spiritual kinship and pragmatic reciprocity with all of nature. Indeed, our species evolved and adapted over millennia to be in deep connection with our earth home, and not until very recently in our species' industrial history have we experienced a radical split from the natural world.

European colonization efforts in the United States and beyond attempted to decimate indigenous peoples, their cultures, and the kinship nature worldview. In its place, western society asserted synthetic fabrication, economic progress, and *Homo sapiens'* dominance over land. Within such an illusionary separation, our world now faces dire circumstances as we confront human-caused climate change and environmental disaster. Much of our earth home is literally on fire at any given moment, with children, women, and people of color the most at risk and vulnerable to the climate and environmental crises (Intergovernmental Panel on Climate Change, 2023). But even with such knowledge and direct experience, western society seems powerless to move beyond our colonized histories. We continue to burn fossil fuels, produce plastic, and contaminate our oceans at an alarming pace. Internalized nature oppression, rooted in a colonial nature worldview and reinforced through capitalistic ideals, can lull us into adopting the belief that we are not part of nature or that nature belongs to the privileged few. Much of western culture remains ignorant of this succumbing as it helplessly consumes the products that personify the good, satiated life. The persisting dominant nature worldview is one of anthropocentric colonization: the land is a commodity to be conquered and exploited with the false promise that everyone can be happy so long as they can allocate the necessary resources.

This disingenuous assurance includes outdoor recreation. The outdoor products industry, for instance, regardless of its commitment to sustainability or broader values around conserving naturally occurring systems, seeks to monetize nature by selling products that make the exploitation of nature achievable, more comfortable, and enjoyable. Take my life passion of steelhead fishing as an example. This activity, and a host of others like mountain biking, kayaking, rafting, sailing, camping, and backpacking requires significant monetary investment. Thus, regardless of intent, accessing nature can appear as though it is intended only for those that have. Culturally, our perceptions of what it means to connect with nature (and who gets to connect with nature) can become limited to the white and affluent faces we see on commercials, social media, or what we encounter immediately inside or outside of our social circles, often at the exclusion of communities of color (Martin, 2004).

Carolyn Finney (2014) cogently highlighted the complex and white-washed relationship between conceptions of nature and mainstream environmentalism in the United States in her book, *Black Faces, White Spaces: Reimagining the Relationship of African Americans to the Great Out-doors*. She articulated how the country's historical roots in slavery and subsequent segregation continue to influence environmental policies and cultural perceptions of nature. In doing so, she shed light on the narra-tives and often adverse experiences of African Americans in relationship to the broader natural world and environmental movement. Research suggests that national parks cater to the behavioral guidelines of white, individualistic cultural norms (Byrne & Wolch, 2009), which may con-tribute to reduced use by black, Latinx, and lower-income populations (Xiao et al., 2022). When it comes to visiting national parks in the US, some communities of color report feeling out of place and unwelcome while also experiencing discrimination and fearing harassment (Byrne, 2012). As such, these natural spaces tend to be most frequently visited by white and economically advantaged populations (Xiao et al., 2018).

In her book, *Intersectional Environmentalism*, Leah Thomas (2022) forwards a framework for adopting socially just environmental policies and practices, promoting an inclusive approach to engaging marginalized groups within environmental efforts and further diversifying conceptions of the natural world. Increasingly, grassroots activists are developing out-door-based organizations (i.e., Outdoor Afro, LatinXhikers, Latino Out-doors, Brown Girls Climb, Unlikely Hikers, and The Venture Out Project) to empower marginalized communities to access the natural world and to do so in culturally empowering and sustaining ways. Similarly, the EcoW-ellness approach illuminated in this book seeks to empower clients to develop awareness and ownership of their unique relationship with the more than human world. Its application includes a stance of not knowing and implores clinicians to approach clients from a perspective of mutual empowerment and liberation. Such a methodology begins with an understanding of the diverse ways clients might view and value nature.

Case Comparisons: Nature Worldview Development in the Urban Context

This section presents comparative case studies of two different cisgender clients, both 35 years old from similar urban backgrounds in Philadelphia, Pennsylvania. The juxtaposition of their lived experiences and factors of positionality demonstrates the profound influence of socioeconomic status, gender, race, physical ability and disability, family values, and personal experiences on an individual's nature worldview. As you read on, I invite you to imagine how you might incorporate the more than human world when working with them while honoring their unique lived experiences and preferences.

Lauren

Lauren is a medical doctor, owns her two-bedroom condo, and has a car. She possesses the financial means to own outdoor recreational gear. Lauren can afford to pay for the gas (or electric charging) to travel to Macungie, a borough located about an hour and a half outside the city that includes recreational opportunities such as hiking and skiing. Paid time off enables her to take extended vacations for mental relaxation and rejuvenation. Lauren is African American and black. She reports that she grew up "working class." Her mother worked full-time at different restaurants throughout her youth, and her father worked in an oil refinery up until his death in her early 20s. Lauren's family rented a two-bedroom home just outside Philadelphia in a predominantly black neighborhood. She was responsible for getting her two younger brothers to and from school each day. She reports that her parents grew up poor, and they endured overt racism based on the color of their skin. They witnessed racial violence in their neighborhood, and her parents experienced multiple hate crimes. Lauren's parents implored her and her siblings to be cautious when walking to and from school and to never walk alone. Additionally, while there was a nearby park, she was not allowed to go there, except for special occasions with family and the broader community. Lauren cherished family birthdays at the park: sunny days with laughter, barbecues, songs, and community.

Lauren's family owned a car. She fondly recalls going camping each summer near Macungie. She remembers the trees, the colorful wildflowers, and playing in the water. Lauren's mother knew many of the names of the trees, the bugs, and the fish, something she admired and came to embody herself as she got older. Both her mother and father viewed nature as a vital resource and something that God gave them to cherish and nurture. Her family was often the only family of color at the campground. Lauren's parents adamantly instructed her and her brothers to stay near the campsite and not to wander far away, which limited her ability to independently explore the surrounding areas as a child. She watched the white children freely explore, why couldn't she?

As Lauren grew older, the annual camping trips continued. She developed a passion for cross-country running in middle and high school, and she came to enjoy trail running on her camping trips. Lauren recalled one significant and traumatic event that occurred when she was 17 that dampened this pursuit. She was running on a trail one late afternoon, and as she rounded the corner, a male-passing individual approached and beckoned her to stop. It quickly became apparent that the individual had ill intentions, and she began to run. The individual chased her, but she was much faster, returning to the family's campsite safe but terrified.

Lauren reports an interest to incorporate EcoWellness into counseling. She enjoys spending time in nature with others, including wilderness or ski trips, but she has not gone trail running or hiking since the time she was attacked. You ask Lauren about her immediate and nearby access to nature, and she indicates discomfort with going to the nearby park alone.

Edgar

Edgar rents a one-bedroom apartment in the city and struggles to make ends meet. He grew up in a single-parent home. Edgar does not have a car and relies on the city rail system for transit. At age 17, Edgar was diagnosed with a rare neurological condition, which affects his gait and makes it difficult to walk on uneven surfaces.

Edgar's parents moved to northeast Philadelphia from Russia when he was an infant. His father tragically passed away shortly after their arrival to the states. Edgar recalls being made fun of at school because of his "accent." He does not recall experiencing discrimination based on the color of his white skin or on account of his gender, though his parents fled Russia because of religious persecution. Edgar remembers his mother always working and not having time or money to take the family on trips or outings. She shared stories about her growing up in a beautiful part of her home country, and he recalled her disdain for the city. Edgar vividly remembers spending time at a nearby park while growing up. He and his siblings would walk and bike there throughout elementary school. He remembered finding snakes, insects, and other critters. He felt safe and comfortable at the park, with few exceptions. As Edgar got older, he would venture to that park on his own, particularly if he felt stressed. The park became a refuge. Edgar also recalls one time where he went to a three-day outdoor school event in middle school near Macungie. He and his classmates spent the night in cabins. That is where he remembers seeing a remote forest for the first time.

Edgar completed high school early through a special diploma program so he could find employment to help support the family. At one point, Edgar thought about pursuing a trade, but he recently had to take on a second job to absorb a significant increase in rent and out-of-pocket medical expenses related to his neurological condition.

While Edgar appreciates the beauty of nature, he does not access what he would consider to be nature with any frequency. He also doesn't feel particularly close with nature on an emotional level, but he is open to exploring this further in counseling. He can no longer easily access the park he used to frequent as a youth and visiting wilderness areas seems entirely out of reach. Besides, he contends, outdoor activities weren't designed for "people like me," referring to his neurological condition.

Case Integration

These cases highlight some of the complexity underlying the development of our nature worldviews and the critical importance of considering the intersecting factors of client positionality prior to engaging clients in nature-based interventions. Economic, gender, racial, and familial differences shaped Edgar's and Lauren's initial connections with the natural world, and subsequent life experiences further molded their outlooks on nature. For Edgar, pragmatic structural barriers such as financial constraints and lack of transportation may limit his present-day ability to engage with nearby and remote forms of nature. For Lauren, although economically positioned to access nature, the potential for re-traumatization in natural settings presents a significant challenge. Thus, nature worldview is not predicated on any one aspect of positionality. Instead, our clients' developing relationships with the natural world are housed within each stage of development, converging within their ever-changing lived and sociocultural contexts.

Conclusion

A person's nature worldview, shaped over their lifespan, is influenced by various factors, including the dominant colonized views of the natural world present in western culture. As such, the integration of nature into traditional clinical settings should be rooted in client positionality and the nuances of the client's relationship with the more than human world. Prior to incorporating an ecotherapeutic paradigm into treatment, it is imperative for clinicians to develop a keen awareness and understanding of client nature worldview and how their unique positionality and lived context shape conceptions of EcoWellness. Similarly, clinicians must maintain awareness of their own nature worldview and how it may impact the ways in which nature is assessed, discussed, and integrated into treatment. In Part II, we review the multidisciplinary research evidence and theory pointing toward the holistic wellness benefits of nature. EcoWellness is introduced as a client-centered and culturally sustaining framework for assessing and addressing the human–nature connection in counseling and psychotherapy.

Chapter 3 Reflection Questions

Self-awareness:

1. Reflect on your understanding of a "colonized nature worldview." How might this perspective influence your relationship with the natural environment and your professional practice?
2. Consider your own nature worldview. How has it been shaped by your cultural context, intersecting identities, and positionality?

3. Identify any personal biases you might have regarding the natural world. How can recognizing and addressing these biases improve your effectiveness as a clinician?

Knowledge:

4. What are the key characteristics of a colonized nature worldview as discussed in this chapter? How does it contrast with other nature worldviews?
5. Explore how a more inclusive approach to nature worldview can benefit the therapeutic process. What are some potential outcomes?

Application:

6. How can counselors use their understanding of diverse nature worldviews to enhance the assessment and incorporation of the more than human world in counseling and psychotherapy?
7. What strategies can be employed to challenge and transform colonized nature worldviews in therapeutic settings?
8. Given the different nature worldviews and life experiences of Lauren and Edgar, how would you tailor ecotherapeutic interventions to meet each of their unique needs? Discuss specific strategies that would respect and utilize their distinct relationships with the natural world.

References

Byrne, J. (2012). When green is white: The cultural politics of race, nature and social exclusion in a Los Angeles urban national park. *Geoforum, 43*(3), 595–611. https://doi.org/10.1016/j.geoforum.2011.10.002

Byrne, J., & Wolch, J. (2009). Nature, race, and parks: Past research and future directions for geographic research. *Progress in Human Geography, 33*(6), 743–765. https://doi.org/10.1177/0309132509103156

Elder, G. H., Johnson, M. K., & Crosnoe, R. (2003). The emergence and development of life course theory. In J. T. Mortimer & M. J. Shanahan (Eds.), *Handbook of the life course* (pp. 3–19). Springer. https://doi.org/10.1007/978-0-306-48247-2_1

Finney, C. (2014). *Black faces, white spaces: Reimagining the relationship of African Americans to the great outdoors.* The University of North Carolina Press.

IPCC. (2023). Sections. In Core Writing Team, H. Lee, & J. Romero (Eds.), *Climate change 2023: Synthesis report. Contribution of working groups I, II and III to the sixth assessment report of the intergovernmental panel on climate change* (pp. 35–115). IPCC. https://doi.org/10.59327/IPCC/AR6-9789291691647

Jung, C. G. (1968). *The archetypes and the collective unconscious* (2nd ed.). Routledge & Kegan Paul.

Martin, D. C. (2004). Apartheid in the great outdoors: American advertising and the reproduction of a racialized outdoor leisure identity. *Journal of Leisure Research*, *36*(4), 513–535. https://doi.org/10.1080/00222216.2004.11950034

Maslow, A. H. (1964). *Religions, values, and peak-experiences.* Ohio State University Press.

Ratts, M. J., Singh, A. A., Nassar-McMillan, S., Butler, S. K., & McCullough, J. R. (2016). Multicultural and social justice counseling competencies: Guidelines for the counseling profession. *Journal of Multicultural Counseling and Development*, *44*(1), 28–48. https://doi.org/10.1002/jmcd.12035

Shultz, P. W. (2002). Inclusion with nature: The psychology of human-nature relations. In P. Schmuck & W. P. Schultz (Eds.), *Psychology of sustainable development* (pp. 61–78). Kluwer Academic Publishers. https://doi.org/10.1007/978-1-4615-0995-0_4

Thomas, L. (2022). *The intersectional environmentalist: How to dismantle systems of oppression to protect people + planet.* Voracious, Little, Brown, and Company.

Wilson, E. O. (1993). Biophilia and the conservation ethic. In S. R. Kellert & E. O. Wilson (Eds.), *The biophilia hypothesis.* Island Press.

Xiao, X., Lee, K. J., & Larson, L. R. (2022). Who visits US national parks (and who doesn't)? A national study of perceived constraints and vacation preferences across diverse populations. *Journal of Leisure Research*, *53*(3), 404–425. https://doi.org/10.1080/00222216.2021.1899776

Xiao, X., Manning, R., Perry, E., & Valliere, W. (2018). Public awareness of and visitation to national parks by racial/ethnic minorities. *Society & Natural Resources*, *31*(8), 908–924. https://doi.org/10.1080/08941920.2018.1448914

PART II
EMPIRICAL AND CONCEPTUAL FOUNDATIONS OF ECOWELLNESS

4

HOLISTIC WELLNESS AND NATURE

A REVIEW OF THE MULTIDISCIPLINARY LITERATURE

Casey, a 26-year-old black and nonbinary client, had been experiencing noticeable auditory hallucinations since age 14. They seldom left their apartment, except for attending our scheduled counseling sessions and other medical appointments. Casey's mother recalled the first time she heard them talking to one of the voices. It seemed Casey had been having an argument with someone on the phone in their room, but when she walked by, Casey would be staring into space engaged in one-way dialogue. Casey recalled being surprised that their mom couldn't hear the voices—they were clear as day. By their late teens, the voices visited Casey with greater frequency and became more intrusive, bordering on violent. The family initially thought that Casey may have been possessed by an evil force, but the family's faith community encouraged them to seek out mental health treatment.

Once the scary voices fully set in, Casey's life drastically changed. One voice, who Casey named "Larry," was primarily present during Casey's waking hours, but sometimes, Larry would wake them up. Larry demanded that Casey cut their body. Self-harming behaviors and emerging suicidal ideation contributed to multiple ER visits and one hospitalization. Casey had been prescribed Risperdal, an antipsychotic, to help reduce the auditory hallucinations. The drug had been effective, overall,

DOI: 10.4324/9781315697437-7

but Casey experienced significant weight gain, affecting their body image, depression, and Casey's desire to engage others socially.

Casey had just moved out of their family home and into an apartment when they began seeing me. Casey's mom was hoping that we could address depressive symptoms, independent living skills, and social anxiety, though Casey was initially ambivalent about coming to therapy. During our first session, I asked Casey about their safe access to nearby green spaces and favorite places. Casey didn't recall having much nearby nature, but they mentioned having a cat. Casey revealed that their one-bedroom apartment had a small porch space that faced a sidewalk, some grass, and a few trees. However, Casey feared accessing the porch because people using the sidewalk might see them. "There's no chance in hell I will go out there," Casey avowed.

I initially didn't spend much time prompting Casey about their connectedness with and access to nature. Over time, however, we began to explore possible strategies for stress management and helping Casey find ways of going to sleep at night. Marijuana had been utilized as a primary pathway to coping, but lately, Casey experienced amplified paranoia after their use. Of course, my mind went to nature. "Have you ever tried listening to nature sounds while going to sleep?" I asked.

"Nature what?" Casey responded.

I pulled up YouTube on my laptop and searched "nature sounds." We spent the remainder of the session exploring rain sounds, ocean waves, birds chirping, waterfalls, creeks, rivers, and nighttime sounds, including frogs croaking, crickets chirping, and cicadas humming. Casey particularly liked water sounds and indicated that they would try listening to them between now and the next session.

"The nature sounds helped!" Casey excitedly reported at our next appointment. Casey expanded upon the different sounds they listened to in the past week, and the ways in which they helped them feel more relaxed before bed and at other times throughout the day. This led to a conversation about the science underlying the possible wellness effects that people can experience through contact with nature, which deeply fascinated Casey.

Casey's initial skepticism about nature's utility in contributing to their own wellness gave way to curiosity and intrigue. Nature sounds opened the door to the immediate experience of EcoWellness for Casey, in part because of the direct calming effects they experienced, and in part because of the fascinating science underlying the effects that nature has on human health and wellness.

While Casey's story is unique to their positionality and context, the multidisciplinary research demonstrates considerable potential for the natural world to have positive effects on our species. The ecopsychology movement at the turn of the 21st century awakened a plethora of multi-disciplinary research examining the human–nature connection relative to human health and wellness, including the development of several theories attempting to explain *how* nature positively impacts wellness. In 2010, when I first started seriously exploring this peer-reviewed literature, it was somewhat manageable to keep track of the published research. Since that time, the scholarship has skyrocketed. In this chapter, we further lay the groundwork for the development of EcoWellness by reviewing the human-wellness research and the associated theory.

Defining Nature and Wellness

Before surveying the literature, let's just briefly clarify a few terms, based on how they are often operationalized in the research. In the studies I directly cite or allude to in this chapter, nature has predominantly been defined as something other than humankind, inclusive of green spaces, blue spaces (e.g., the ocean or freshwater streams), or a combination. Frequently, nature definitions include urban forms of nature, such as neighboring trees or plants, or in the form of parks. In some of the literature I reference, nature encapsulates wilderness settings or unbuilt environments, where humans have had limited influence on the landscape. Nature is also conceptualized as "nature connectedness," the degree to which an individual affectively connects with the natural world. Additional research has examined technological forms and sensory forms of nature, including nature sounds, images of nature on a computer screen, virtual reality environments, and aromatherapies.

In this book, I conceptualize wellness as the integration of mind, body, and spirit, inclusive of all health domains. In the discussion of the wellness research in this chapter, we'll predominantly reference specific domains of wellness, conceptualized as health. For our purposes, I'll classify the health effects of the nature literature into four areas: physical health, cognitive health, mental and emotional health, and transcendence.

Physical Health

In his seminal study, Roger S. Ulrich (1984) examined the records of 46 patients who underwent gallbladder surgery at a hospital. He was curious how a window view of nature might affect patient stay, nurse observations, and medication consumption. Half of the sample had a view of a brick wall outside their window during recovery and half of the sample had a view of a natural scene that included deciduous trees. Patients with a nature view experienced significantly shorter hospital stays, took fewer pain medications, and reported fewer complaints to nurses (e.g., reduced anxiety and pain). Ulrich's study was one of the first to find that viewing natural landscapes might positively impact physical health outcomes.

Ulrich developed evolutionary stress reduction theory (SRT) to explain nature's ability to elicit an unconscious emotional response within humans, thus bearing a significant influence on physiological response and stress reduction. He hypothesized that vegetative elements such as trees, gardens, and other plants and natural settings including "calm or slowly moving water, verdant vegetation, flowers, savanna-like or park-like properties" can have stress reducing properties (Ulrich, 2008, p. 90). He contended,

> For individuals experiencing stress or anxiety, most unthreatening natural views may be more arousal reducing and tend to elicit more positively toned emotional reactions than the vast majority of urban scenes, and hence are more restorative in a psychophysiological sense.
>
> (Ulrich, 1983, p. 116)

Forty years later, researchers have not only corroborated Ulrich's findings and theory, but they've also built upon them in significant ways. Time spent in nature can reduce blood pressure and heart rate (Kondo et al., 2018), pulse rate (Li et al., 2016), and reduce the stress response measured via salivary cortisol (Hunter et al., 2019). Residential proximity to green spaces and parks has been associated with decreased childhood obesity and sedentary behaviors (Dadvand et al., 2014) and may reduce the risk of respiratory health issues across the lifespan (Jimenez et al., 2021). Additionally, activities that include frequent interaction with the soil (i.e., gardening) may help to improve immune response on account of the natural elements present in soil bacteria (Mills et al., 2017). Short-term sunlight exposure (i.e., 15–20 minutes) has also been associated with vitamin D production (Akpınar et al., 2022), a nutrient critical to immune function, mood regulation, and bone health. Daytime sunlight helps regulate circadian rhythm, which in turn may positively contribute to sleep and mood regulation (Burns et al., 2021). As we know, physical activity can also play a critical role in cardiovascular and immune function and reduce the risk for chronic disease, and these effects seem greater when exercise occurs within natural settings (Brito et al., 2021).

Without our conscious awareness, nature holds the potential to significantly and positively impact physical health. Collectively, the research supporting SRT underscores the utility of nature in preventing immune, respiratory, cardiovascular, and stress-related illnesses. Similarly, nature can positively and unconsciously affect cognitive health.

Cognitive Health

In 1989, Stephen and Rachel Kaplan proposed Attention Restoration Theory (ART). They theorized that exposure to nature has significant potential to restore psychological attention (i.e., concentration or mental fatigue) via effortless fascination with nature. Viewing natural landscapes or immersion in nature engages one's effortless or "soft" fascination, thereby restoring focus and concentration. Much like Ulrich contended, they believed that the attention restoration process occurs involuntarily and demands minimal effort or energy. They contrasted soft fascination with "hard" fascination, defined as the directed attention placed toward activities or tasks requiring full attention and effort to maintain concentration (e.g., staring at a computer or smart phone screen for long periods of time). To be restorative, they believed environments must include four features: fascination, a sense of being away, extent, and compatibility.

Soft fascination tends to occur without effort in the presence of natural stimuli. Being away encompasses what it sounds like: a "change in one's thoughts from the pressures and obligations of everyday life"

(Scopelliti & Giuliani, 2004, p. 424). One doesn't necessarily need to be hours away from their home, but they do need to perceive being away from their typical environment. Extent refers to the perceived vastness and richness of the environment and how its different elements interconnect. If an environment has much to explore, it may invoke further motivation to discover the elements therein. Thus, extent prompts a sense of fascination within nature, which enables the ability of nature to capture one's attention involuntarily. Lastly, compatibility is the perceived fit between an environment's attributes and the individual's purposes for immersing within a particular setting.

Much of the excitement surrounding contact with green spaces has resulted from literature suggesting that access to nature may serve as a protective factor in children developing attention deficit hyperactivity disorder (ADHD; Donovan et al., 2019). Andrea Faber Taylor and Frances E. Kuo (2009, 2011) published several small-scale studies contributing to pediatricians and family doctors encouraging families to spend more time in parklike settings. In one correlational study, they found that children playing in green settings experienced milder symptoms of ADHD as compared to children playing in indoor environments (controlling for both gender and income status). In a convenience sample of 17 children who met criteria for ADHD, they used a quasi-experimental design in investigating the effects of three different settings, including a park, downtown area, and neighborhood. The participants completed several attentional measures, including the Digit Span Backwards test, which instructs the participant to listen to a sequence of numbers, two to eight digits in length, and repeat the sequence in reverse. They found that children diagnosed with ADHD concentrated significantly better after a walk in the park than either the downtown or neighborhood walks.

The enthusiasm of ADHD research should be tempered, however. More recently, researchers employing a similar design have not identified the same effect of nature on reducing ADHD symptoms (Stevenson et al., 2021). Instead, they found that medication helped mitigate ADHD symptoms and there was no effect from the environment. Thus, more substantive research is needed to determine the extent to which green spaces might serve as a legitimate prescription to address ADHD symptomology in children.

Research with adult populations has demonstrated similar results on focus and concentration, providing additional support for ART. Scholars in one study examined the effects of nature on cognitive performance tasks and demonstrated that undergraduate students with a view of nature performed better than participants without a nature view (Tennessen & Cimprich, 1995). In two separate studies, Berman and colleagues (2008) explored the effects of nature on several different attentional tasks. In the first study, they compared the cognitive benefits of a 50-minute walk in a downtown arboretum or in a downtown urban setting. In experiment two, they assigned participants to view pictures of natural images or images of cities. Participants across both experiments first engaged in attention-depleting tasks. Participants then received the urban or nature conditions. In both experiments, the study authors found that the nature conditions improved directed attention abilities.

As with SRT, ART and its coinciding research provide both compelling evidence and a convincing argument for how nature positively impacts cognitive health. In my evaluation, these two theories have the most convincing evidence in the peer-reviewed scientific literature. In addition to the physical and cognitive benefits of nature, these theories are often discussed as possible theoretical mechanisms underlying the positive mental and emotional outcomes.

Mental and Emotional Health

In non-applied settings, scholars frequently measure the mental and emotional health effects of nature using survey designs. Arola and colleagues (2023) conducted a systematic literature review spanning two decades on the impacts of nature connectedness on children's well-being. The reviewed studies included the exploration of nearby nature, murals in hospitals, and blue spaces. Findings pointed toward the experiences of reduced stress, decreased anger and depression, enhanced feelings of happiness, mindfulness and spiritualty, and perceptions of self-efficacy, self-esteem, and emotional well-being. The authors concluded that there is a clear and often positive relationship between nature connectedness and various indicators of mental health. Similarly, meta-analytic studies in adult participants have demonstrated that connectedness with nature positively impacts perceptions of both mental and emotional health (Capaldi et al., 2014; Pritchard et al., 2020).

While SRT and ART are often used to explain the mental and emotional benefits of nature, place attachment might also serve as a complementary theoretical explanation. Attachment forms from early bonds between the caregiver–child relationship, thus influencing early mental images of self and others. Such representations assist in the interpretation of social stimuli that serve as a foundation for the individual's expectations and experiences in future relationships (Bowlby, 1982). In my clinical experience, I've found that early, sustained, and positive experiences with nature are critical in fostering client connectedness to nature as they progress through life. Such contact seems to enhance motivation to spend time with nature, care for nature, and contribute to perceptions of mastery over nature-based skills. Having a primary caregiver who valued and prioritized time in nature can also play a critical role in fostering nature connectedness. Clients with consistent childhood access and positive memories with nature are more prone to developing an emotional attachment to the natural world. Participating in nature-based activities and viewing nature as part of one's identity may become part of a schema or mental framework for stress management, lifestyle, and coping. In one retrospective analysis, Wells and Lekies (2006) found that childhood activities in nature were associated with the development of pro-environmental attitudes as adults. Specifically, time spent in wilderness settings prior to the age of 11 increased the likelihood of pro-environmental beliefs amongst adults, possibly because such experiences influenced the incorporation of nature within self-concept.

Place attachment theorists posit that health benefits occur through an emotional bond or attachment with the natural places in which people reside and visit (Hernandez et al., 2007; Mazumdar, 2005). Williams and colleagues (1992) described the "functional meaning of a place as the tendency to see the environment as a collection of attributes that permit the pursuit of a focal activity" (p. 31). Similarly, attachment to place (or place attachment) is the emotional bond that takes place between person and environment (Mazumdar, 2005). Hernandez and colleagues defined it as the "affective link that people establish with specific settings, where they tend to remain and where they feel comfortable and safe" (p. 310).

I find the conceptualization of place attachment offered by Ramkissoon et al. (2012) to be particularly useful. They described place attachment as a combination of place identity, place dependence, place affect, and place social bonding. Place identity includes the processes underlying conscious and unconscious identification one experiences with a physical environment. Place dependence is the functional attachment between the individual and the specific place or the bond established between the person and the physical characteristics of the place. Place affect is the emotional bond individuals experience with different settings, and place social bonding is the tendency for people to become emotionally attached to settings where they experience interpersonal relationships and belongingness.

While SRT and ART suggest the unconscious influences of nature on indicators of health, place attachment implies that one's propensity to benefit from nature may be rooted within developmental contexts that likely progress through the lifespan. The nature connectedness research suggests that those who feel more connected with nature tend to report greater mental and emotional health. Said another way: clients less connected with nature may experience reduced emotional and mental health. Seeing oneself within nature, having the ability and confidence to traverse nature, emotionally attuning with nature, and experiencing belongingness in nature may be critical in facilitating positive mental frameworks and coinciding emotional experiences with the natural world.

Transcendent Health

Nature also offers an avenue for self-transcendence and the potential for developing a greater sense of kinship with other entities. Themes of social connectedness span the nature–wellness literature, whether researchers investigated the effects of community gardens on wellness, reduced incidences of violence in urban settings, the ability of virtual reality environments to invoke selflessness, nature-based group interventions (i.e., wilderness therapy), or quasi-experimental studies. Similarly, spiritual enhancement is consistently discussed as a primary motivation to access the natural world and a key outcome when studying the wellness effects of nature.

One of my favorite studies on nature and social connectedness was orchestrated by Netta Weinstein and her colleagues in 2009. They conducted four studies in researching the effects of nature on intrinsic and extrinsic value aspirations. The researchers randomly assigned participants to a nature condition (i.e., pictures of natural landscapes in the first three studies or a room with four plants in the fourth study), or to a non-nature condition (i.e., pictures of urban environments in the first three studies or a room without the four plants in the fourth study). Participants in the nature conditions self-reported higher intrinsic value aspirations that focused on relationship and community wellness and demonstrated lower value aspirations placed on extrinsic values (i.e., fame and money). In one of the studies, researchers instructed participants to distribute a $5 prize however they preferred (e.g., they could keep the money or give it to a fellow research participant). Interestingly, participants in the nature condition evidenced greater generosity than those in the non-nature condition. The researchers concluded: "Together these findings suggest that full contact with nature can have humanizing effects, fostering greater authenticity and connectedness and, in turn, other versus self-orientations that enhance valuing of and generosity toward others" (p. 1328).

When I discuss the nature–wellness literature with clients, students, and consultees, the aspect of the more than human nature connection that seems the most apparent is nature's ability to evoke conceptions of spirituality. Cross-culturally, people tend to experience a sense of closeness to their individual, community, and ancestral life guiding beliefs and values in or near revered natural places. Individuals transcend the self and experience kinship and cultural meaning when interacting with specific landscapes or species of nature. Robin Wall Kimmerer's (2013) beloved *Braiding Sweetgrass* brilliantly and beautifully weaved together indigenous wisdom, scientific knowledge, and her own personal reflections about the relationship between humanity and nature. Throughout Kimmerer's memoir, she describes sweetgrass (and other nonhuman entities) as having specific cultural significance and meaning. She argues that the degradation of nature can translate into the elimination of shared meaning and collective purpose. Thus, developing not only an affinity for nature but taking action to protect it might serve as an important aspect of spiritual connectedness.

Miles Richardson (2022), a scholar at the University of Derby, found that intentional interactions with nature, and not just exposure, may be critical to facilitating both connectedness with and caring for nature. Within a UK sample, he and colleagues (Martin et al., 2020) investigated three different types of nature contact on nature connectedness, health, subjective well-being, and environmental behaviors. Living in a "greener" neighborhood was not associated with well-being or sustainability. Rather, a visit to nature at least once a week was associated with general health and an increase in pro-environmental behaviors. Barragan-Jason and colleagues (2023) conducted a systematic review of 16 meta-analyses that included a total of 832 studies. Across them, connection with nature was associated with enhanced human cognition, social skills, psychology, and mental health. Psychological connectedness with nature also had a significant and positive impact on environmental attitudes and behaviors.

Nature's tendency to invoke self-transcendence in the form of caring for others and nonhuman nature is often discussed within transpersonal and depth psychology. Transpersonal psychology is "concerned with the study of humanity's highest potential, and with the recognition, understanding, and realization of unitive, spiritual, and transcendent states of consciousness" (Lajoie & Shapiro, 1992, p. 79). In the 1960s and 70s, "peak experiences" with nature were popularized with the purposes of expanding the self and helping one reach their highest potential. Abraham Maslow (1971) believed peak experiences could bring about deep feelings of interconnectedness and unity with all things. Jung suggested that the collective unconscious includes archetypes such as instincts, behavior, emotion, and imagery (Schroeder, 1992). Embedded in humanity's collective history, he believed that such archetypes passed on to each generation and emerge within interpersonal interactions and the world more broadly through projection, thought to inspire deep feelings of interconnectedness with all living beings. Relatedly, Roszak's (1992) initial conception of ecopsychology included the notion of the ecological unconscious, rooted in psychoanalytic theory. Roszak likened the ecological unconscious to the id in psychoanalytic theory, wherein the id played a primary role in selecting instincts and traits that helped humans to adapt to their surroundings. He contended, however, that the id is not solely driven by pleasure but instead enacts itself through inherent knowledge about and connectedness with nature. Interaction between the ecological unconscious and our conscious selves fosters the ecological ego, wherein people view themselves and their health as part of an inter-dependent whole with the natural world.

To date, transpersonal and depth psychology have been difficult to operationalize in the nature–wellness research. They face similar challenges as the biophilia hypothesis: they aren't readily testable using quantitative designs. A not-so-distant construct in the literature includes non-ordinary states of consciousness (NOSC). NOSC experiences include forms of awareness differing from our typical waking moments, such as altered sensory perception. NOSC are thought to be a primary driver of change within the psychedelic therapies. For instance, ingesting magic mushrooms, fungi containing psilocybin, has been shown to amplify the visual and auditory cortices while quieting what is referred to as the default mode network, a web of brain regions responsible for activities like self-reflection, mind-wandering, and rumination. Quieting this typically active network is thought to contribute to a temporary shift in consciousness that facilitates greater openness, interconnection, and introspection. During such experiences, certain emotions might be amplified while others might be less pronounced; our ways of thinking can become less rigid. This theoretical process isn't far different from what has been identified within the nature–wellness literature. In one fascinating study, Gregory Bratman and colleagues (2015) investigated the effects of a 90-minute walk in nature in comparison to the same walk in an urban area. The researchers found that those who walked in the natural setting reported reduced levels of negative thinking and demonstrated lower neural activity in the subgenual prefrontal cortex, an area of the brain associated with rumination.

Moreover, forms of nature immersion focusing on mindfulness, such as shinrin-yoku, bring us into greater contact with the colors, shapes, sounds, tastes, and physical sensations of the immediate environment. Our perceptions of time, our cognitions, and our emotions can shift. Boundaries between the self and nature blur, and we feel like we are part of an interconnected whole. Mindfulness, an application of NOSC, includes purposefully attending to the present moment and doing so without judgment. For example, focusing on one's breath, noticing when the mind wanders, and gently returning the focus back to the breath. Research demonstrates a strong and significant relationship between conceptions of nature connectedness and mindfulness. Schutte and Malouff (2018) conducted a meta-analysis including 12 studies that focused on mindfulness and connectedness with nature. They found a moderate and significant relationship between mindfulness and nature connectedness, suggesting that these concepts are highly related. Other researchers (e.g., Barbaro & Pickett, 2016) have found that people who are mindfully observant of their surroundings are also more connected with their surroundings, which might in turn positively impact environmental stewardship. Thus, those who are more mindful seem to experience greater connectedness to nature, and those who are more connected with nature tend to be more mindful.

In my clinical experience, I notice that clients often engage in therapy with greater openness, curiosity, and self-compassion when counseling sessions occur in natural settings. In nature, we tend toward thinking about life's challenges in novel and creative ways; there's often greater openness and decreased guardedness. By contrast, I haven't noticed this same shift in consciousness when walking with clients in urban settings with limited nearby vegetation. Such observations are consistent with the literature.

Is it conceivable that nature elicits NOSC? I certainly think so. Indirect research seems to support the NOSC hypothesis as a possible pathway for nature's transcendent effects on human consciousness. Nature contact contributes to expanding our vision beyond ourselves and experiencing enhanced interconnectedness, including greater generosity, social cohesion, and feeling small and big at the same time as we reflect on our individual places in this world. Nevertheless, while potentially promising, additional research is needed that directly tests the NOSC hypothesis, particularly studies investigating how different regions of the brain respond to nature-based experiences.

Summary of the Nature–Wellness Literature

The natural world has compelling effects on human health and wellness. Our species adapted alongside all other aspects of nature, and only in our recent history have we experienced advancements in technology enabling us to disembody ourselves from the more than human world. Scholars and practitioners often describe the biophilia hypothesis and ecological unconscious as contributing to humanity's connectedness and need for nature. However, these concepts are challenged within reductionistic, scientific paradigms necessitating theory to be falsifiable.

The theories discussed in this chapter, particularly stress reduction theory and attention restoration theory, have been widely grounded in the literature. Nature seems to provide unconscious relief from stress and mental fatigue through psychophysiological mechanisms enacting both stress reduction and attention restoration. Connectedness with nature might be facilitated through the development of place attachment, suggesting the potential importance of fostering positive and consistent nature encounters early in human development so that affinity toward nature might continue to flourish from childhood to adulthood. An additional pathway for experiencing the benefits of nature might occur through nature's ability to provoke NOSC, though further empirical inquiry is needed to examine this possible theoretical mechanism. Regardless, compelling evidence points toward nature's profound capacity for impacting human physical, cognitive, mental, emotional, and transcendent health, enhancing compassion toward self and others while facilitating a greater sense of interconnectedness with other living and nonliving entities.

Implications for Counseling and Therapy

Despite the positive trajectory of the nature–wellness scholarship, clinicians must be cautious not to overextend findings from non-applied research. In Chapter 1, I implored a similar level of caution when considering possible applications of ecotherapy in licensed clinical settings. Much of the multidisciplinary research has not been experimental or quasi-experimental in design, and many of the studies I cited utilized correlational methods, which do not imply causality. Additionally, this literature often lacks finesse in parsing out the wellness effects of nature based on client identities, life histories, and cultural context (i.e., positionality). In highlighting this limitation I'm not suggesting that this research is poorly constructed. Rather, I'm emphasizing how difficult it can be to isolate variables within the vastness of nature while also trying to assess the limitlessness of human wellness.

As we round out this chapter, let's return to Casey. Casey benefited from incorporating nature sounds into their bedtime routines. We also identified ways of applying mindful interaction with their cat, wherein

Casey focused on the physical sensations of touching the cat's fur and listening to it purr. Over time, their fear around accessing outdoor spaces near their home began softening. I recall the first session when we headed outdoors and walked the short block around the office. Casey slowed as they approached a large willow oak tree, in admiration. "I wonder how old it is," Casey pondered. They inhaled deeply, eager to absorb the tree's essence. Casey picked up a leaf, exploring its veins with their eyes and fingers and then raising it to their nostrils. We stood there for several minutes, during which a handful of pedestrians passed by. I marveled at Casey's nonresponse to seeing other people. Intuiting what I was about to reflect outward in that moment, Casey smiled and said, "I never thought I could do what we are doing right now."

As our counseling relationship concluded, Casey's depressive symptoms reduced, and the self-harming behaviors subsided. Accessing nearby green spaces and developing a plan for purposeful connection with nearby nature significantly contributed to Casey's wellness. We had curated a daily routine for accessing nature that brought about tranquility, peace, and wholeness. Nature sounds permeated their bedtime routine, mindfulness enhanced the relationship with their furry feline, and courage enabled Casey to sit on their apartment porch to breathe fresh air each day.

Conclusion

The voluminous research and theory reviewed in this chapter suggest that the more than human world positively impacts just about every domain of human wellness, including both hedonic (e.g., increases in pleasant emotions and reductions in stress) and eudemonic (e.g., facilitating purpose, care for others and nature) well-being. While the EcoWellness framework emerged from this literature base, we have the most to learn about nature from our clients. Clinicians partner with their clients in identifying where and how addressing EcoWellness may serve the client's broader treatment goals. Casey educated me about what nature was and meant to them, and jointly, we collaboratively developed ways of incorporating their connection with the natural world to promote optimal wellness. In Chapter 5, we delve into the foundations of EcoWellness. By exploring its development and examining its underlying constructs,

I aim to provide a holistic understanding of how EcoWellness aligns with the established wellness models in the field of professional counseling. This exploration lays the groundwork for the practical applications and EcoWellness-based interventions examined in Part III.

Chapter 4 Reflection Questions

Self-awareness:

1. In what ways has this chapter influenced your personal or professional perspectives on the role of nature in wellness, if at all?
2. Reflect on a study discussed in the chapter that particularly resonated with you. What implications does it have for your clinical practice and setting(s)?

Knowledge:

3. How do the definitions of nature and wellness discussed in this chapter influence our understanding of their relationship in therapy?
4. How might you incorporate literature-based strategies to promote self-transcendence in your therapeutic setting(s)?
5. What might be some of the considerations and possible limitations when applying non-applied research findings to clinical practice?

Application:

6. What skills are necessary for counselors and psychotherapists to effectively integrate the discussed multidisciplinary literature into applied practice?
7. How can clinicians assess the impact of nature on cognitive and emotional wellness in their clients?
8. Consider the role of physical health in your current or future practice. How might the insights from the nature-related studies enhance your approach?

References

Akpınar, Ş., & Karadağ, M. G. (2022). Is vitamin D important in anxiety or depression? What is the truth? *Current Nutrition Reports*, *11*(4), 675–681. https://doi.org/10.1007/s13668-022-00441-0

Arola, T., Aulake, M., Ott, A., Lindholm, M., Kouvonen, P., Virtanen, P., & Paloniemi, R. (2023). The impacts of nature connectedness on children's well-being: Systematic literature review. *Journal of Environmental Psychology*, *85*, 101913. https://doi.org/10.1016/j.jenvp.2022.101913

Barbaro, N., & Pickett, S. M. (2016). Mindfully green: Examining the effect of connectedness to nature on the relationship between mindfulness and engagement in pro-environmental behavior. *Personality and Individual Differences*, *93*, 137–142. https://doi.org/10.1016/j.paid.2015.05.026

Barragan-Jason, G., Loreau, M., de Mazancourt, C., Singer, M. C., & Parmesan, C. (2023). Psychological and physical connections with nature improve both human well-being and nature conservation: A systematic review of meta-analyses. *Biological Conservation*, *277*, 109842. https://doi.org/10.1016/j.biocon.2022.109842

Berman, M. G., Jonides, J., & Kaplan, S. (2008). The cognitive benefits of interacting with nature. *Psychological Science*, *19*(12), 1207–1212. https://doi.org/10.1111/j.1467-9280.2008.02225.x

Bowlby, J. (1982). *Attachment and loss: Separation-anxiety and anger* (Vol. 2). Basic Books.

Bratman, G. N., Hamilton, J. P., Hahn, K. S., Daily, G. C., & Gross, J. J. (2015). Nature experience reduces rumination and subgenual prefrontal cortex activation. *Proceedings of the National Academy of Sciences*, *112*(28), 8567–8572. https://doi.org/10.1073/pnas.1510459112

Brito, H. S., Carraca, E. V., Palmeira, A. L., Ferreira, J. P., Vleck, V., & Araujo, D. (2021). Benefits to performance and well-being of nature-based exercise: A critical systematic review and meta-analysis. *Environmental Science & Technology*, *56*(1), 62–77. https://doi.org/10.1021/acs.est.1c05151

Burns, A. C., Saxena, R., Vetter, C., Phillips, A. J., Lane, J. M., & Cain, S. W. (2021). Time spent in outdoor light is associated with mood, sleep, and circadian rhythm-related outcomes: A cross-sectional and longitudinal study in over 400,000 UK biobank participants. *Journal of Affective Disorders*, *295*, 347–352. https://doi.org/10.1016/j.jad.2021.08.056

Capaldi, C. A., Dopko, R. L., & Zelenski, J. M. (2014). The relationship between nature connectedness and happiness: A meta-analysis. *Frontiers in Psychology*, *5*, 976. https://doi.org/10.3389/fpsyg.2014.00976

Dadvand, P., Villanueva, C. M., Font-Ribera, L., Martinez, D., Basagaña, X., Belmonte, J., Vrijheid, M., Gražulevičienė, R., Kogevinas, M., & Nieuwenhuijsen, M. J. (2014). Risks and benefits of green spaces for children: A cross-sectional study of associations with sedentary behavior, obesity, asthma, and allergy. *Environmental Health Perspectives*, *122*(12), 1329–1335. https://doi.org/10.1289/ehp.1308038

Donovan, G. H., Michael, Y. L., Gatziolis, D., Mannetje, A. T., & Douwes, J. (2019). Association between exposure to the natural environment, rurality, and attention-deficit hyperactivity disorder in children in New Zealand: A linkage study. *The Lancet Planetary Health*, *3*(5), e226–e234. https://doi.org/10.1016/S2542-5196(19)30070-1

Faber Taylor, A., & Kuo, F. E. (2009). Children with attention deficits concentrate better after walk in the park. *Journal of Attention Disorders*, *12*(5), 402–409. https://doi.org/10.1177/1087054708323000

Faber Taylor, A., & Kuo, F. E. (2011). Could exposure to everyday green spaces help treat ADHD? Evidence from children's play settings. *Applied Psychology: Health and Well-Being*, *3*(3), 281–303. https://doi.org/10.1111/j.1758-0854.2011.01052.x

Hernandez, B., Hidalgo, M. C., Salazar-Laplace, M. E., & Hess, S. (2007). Place attachment and place identity in natives and non-natives. *Journal of Environmental Psychology*, *27*, 310–319. https://doi.org/10.1016/j.jenvp.2007.06.003

Hunter, M. R., Gillespie, B. W., & Chen, S. Y. P. (2019). Urban nature experiences reduce stress in the context of daily life based on salivary biomarkers. *Frontiers in Psychology*, *10*, 722. https://doi.org/10.3389/fpsyg.2019.00722

Jimenez, M. P., DeVille, N. V., Elliott, E. G., Schiff, J. E., Wilt, G. E., Hart, J. E., & James, P. (2021). Associations between nature exposure and health: A review of the evidence. *International Journal of Environmental Research and Public Health*, *18*(9), 4790. https://doi.org/10.3390/ijerph18094790

Kimmerer, R. W. (2013). *Braiding sweetgrass: Indigenous wisdom, scientific knowledge, and the teachings of plants*. Milkweed Editions.

Kondo, M. C., Jacoby, S. F., & South, E. C. (2018). Does spending time outdoors reduce stress? A review of real-time stress response to outdoor environments. *Health & Place*, *51*, 136–150. https://doi.org/10.1016/j.healthplace.2018.03.001

Lajoie, D. H., & Shapiro, S. I. (1992). Definitions of transpersonal psychology: The first twenty-three years. *Journal of Transpersonal Psychology*, *24*, 79–98. http://www.atpweb.org/journal.aspx

Li, Q., Kobayashi, M., Kumeda, S., Ochiai, T., Miura, T., Kagawa, T., Imai, M., Wang, Z., Otsuka, T., & Kawada, T. (2016). Effects of forest bathing on cardiovascular and metabolic parameters in middle-aged males. *Evidence-Based Complementary and Alternative Medicine*, *2016*. https://doi.org/10.1155/2016/2587381

Martin, L., White, M. P., Hunt, A., Richardson, M., Pahl, S., & Burt, J. (2020). Nature contact, nature connectedness and associations with health, wellbeing and pro-environmental behaviours. *Journal of Environmental Psychology*, *68*, 101389. https://doi.org/10.1016/j.jenvp.2020.101389

Maslow, A. H. (1971). *The farther reaches of human nature*. Viking.

Mazumdar, S. (2005). Religious place attachment, squatting and "qualitative" research: A commentary. *Journal of Environmental Psychology*, *27*(1), 87–95. https://doi.org/10.1016/j.jenvp.2004.09.003

Mills, J. G., Weinstein, P., Gellie, N. J., Weyrich, L. S., Lowe, A. J., & Breed, M. F. (2017). Urban habitat restoration provides a human health benefit through microbiome rewilding: The microbiome rewilding hypothesis. *Restoration Ecology*, *25*(6), 866–872. https://doi.org/10.1111/rec.12610

Pritchard, A., Richardson, M., Sheffield, D., & McEwan, K. (2020). The relationship between nature connectedness and eudaimonic well-being: A meta-analysis. *Journal of Happiness Studies*, *21*, 1145–1167. https://doi.org/10.1007/s10902-019-00118-6

Ramkissoon, H., Weiler, B., & Smith, L. D. G. (2012). Place attachment and pro-environmental behaviour in national parks: The development of a conceptual framework. *Journal of Sustainable Tourism*, *20*(2), 257–276. https://doi.org/10.1080/09669582.2011.602194

Richardson, M., Hamlin, I., Butler, C. W., Thomas, R., & Hunt, A. (2022). Actively noticing nature (not just time in nature) helps promote nature connectedness. *Ecopsychology*, *14*(1), 8–16. https://doi.org/10.1089/eco.2021.0023

Roszak, T. (1992). *The voice of the earth: An exploration of ecopsychology*. Phanes Press, Inc.

Schroeder, H. W. (1992). The spiritual aspect of nature: A perspective from depth psychology. In G. A. Vander Stoep (Ed.), *Proceedings of the 1991 Northeastern recreation research symposium* (pp. 25–30). U.S. Department of Agriculture, Forest Service, Northeastern Forest Experiment Station.

Schutte, N. S., & Malouff, J. M. (2018). Mindfulness and connectedness to nature: A meta-analytic investigation. *Personality and Individual Differences*, *127*, 10–14. https://doi.org/10.1016/j.paid.2018.01.034

Scopelliti, M., & Giuliani, M. V. (2004). Choosing restorative environments across the lifespans: A matter of place experience. *Journal of Environmental Psychology*, *24*, 423–437. https://doi.org/10.1016/j.jenvp.2004.11.002

Stevenson, M. P., McEwan, J., Bentsen, P., Schilhab, T., Glue, P., Trani, P., Wheeler, B., & Healey, D. (2021). Nature walks versus medication: A pre-registered randomized-controlled trial in children with attention deficit/hyperactivity disorder. *Journal of Environmental Psychology*, *77*, 101679. https://doi.org/10.1016/j.jenvp.2021.101679

Tennessen, C. M., & Cimprich, B. (1995). Views to nature: Effects on attention. *Journal of Environmental Psychology*, *15*, 77–85. https://doi.org/10.1016/0272-4944(95)90016-0

Ulrich, R. S. (1983). Aesthetic and affective response to natural environments. In I. Altman & J. F. Wohlwill (Eds.), *Human behavior and environment* (Vol. 6, pp. 85–125). Plenum Press.

Ulrich, R. S. (1984). View through a window may influence recovery from surgery. *Science*, *224*, 420–421. https://doi.org/10.1126/science.6143402

Ulrich, R. S. (2008). Biophilic theory and research for healthcare design. In S. R. Kellert, J. H. Heerwagen, & M. L. Mador (Eds.), *Biophilic design: The theory, science, and practice of bringing buildings to life* (pp. 87–106). John Wiley & Sons.

Weinstein, N., Przybylski, A. K., & Ryan, R. M. (2009). Can nature make us more caring? Effects of immersion in nature on intrinsic aspirations and generosity. *Personality and Social Psychology Bulletin*, *35*(10), 1315–1329. https://doi.org/10.1177/0146167209341649

Wells, N. M., & Lekies, K. S. (2006). Nature and the life course: Pathways from childhood nature experiences to adult environmentalism. *Children, Youth, and Environments*, *16*, 1–24. https://doi.org/10.1353/cye.2006.0031

Williams, D. R., Patterson, M. E., Roggenbuck, J. W., & Watson, A. E. (1992). Beyond the commodity metaphor: Examining emotional and symbolic attachment to place. *Leisure Sciences*, *14*, 29–46. http://www.tandfonline.com/loi/ulsc20

5

ECOWELLNESS

Teran's mom left when she was 14, and her dad wasn't around much. She remembers her youth wandering the world with minimal guidance and connection. At age 16, she went rock climbing for the first time. She was immediately hooked. Climbing quickly became her escape, her way to experience community, and a pathway for connecting with something bigger than herself. In her late teens, she began traveling the world in pursuit of climbing some of the most well-known and challenging peaks. She started gaining notoriety in the sport and secured several financial sponsorships.

Teran reached out to me seven months pregnant and amid a breakup. Her OBGYN recently advised against rock climbing for the remainder of her pregnancy, and she just learned that a good friend and former climbing buddy recently fell to her death during an ascent gone wrong.

Teran couldn't recall the last time she felt this lost and this devastated. Emotional numbness permeated Teran's voice and an emptiness filled her gaze. "Climbing is my life," she stated. "I've always been a climber. Now I can't climb, but even if I could, I'm too devastated." While she had peripherally known other climbers who had died pursuing their passion, the direct loss of her friend had been traumatic.

"That could have been me and my baby," she said, staring blankly into space. Teran went on to describe the bewildering prospect of caring for a

DOI: 10.4324/9781315697437-8

child, and in her words, needing to find a "real" job. Teran couldn't fathom moving forward in her life without rock climbing. It permeated every fiber of her being and was embedded within her spirit. Nature, through rock climbing, had been core to her identity and to her holistic wellness. In our initial sessions Teran reflected on the many ways she felt positively affected by the natural world: calm, soothed, relaxed, focused, mindful, rejuvenated, interconnected, selfless, outside herself, inspired, challenged, needed, valued, authentic—there was no scarcity in the variety of ways she felt touched by the more than human world. However, as she concurrently faced the trauma of losing her friend and layering on her developing identity as a mother, she didn't know how to navigate the burgeoning new chapter in her relationship with herself and the natural world.

Without a guiding conceptual or theoretical framework, it's difficult to know where to begin in assessing Teran's connection with nature and how we might incorporate the more than human world into treatment. As we've discussed, the ecotherapies lack well-formulated theories of change. Often, the biophilia hypothesis or ecological unconscious are described in this literature, but these general guiding principles lack much specificity for what to explore relative to the human–nature connection during the assessment stages of counseling. Likewise, we can only glean so much from the non-applied nature–wellness multidisciplinary literature and their underlying theories when attempting their application to counseling and psychotherapy settings.

The EcoWellness framework was developed to assist clinicians in assessing and incorporating nature into treatment planning processes in traditional clinical settings. It coalesces the multidisciplinary scholarship focused on nature and human wellness and addresses a gap within the counseling profession's wellness frameworks, which do not explicitly address the human–nature connection in their structures. In this chapter, we review the development of the EcoWellness framework, which was formulated with the holistic wellness models in mind.

Holistic Wellness

I was drawn to the counseling profession on account of its roots in human development and holistic wellness. That is, counselor preparation programs have historically trained their students to view clients through a holistic and non-pathological lens and conceptualize presenting problems within a client's developmental context.[1] Jane Myers et al. (2000) defined wellness as

> a way of life oriented toward optimal health and well-being, in which body, mind, and spirit are integrated by the individual to live life more fully within the human and natural community. Ideally, it is the optimum state of health and well-being that each individual is capable of achieving.
>
> (p. 252)

Jane Myers (1991) argued that wellness philosophy is the cornerstone of the counseling profession. At that same time, counseling scholars developed the first wellness model in the field, the Wheel of Wellness (Witmer & Sweeney, 1992). These researchers grounded the framework (see Figure 5.1) in Adlerian philosophy. Austrian psychiatrist, Alfred Adler, created Individual Psychology, an approach to psychotherapy that refers to the Latin *individuals*, meaning "indivisible" and "inseparable" (King & Shelley, 2008). Adler believed that all aspects of the self are interconnected and disseminated the notion that the whole of the individual is greater than the sum of their parts. He (1954) used the term *Gemeinschaftsgefuhl* to describe an individual's need for community and belongingness (i.e., social interest) and argued that a person's lived context is critical to their overarching wellness. Adler also described several life tasks critical to human development: spirituality, self-regulation, work and leisure, friendship, and love. Humans attain wellness through the development of a meaning-making framework, the ability to purposefully manage their physical, mental, and emotional self, having meaningful opportunities for work and play, and engaging in growth-fostering relationships. Witmer and Sweeney (1992) incorporated each of these life tasks into their Wheel of Wellness, contending that all aspects of holistic wellness are interconnected and indivisible within the self.

Spirituality lies at the center (or hub) of the wheel, suggesting that spirituality is the most critical component of wellness. From there, self-direction, or having the purposeful ability to pursue

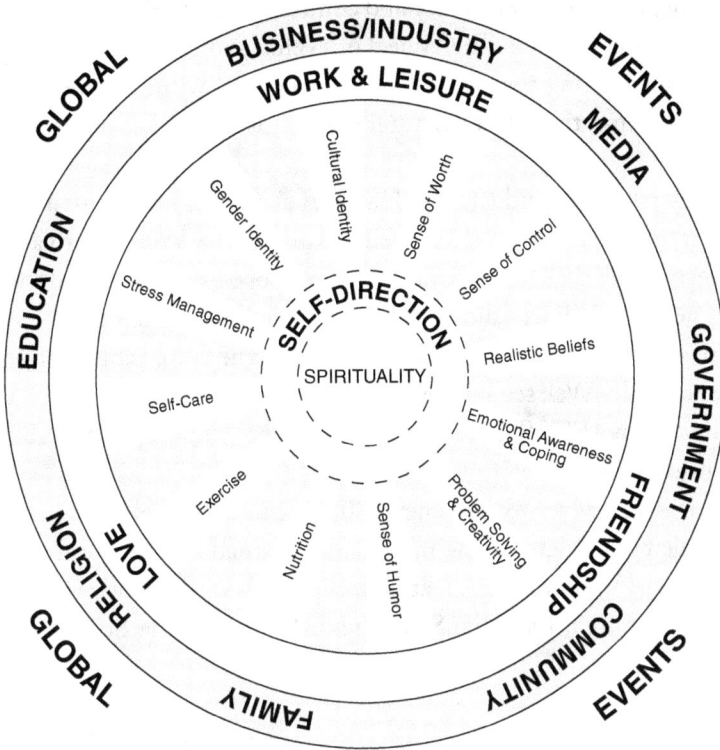

Figure 5.1 The Wheel of Wellness

Note: Copyright 1998 by J. M. Whitmer, T. J. Sweeney, and J. E. Myers

short- and long-term goals, is the second life task. The wheel spokes extending from self-direction to the outer part of the wheel include exercise, nutrition, sense of humor, problem-solving and creativity, emotional awareness and coping, realistic beliefs, sense of control, sense of worth, cultural identity, gender identity, stress management, and self-care.

The wheel's outer part includes Adler's final three life tasks: work and leisure, friendship, and love. The Wheel of Wellness authors conjured that work and leisurely pursuits provide opportunities for intrinsic achievement and self-directed fulfillment. Similarly, friendship and love (i.e., social interest) are what allow the wheel to ultimately move, providing greater motivation for and commitment to self-directed behaviors facilitating wellness. The Wheel of Wellness included contextual factors, acknowledging that an individual functions within immediate and broader systems, though the natural world was not conceptualized in the model.

Survey research conducted by Hattie et al. (2004) investigated the factor structure of the Wheel of Wellness using the Wellness Evaluation of Lifestyle (WEL) Inventory, but the proposed factor structure within the Wheel of Wellness didn't hold up. Their findings led to Myers and Sweeney (2005) developing a revised model, the Indivisible Self Model of Wellness (IS-Wel; see Figure 5.2), and the associated Five Factor Wellness Inventory (FFWEL), a 73-item assessment that operationalizes its conceptual structure.

The IS-Wel (Myers & Sweeney, 2005) includes the Self as the core and indivisible component of the model and retained all the key features of the Wheel of Wellness. Five factors compose the framework: the Coping Self, Creative Self, Essential Self, Physical Self, and the Social Self. The

CONTEXTS:

Local (safety)
Family
Neighborhood
Community

Institutional (policies & laws)
Education
Religion
Government
Business/Industry

Global (world events)
Politics
Culture
Global Events
Environment
Media

Chronometrical (lifespan)
Perpetual
Positive
Purposeful

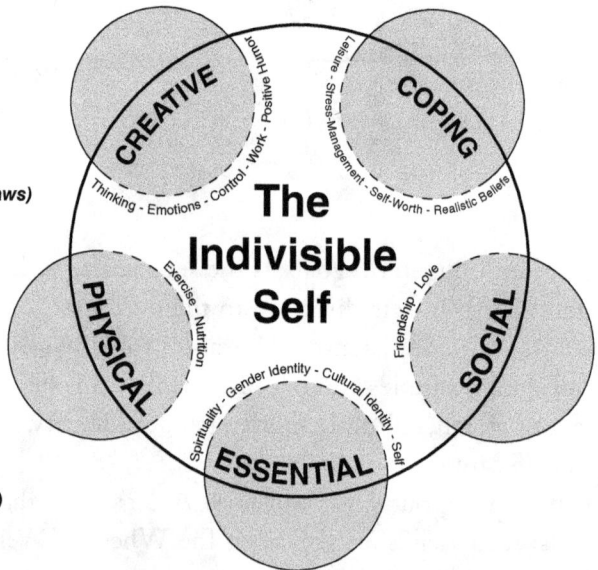

Figure 5.2 The Indivisible Self Model of Wellness

Note: Copyright T.J. Sweeney and J.E. Myers, 2003

Coping Self includes facets of wellness that contribute to one's overall resilience. These components include leisure, self-worth, stress management, and realistic beliefs. The Creative Self encompassed the facets of thinking, emotions, control, work, and positive humor. The Social Self includes two of Adler's life tasks, love and friendship. The Essential Self incorporates spirituality, gender identity, cultural identity, and self-care. Lastly, the Physical Self includes exercise and nutrition.

Nearly 20 years later, the IS-Wel is the most widely referenced and well-researched wellness model in the counseling profession (Nice et al., 2023) and the FFWEL has been translated into Turkish, Chinese, Spanish, Lithuanian, and German. Notably, while Myers and Sweeney (2005) included contextual variables within their framework (e.g., local, institutional, global, and chronometrical), researchers have yet to empirically validate them. Additionally, there is no explicit mention of the natural environment within the IS-Wel. As I began my doctoral studies in 2010, I observed the glaring absence of nature within counseling's wellness models. With little to no research on the topic in counseling, I began exploring the non-applied multidisciplinary literature outside the field (much of which I reviewed in Chapter 4), forming the foundation of the EcoWellness framework.

The Development of EcoWellness

I was fortunate to have an immeasurably supportive mentor during my doctoral studies. She also happened to be the co-author of the IS-Wel model and an avid lover of nature. I met Jane Myers in the first term of my doctoral program. She taught the advanced counseling theories course and highlighted the wellness models she and her husband, Tom Sweeney, developed. In one class, I couldn't help but point out the obvious nature deficit within the IS-Wel framework. "Hmm," she shrugged. "You're right." The conversation continued without skipping a beat.

I began visiting Jane during her office hours and we commiserated over our shared fondness of the natural world. I got to know her first as a fellow nature lover, but over time, she became my mentor and collaborator. When it came time to select a dissertation chair, I approached her about developing an EcoWellness Inventory and insisted that I needed her expertise in addressing the gap in the IS-Wel model. It didn't take much to convince her, and I quickly set out to explore what the multidisciplinary literature might suggest about the interrelationships between nature and wellness.

Something I appreciate about the counseling profession's core definition of wellness is its focus on *lifestyle*. While an optimum state of wellness is certainly ideal, the maintenance of wellness has much more to do with fulfilling life tasks that contribute to feelings of wholeness. In my way of thinking, EcoWellness functioned as an overlooked life task and an extension of Adler's conception of social interest. In addition to being in relationship with people, people have the inherent need to be in community with and experience a sense of belonging within their natural world. We (Reese & Myers, 2012) defined EcoWellness as "a sense of appreciation, respect for, and awe of nature that results in feelings of connectedness with the natural environment and the enhancement of holistic wellness" (p. 400). To maximize the construct's cultural relevance, I incorporated a broad definition of nature within the framework. I defined nature as

an individual's purposeful, direct or indirect, engagement with other living systems and non-human species (e.g., public parks, national forest, personal and community gardens, or domesticated and undomesticated animals). Such interactions are culturally bound and assumed to be contingent upon the values and lived experiences of the individual.

(Reese, 2013, p. 12)

In this way, the definition of nature is client-centered, rooted within their unique worldview, not the clinician's.

The EcoWellness model has undergone multiple iterations. We'll briefly review each here. The first formulation was based on a cursory review of the literature early in my doctoral studies (Reese & Myers, 2012). I grounded the second iteration of the model in a much more in-depth literature review and a factor analytic study, which resulted in a seven-factor model (Reese et al., 2015). The most recent composition—a three-factor model—emerged after nearly a decade of continued research and applied practice (Reese et al., 2022). Across each iteration,

EcoWellness has been conceptualized and measured as a *trait*, reflecting a person's stable, enduring relationship with ecological aspects of well-being.

Iteration #1: The Theoretical Model of EcoWellness

Based on an initial review of the multidisciplinary literature, I identified three overarching facets of EcoWellness: access to nature, environmental identity, and transcendence. I reasoned that *Access* to nature demonstrated profound impacts on attention restoration and stress reduction; without nature access, people tend to be less well. I conceptualized *Environmental identity* as the degree to which an individual identifies with and incorporates the natural environment into self-concept. Across survey studies, the more people experience feelings of connectedness with nature (including attachment to place), the more people care for nature; and the more people care for nature, the more they tend to report positive perceptions of wellness. *Transcendence* included the ability to connect with entities outside one's self-perceptions when accessing nature, including an expanded awareness about one's sense of meaning in and interconnectedness with the broader landscape of the human and nonhuman communities. Transcendence included two sub-domains. *Spirituality* is the experience of one's life-guiding values or connection with a power outside themselves when in the presence of nature. *Community connectedness* is "the propensity for individuals to consider the needs of other living things as much as one's own needs when exposed to natural environments" (Reese & Myers, 2012, p. 403).

Iteration #2: The Seven-factor Model of EcoWellness

As I began looking toward developing a quantitative measure (i.e., paper and pencil assessment) of EcoWellness (Reese, 2013), I revisited the multidisciplinary literature, which resulted in an expansion of the theoretical EcoWellness model. While the proposed transcendence domain and sub-domains remained intact, I identified two potential sub-domains within the proposed access facet and three sub-domains of the environmental identity facet.

I parsed access into two sub-domains because of what appeared to be two distinctive themes in the literature. One area of research, *physical access*, explored the effects of direct, physical contact with nature, including living in or with one's conception of the more than human world. The other area, *sensory access*, included having the ability to see, touch, smell, or hear nature, even in the absence of physical nature. This might include viewing nature outside a window, virtual reality experiences of nature, or listening to nature sounds.

I further hypothesized that environmental identity included three related areas including connection, protection, and preservation. *Connection* is the experience of pleasant cognitions or emotions when recalling one's interactions with or in directly engaging nature experiences. *Protection*, or nature-self-efficacy, is the incorporation of nature into one's lifestyle that can be of direct benefit to one's survival, including having the working knowledge and skills enabling one to navigate a particular natural environment safely. Lastly, *preservation*, or environmental agency, includes having a pro-environmental stance toward nature and taking direct action relative to an environmental cause (e.g., individual efforts to recycle or compost, community involvement, or advocacy). Thus, I predicted a complicated higher order factor structure of EcoWellness that included the second-order factors of Access, Environmental Identity, Transcendence, and their proposed associated lower-order factors (see Figure 5.3).

To test this proposed factor structure of EcoWellness, I developed the 61-item EcoWellness Inventory (EI-61) using a six-step instrument development procedure based in item-response theory and classical test theory (Crocker & Algina, 1986; DeVellis, 2003). For our purposes here, I'm not going to dive super deep into this six-step process, but for those wanting to do so, please refer to Reese (2013) or Reese and colleagues (2015). The EI-61 is answered using a four-point Likert Scale, ranging from Strongly Agree (4) to Strongly Disagree (1). Scores on the EcoWellness scale and subscales are created by calculating the mean item ratings for each subscale and modifying them by using a linear transformation (i.e., taking the average scale/subscale score and multiplying by 25). Scores range between 25 to 100 with higher scores indicating stronger perceptions of EcoWellness. You can find the EI-61, including directions and the scoring guide, in Appendix A.

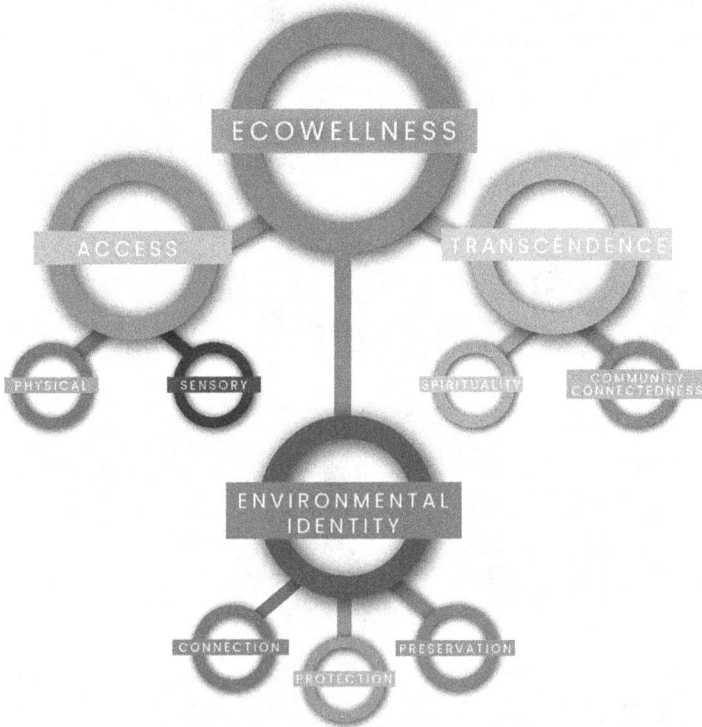

Figure 5.3 The Proposed Model of EcoWellness
Note: Copyright Ryan F. Reese, 2013

I field tested the EI-61 and investigated its initial validity and reliability with a national sample of 853 participants in the United States (Reese et al., 2015). Given that I had a theoretical basis for the model, I ran what's called a confirmatory factor analysis (CFA) on the data. However, the correlations between the seven lower-level factors (i.e., hypothesized subscales) were so high that the analysis couldn't compute. This suggested that a third-order factor model, while theoretically plausible, was not supported by the data. This finding contradicted the proposed second-order factors of Access, Environmental Identity, and Transcendence, and thus, they were eliminated from the EcoWellness model.

Next, I tested a second-order factor model wherein seven lower-level factors (Physical Access, Sensory Access, Connection, Protection, Preservation, Spirituality, and Community Connectedness) loaded onto a

Figure 5.4 The Seven-factor Model of EcoWellness
Note: Copyright Ryan F. Reese, 2013

single factor of EcoWellness. Despite high correlations between some of the seven subscales, the empirically grounded EcoWellness framework demonstrated acceptable model fit and good to excellent internal consistency (see Figure 5.4).

Following its development and clarification of the underlying seven-factor structure, we began testing the validity of the EI-61. The assessment demonstrated compelling relationships with the FFWEL, the measure that operationalizes the IS-Wel (Reese & Lewis, 2019). Using a correlational design (specifically, a multivariate canonical correlation analysis), we assessed the different ways in which the two models relate. The Protection, Preservation, and Spirituality subscales of EcoWellness seemed to have the greatest effect on the IS-Wel. That is, feeling effective in nature and having a sense of environmental agency were most closely associated with navigating difficult life events (Coping Self), fostering creativity (Creative Self), and reporting higher physical health (Physical Self). Additionally, those who possessed strong values or beliefs surrounding their cultural and spiritual practices in the sample tended to report enhanced spirituality with nature.

We (Holden et al., 2020) also explored which aspects of personality and mindfulness seem most associated with EcoWellness. The personality factors of extroversion, agreeableness (i.e., warmth and cooperation), and openness demonstrated some of the strongest relationships with EcoWellness, overall. Relative to mindfulness, the ability to observe and then describe internal mental states was associated with higher EcoWellness. In this same study, we also found that people who scored higher on naturalness (i.e., a trait wherein nature is viewed on a continuum from wilderness to technological nature) also scored higher on EcoWellness. We've (Reese et al., 2020) also identified sex-based differences and generational differences in EcoWellness. Consistent with the broader literature, females assigned at birth who were later in the lifespan tended to report greater EcoWellness than males in the sample, as well as younger females.

Overall, the EcoWellness research using the EI-61 has demonstrated compelling validity evidence in support of the seven-factor structure. Additionally, much of our research using this assessment utilized samples of participants well-represented in the United States. Nevertheless, the measure also has its limitations. The EI-61 has been of limited utility outside research settings on account of its length, which is just too cumbersome to administer in traditional counseling and psychotherapy settings. Additionally, while the model fit indices of the seven-factor structure were acceptable in our initial validation of the assessment, they were marginal. When attempting to predict mental health outcomes in a recent study, we couldn't get the seven-factor structure to replicate, which posed a significant predicament. Sure, the EI-61 could be used with research utilizing correlational designs bearing in mind its limitations, but if I wanted to begin investigating the EcoWellness construct in applied research, or research using predictive models, we would need a more robust framework.

Iteration #3: The Three-factor Model of EcoWellness

We (Reese et al., 2022) developed the third iteration of the EcoWellness Inventory using the original items from the EI-61. We conducted multiple studies using both exploratory and confirmatory factor analysis to iteratively eliminate statistically redundant and noncontributory items and retain items that loaded strongly onto discrete factors. We identified several possible factor solutions, though ultimately, only a three-factor solution replicated across samples (see Figure 5.5). Thus, we landed on a 15-item, three-factor version of EcoWellness, the EI-15.

Items on the original Physical Access, Sensory Access, and Connection domains were entirely removed while varying items of the Protection, Preservation, Spirituality, and Community Connectedness factors were retained in the EI-15. The retained items across the three factors maintain a transcendental focus. They span experiences of interconnectedness with

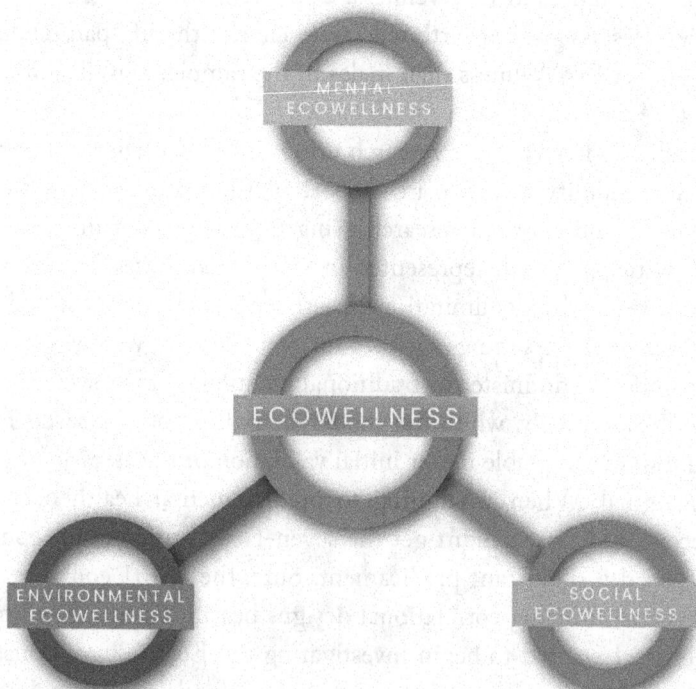

Figure 5.5 The Three-factor Model of EcoWellness
Note: Copyright Ryan F. Reese, 2022

others and the natural world, seeing beyond oneself to care for the environment, and seeking mental restoration and stress reduction through accessing nature. Access to nature is directly mentioned or inferred in most of the retained items (e.g., "When I am in nature, I find myself thinking about others in my life"). Nature connection, while no longer directly assessed in the EI-15, is inferred across multiple items (e.g., "I go to nature to find peace," and "I experience a sense of privacy in nature").

We labeled the factors that emerged *Social EcoWellness*, *Environmental EcoWellness*, and *Mental EcoWellness*. The Social EcoWellness factor encompassed five out of the six items within the original Community Connectedness domain. Thus, this factor still addresses the propensity for one to experience emotional closeness and community with others in natural settings. Environmental EcoWellness merged two items from the Protection factor and three items from the Preservation factor. The items within this new subscale represent an action orientation toward addressing environmental sustainability and climate change, what might be described as an ethic of care for the natural world. Mental EcoWellness includes all but two items from the original Spirituality factor. However, the removal of two items that focused specifically on spirituality resulted in a broader focus on mental health. Nevertheless, spiritual components lie at the heart of Mental EcoWellness. That is, the items of this factor address connecting with something bigger than oneself for the purposes of mental restoration and stress reduction. Thus, Mental EcoWellness is "the expansion of self-concept to include and feel part of a larger whole in nature for reducing stress and achieving mental clarity and balance" (Reese et al., 2022, p. 9).

The EI-15 is answered on the same Likert scale as the EI-61. Similarly, scale and subscale scores range between 25 to 100. The EI-15, its directions, and scoring can be found in Appendix B. The assessment has demonstrated initial convergent validity evidence with measures of resilience, self-efficacy, and self-esteem. Additional research is needed exploring its replicability as well as additional convergent and divergent validity evidence.

Dismantling the EI-61 was not an easy emotional process for me. However, as we'll discuss in the coming chapters, the seven-factor framework maintains practical utility—particularly for treatment planning and intervention development—even though the EI-15 is a stronger and more refined instrument for future research.

Limitations and Considerations

I critiqued the ecotherapy literature and the multidisciplinary nature–wellness literature for its reliance on correlational research designs. Well, I have a similar critique of the EcoWellness research I've conducted. The EcoWellness constructs and their corresponding items were based in correlates of the nature–wellness literature. Similarly, research underlying the development of the EcoWellness framework relied solely on survey research.

Another limitation of EcoWellness resides within its Eurocentric overtones. Aspects of my lived experiences and positionality undoubtedly contributed to biases within the EcoWellness framework. I could argue that by engaging in rigorous methodological and peer-reviewed practices that EcoWellness possesses significant scientific merit, but these processes were established within western, reductionistic conceptions of science. Just because EcoWellness has passed muster at different points of the scientific process, it doesn't mean that all items are impartial or bear cultural relevance to all client communities. One item and an associated experience comes to mind. Several years ago, I was discussing the EcoWellness Inventory with a dear colleague of mine born and raised within a neighboring Native American community. In reviewing the assessment, she highlighted the item, "I make it a priority to recycle." It was an impossibility for her community of origin. "We don't have the community resources to recycle on the reservation," she revealed. "Does this mean my people aren't EcoWell?" This experience has stuck with me. The cultural limitations of EcoWellness are not to say that the framework lacks broad applicability to client populations. Rather, we must enact intentionality and cultural humility when incorporating EcoWellness into counseling settings.

These potential limitations of the EcoWellness framework give rise to several important considerations. While EcoWellness assumes that the natural world is needed for humans to achieve optimal holistic wellness, the approach does not pre-suppose that the natural world should be incorporated into counseling and psychotherapy. Thus, EcoWellness serves as a guiding framework when assessing nature connection in counseling and is intended to reduce the risk of imposing clinician bias when incorporating nature into therapeutic processes. From their initial appraisal, counseling professionals partner together with clients to incorporate EcoWellness into the treatment plan based on an overall assessment of a client's wellness, as well as the client's own preferences for treatment. Thus, EcoWellness should be client-centered and culturally sustaining in its application and merged with evidence-based and/or theoretically driven counseling paradigms.

An Initial Glimpse at Addressing EcoWellness in Counseling

Okay, so how do we incorporate EcoWellness into counseling and psychotherapy? Do we need to administer, score, and interpret the EI-61 or EI-15? We'll discuss this question in much greater depth in Part III. For now, let's return to Teran, and take an initial look into what it might look like to integrate the EcoWellness framework into counseling.

During Teran's holistic intake interview (i.e., session number one), I informally assessed the seven original factors of EcoWellness. I started by asking Teran about her definition of nature. She responded, "You know, the wilderness, places mostly untouched by humans."

I explored her immediate access to nature, both physical and sensory. "It's not really nature, but there's a park down the street from my apartment." She could see some of the park's trees through a window in her bedroom. Teran had a lot to say about her connection with nature, but the pain of losing her friend brought about a somatic block that seemed to interfere with her recollection of some of her most cherished memories and experiences. She recalled a prior love for getting youth into rock climbing. "Leave no trace" was a key component to her ethos, which included clean ups at some of her favorite climbing areas. She felt helpless regarding her present level of connectedness with nature. Without rock climbing, she no longer had a pathway for feeling effective with accessing nature or having opportunities to care for it.

We also discussed how much she could connect with something bigger than herself now that she was no longer rock climbing. "Very little," she asserted. "I haven't gone to my sacred places in a while; I've disconnected from my rock climbing people."

In treatment, our EcoWellness focus complemented the primary aim of trauma processing. Specifically, nearby access to nature proved to be a critical starting point in Teran's healing process. She learned stress reduction techniques, including guided imagery, and began using a smart phone app to incorporate mindfulness into her daily routines. I invited Teran to consider a broader conceptualization of nature so she could get outdoors with added frequency. "What if nature is more expansive than wilderness?" I pondered. "You mentioned living by a park, would you ever consider going there to check it out?"

She hadn't thought much about going to the park because she hadn't considered a city park being nature. While initially resistant, Teran humored my curiosity. Besides, she reasoned, going to the park might help her apply what she had been learning about mindfulness.

Teran's first visit to the park was a success. She noticed birds, flowers, and plants. She also saw children climbing about the playground. Seeing them laughing and playing gave her a sense of hope and positive anticipation for welcoming her baby into the community. She began visiting the park nearly every day as she approached her due date.

We addressed Teran's trauma using eye movement desensitization and reprocessing (EMDR). After multiple months of processing and two months after the birth of her child, she announced that she felt ready to visit the location where her friend had fallen. She was accompanied by a group of friends. When she returned to counseling the following week, she reported feeling more connected to her friend; she felt her spiritual presence in the desert. Within several months, Teran was again returning to the spaces where she climbed, newborn in tow. They continued visiting the nearby park. She loved seeing her daughter's reactions to the birds and squirrels and observing her daughter's developing curiosity for the more than human world.

While many of our counseling sessions centered on Teran's relationship with nature, we never once stepped outdoors together. I collaboratively assessed Teran's relationship with nature using EcoWellness as our guide, which informed treatment planning. Teran expanded her notion of nature to include nearby physical access, which provided an initial source of self-efficacy in attaining stress reduction. As Teran began to heal from trauma, her motivation to revisit sacred natural places with important others resurfaced. Confidence reemerged to rock climb. As her shifting identity accommodated becoming a mother, she began seeing nature through her daughter's eyes, and at a city park no less.

Conclusion

The EcoWellness framework provides a starting point for assessing and then incorporating the more than human world into counseling and psychotherapy. It has received empirical support, and in the process, undergone three different iterations. An EcoWellness philosophy is not employed in isolation, and, importantly, it takes into consideration a client's cultural lens, context, and client-specific preferences. EcoWellness complements the traditional modalities employed by counselors and psychotherapists, and the framework does not require setting foot outdoors during therapy. As we dive into the latter part of this text, let's first take an in-depth gander at incorporating EcoWellness into holistic intake assessment procedures.

Chapter 5 Reflection Questions

Self-awareness:

1. Reflect on the evolution of the EcoWellness counseling framework. How have the modifications across its iterations improved its applicability in clinical settings?
2. Consider the underlying concepts of the varying conceptions of EcoWellness. Which of the three EcoWellness iterations resonate with you most and why?
3. Analyze how personal and professional experiences with nature can influence a counselor's application of the EcoWellness framework in their practice.

Knowledge:

4. How does the EcoWellness framework align and diverge with traditional models of holistic wellness in professional counseling?

5. Explore the significance of the EcoWellness framework in therapeutic settings. How might the EcoWellness model aid clinicians in formulating treatment plans that incorporate nature?

6. Reflect upon the role of empirical research in shaping the development of the EcoWellness framework. How does its methodological strengths and limitations influence its credibility and acceptance in the counseling and psychotherapy communities?

Application:

7. Consider the implications of integrating EcoWellness into your routine therapeutic practice. What challenges might you face when incorporating EcoWellness within your setting(s) and the population(s) you serve?

8. Bearing in mind the multidisciplinary nature of the EcoWellness framework, how can clinicians ensure they maintain cultural humility when applying these concepts in their work with clients?

Note

1 This is not to say that other helping professions such as social work, clinical psychology, and counseling psychology do not have a focus on wellness in their training programs or disciplines more broadly. For example, the closely related notion of Positive Psychology, a construct rooted on human flourishing and optimal wellness, emerged within mainstream psychology in 1998 during Martin Seligman's presidency within the American Psychological Association.

References

Adler, A. (1954). *Understanding human nature.* Fawcett. (Original work published 1927)

Crocker, L., & Algina, J. (1986). *Introduction to classical and modern test theory.* Harcourt Brace Jovanovich.

DeVellis, R. F. (2003). *Scale development theory and applications.* Sage.

Hattie, J. A., Myers, J. E., & Sweeney, T. J. (2004). A factor structure of wellness: Theory, assessment, analysis, and practice. *Journal of Counseling & Development, 82*(3), 354–364. https://doi.org/10.1002/j.1556-6678.2004.tb00321.x

Holden, C., Reese, R. F., & Seitz, C. (2020). Naturalness, personality traits, and mindfulness predict EcoWellness: Implications for counseling practice. *International*

Journal for the Advancement of Counselling, 42(4), 439–454. https://doi.org/10.1007/s10447-020-09414-w

King, R. A., & Shelley, C. A. (2008). Community feeling and social interest: Adlerian parallels, synergy, and differences with the field of community psychology. *Journal of Community & Applied Social Psychology, 18,* 96–107. https://doi.org/10.1002/casp.962

Myers, J. E. (1991). Wellness as the paradigm for counseling and development: The possible future. *Counselor Education and Supervision, 30*(3), 183–193. https://doi.org/10.1002/j.1556-6978.1991.tb01199.x

Myers, J. E., & Sweeney, T. J. (2005). *The five factor wellness inventory, adult (5F-Wel-A).* Mind Garden.

Myers, J. E., Sweeney, T. J., & Witmer, J. M. (2000). The wheel of wellness counseling for wellness: A holistic model for treatment planning. *Journal of Counseling & Development, 78*(3), 251–266. https://doi.org/10.1002/j.1556-6676.2000.tb01906.x

Nice, M. L., Brubaker, M. D., Gibson, D. M., McMullen, J. W., Asempapa, B., Kennedy, S. D., Fullen, M. C., & Moore, C. M. (2023). Wellness and well-being in counseling research: A 31-year content analysis. *Journal of Counseling & Development, 101*(3), 251–263. https://doi.org/10.1002/jcad.12467

Reese, R. F. (2013). *EcoWellness: Construction and validation of the Reese EcoWellness inventory* [PhD dissertation, The University of North Carolina]. ProQuest Digital Dissertations (UMI 3568902).

Reese, R. F., Holden, C., Hall, C., & Wingrove, T. (2022). Replicability and revision of the EcoWellness inventory: Development of a brief measure of EcoWellness. *Measurement and Evaluation in Counseling and Development, 55*(4), 266–285. https://doi.org/10.1080/07481756.2021.2022984

Reese, R. F., & Lewis, T. F. (2019). Greening counseling: Examining multivariate relationships between EcoWellness and holistic wellness. *Journal of Humanistic Counseling, 58*(1), 53–67. https://doi.org/10.1002/johc.12089

Reese, R. F., Lewis, T. F., & Kothari, B. (2020). Nature connection changes throughout the lifespan: Generation and sex-based differences in EcoWellness. *Adultspan Journal, 19*(2), 94–106. https://doi.org/10.1002/adsp.12098

Reese, R. F., & Myers, J. E. (2012). EcoWellness: The missing factor in holistic wellness models. *Journal of Counseling and Development, 90*(4), 400–406. https://doi.org/10.1002/j.1556-6676.2012.00050.x

Reese, R. F., Myers, J. E., Lewis, T. F., & Willse, J. T. (2015). Construction and initial validation of the Reese EcoWellness inventory. *International Journal for the Enhancement of Counselling, 37*(2), 124–142. https://doi.org/10.1007/s10447-014-9232-1

Witmer, J. M., & Sweeney, T. J. (1992). A holistic model for wellness and prevention over the lifespan. *Journal of Counseling & Development, 71,* 140–148. https://doi.org/10.1002/j.1556-6676.1992.tb02189.x

PART III
ECOWELLNESS COUNSELING

6

ECOWELLNESS ASSESSMENT

Cultural and professional values lie at the heart of any form of clinical assessment. Our individual, systemic, and sociocultural principles and norms influence the language we use when talking with clients about their presenting problems, their mental illness, or their symptoms. Conceptualized through a strength-based lens, our values influence the language we use when talking with clients about their wellness goals, their strengths, and their internal and external resources. When we look toward assessing EcoWellness as part of a client's broader holistic wellness, the client's unique factors and lived experiences should influence the specific questions we ask, and how we ask them.

In this chapter, I introduce a three-tiered approach to EcoWellness assessment (see Figure 6.1). As we progress through the tiers, the level of specificity and time taken to assess EcoWellness increases. Tier 1 includes a broad appraisal of EcoWellness within the initial intake assessment process. Tier 2 comprises a more robust informal assessment of the EcoWellness facets. Tier 3 assessment encompasses formally assessing EcoWellness using the EI-15. I'll initially discuss each tier with the assumption of working with adult populations. We'll then explore special considerations for assessing EcoWellness with adolescents and children.

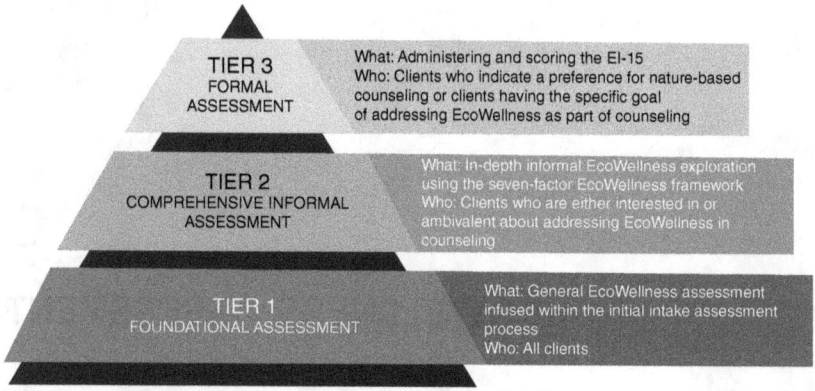

Figure 6.1 Tiered EcoWellness Assessment

Note: Copyright Ryan F. Reese, 2024

Tier 1 EcoWellness Assessment

Regardless of theoretical orientation or the clinical modalities employed in therapy, most clinicians in agency and private practice settings engage in holistic intake and bio-psycho-social assessment processes. Many of us work within managed care systems that require a global intake assessment leading to a clinical diagnostic formulation and an associated measurable treatment plan. This initial assessment helps us view clients as holistic beings functioning across micro- and macro-level systems. The following list includes some of the areas of holistic wellness commonly explored with clients and/or their families:

- Presenting Problem(s)
- Basic Needs (e.g., economic, housing, nutritional, and environmental security)
- Family Background
- Medical and Mental Health Diagnostic History
- Physical and Nutritional Health
- Social Support System and Relationship History
- Cultural Heritage and Identities
- Academic and Career History
- Substance Use History
- Trauma and Adverse Life Experiences

- Experiences of Discrimination or Oppression
- Self and Other Harm History
- Self-care Strategies
- Internal Strengths and Resources
- Existential Information

The primary goal of Tier 1 EcoWellness assessment to is to clarify a client's conception of nature within the context of the broader intake assessment. It should be brief, thus enabling clinicians to generally assess EcoWellness with every client. In my own clinical practice, I've added several EcoWellness-based questions to the intake form that clients complete prior to the initial appointment. Specifically, I ask clients to identify positive and adverse experiences with the natural world and the degree to which a client may want to incorporate EcoWellness as part of their treatment plan. Here is what it looks like in my context:

> One area of specialization in my practice includes EcoWellness, which addresses the extent to which the natural world affects health and wellness. As you respond to the three following questions, please consider your own ways of experiencing or defining nature.
>
> 1. How have your experiences with nature **positively** influenced your overall wellness, if at all?
> 2. How have your experiences with nature **negatively** influenced your overall wellness, if at all?
> 3. Would you like to explore incorporating EcoWellness into your treatment plan? If so, how might you like to address it?

I like these template questions for several reasons. First, they alert clients of the specialty area of EcoWellness within my practice. While I will have already likely shared about this focus during the initial phone or email exchanges with a client or family, these questions serve as an additional layer of informed consent. Second, these questions cue clients to discuss pleasant and adverse experiences with nature. Lastly, all three questions use tentative language (". . . if at all" and "if so . . ."), which empowers the client to answer the questions honestly and based on their own lived experiences and worldview.

When possible, I review the completed intake assessment prior to the first appointment. This enables me to consider the possible ways I might adjust the language I use to inquire further about EcoWellness and other areas of holistic wellness within the intake. Specific to EcoWellness, I look for how the client seems to be defining nature within their responses and the possible value orientations that may be present within the experiences shared (e.g., ecocentric, anthropocentric, etc.). I consider how other reported aspects of client positionality, identity, and life experiences influence their preferences of nature, including whether the client has reported any adverse experiences or traumas within the natural world.[1] From this review, I also develop an initial understanding of whether the client seems favorable, ambivalent to, or uninterested in addressing EcoWellness in counseling.

If a client reports a lack of interest in further addressing EcoWellness in counseling, and they assert something to that effect on the intake paperwork, I will still minimally revisit that during the first appointment. Here are some examples of how a clinician might prompt the client in such instances:

"I noticed on the intake questionnaire that you indicated EcoWellness having a minimal effect on your overall wellness. Is there anything else you want to share about that?"

"You reported having some unpleasant experiences in nature and that you would prefer not to address EcoWellness as part of our work together in counseling. Is there anything about these adverse experiences that you feel would be relevant to our work together?"

"While you reported EcoWellness as a positive aspect of your wellness, overall, you mentioned that it didn't seem relevant to your counseling experience. Can you tell me more about that?"

Moreover, I find it important to revisit Tier 1 EcoWellness questions during the initial meeting because clients may lack a clear understanding of what *incorporating* EcoWellness into the treatment plan means. Clients might interpret questions about EcoWellness equating to spending time outdoors during counseling sessions or as part of their everyday lives. Thus, revisiting these questions during the initial appointment serves as an important opportunity to clarify client expectations for what it might look like to address EcoWellness in counseling or psychotherapy. I clarify with clients that embedding EcoWellness into treatment planning varies based on the client, and that it doesn't always include outdoor sessions. Rather, EcoWellness often shows up in the treatment plan when helping clients identify coping mechanisms and self-care strategies. When this is the case, I'll often progress to Tier 2 strategies in further assessing the different dimensions of client EcoWellness.

Tier 2 EcoWellness Assessment

In Tier 2 EcoWellness assessment, it's assumed that the clinician has determined a client is either interested in or at least ambivalent about addressing EcoWellness in counseling. Within this layer, we informally assess the different facets of EcoWellness during the clinical interview relative to the other areas of the holistic wellness or psychodiagnostic intake assessment. Tier 2 includes elements of both assessment and psychoeducation, most often occurring during the first or second meeting with the client, though this appraisal can happen at any point in a clinician's process when working with clients.

In Chapter 5, we discussed the different iterations of the EcoWellness framework. While the three-factor model of EcoWellness is the most statistically robust when it comes to the research, I prefer using the seven-factor framework when informally assessing EcoWellness.[2] The seven-factor framework is particularly useful when considering aspects of client positionality and developing culturally relevant EcoWellness-based interventions. I've included template informal assessment questions in Appendix C that can be further adapted for use with individual clients and population(s).

Connection

Emotional, cognitive, and ancestral connection with nature is the place I like to start when informally assessing client EcoWellness. Here is where I begin to develop an initial sense of a client's nature worldview (i.e., how they define nature and how they define themselves relative to the more than human world). I revisit areas of the intake questionnaire wherein clients reported the benefits or adverse experiences of nature within their history. I like to know who these experiences were with, including important caregivers, friends, family members, or romantic partners. I explore early recollections in or with nature contributing to current conceptions of nature, and how it is defined by the client. I further work toward helping clients explore their current level of connectedness with the natural world. I ask about sacred places or spaces in nature, sacred nonhuman species, and their level of connectedness to conceptions of immediate nearby nature.

Where possible and appropriate, I explore with clients their ancestral connections with nature. Some clients will report a rich history of ancestral positive connectedness with the natural world, and often, associated intergenerational tragedy and trauma. Gaining understanding of ancestral experiences with nature provides one window into the client's current nature worldview. In my experience, the more on the margins one's positionality, the more I hear trauma narratives occurring in the natural world within their ancestral lineage. For example, within some BIPOC client communities, there can be a learned trepidation for accessing the outdoors. Clients sometimes reference their ancestral history of forced enslavement, stories of public lynching, forced internment, genocide, and the loss of cultural, familial, and spiritual traditions and places. Adverse ancestral experiences are further reinforced through a client's lived and direct experiences of discrimination, intimidation, and violence in and around natural environments. This isn't to say that all clients with marginalized identities will report immediate, ancestral, or cultural trauma in and around natural spaces. Rather, we must be alert and open to a range of experiences with the natural world and assess nature connectedness in tandem with the client's holistic developmental background.

Physical and Sensory Access

Developing a clear sense for how a client defines nature is paramount to understanding how they categorize nature access. This includes assessing the frequency and quality of accessing what the client considers nature, as well as whether the client perceives such access as being restorative, accessible, and safe. Thus, I ask clients about their nearby, safe access to nature, and their transportation, including any possible barriers and facilitating factors. Moreover, I assess the nature that is often right in front of our client's noses—literally. I ask about the presence of indoor plants, domesticated animals, and whether one has windows in their place of residence. I explore whether clients have pictures or murals of nature, whether they have favorite aromas or scents of nature, and whether they have any preferences of nature sounds.

One of the most common themes I've identified with clients over the years is that, regardless of positionality and context, clients often define nature as being "out there," something that is remote, the untouched wilderness. As I emphasized in Chapter 3, this divorced nature perspective further disconnects us from the more than human world. In this way, we can miss out on benefitting from what is most near us. Thus, probing clients about their access to nature can be a significant opportunity for psychoeducation wherein we can share the holistic wellness benefits of accessing proximal forms of nature.

Once again, the approach to such assessment should be rooted in a client's developmental history, positionality, and community context. Therefore, we can't assume that nearby nature is accessible for all of us. Such a position ignores the obvious inequitable fact that many of the client communities we serve in the United States, particularly brown and black communities, reside in nature deserts, communities embedded within the urban sprawls of our industrial and capitalistic culture. This includes generations of families exposed to environmental hazards such as air pollution, toxic waste, and water contamination, families lacking safe access to nearby parks where their children can play and where they can join with others in community. As we'll further deconstruct in Chapter 10, these same communities are disproportionately affected by the impacts of climate change, and together, environmental and climate hazards merge to adversely affect both physical and mental health outcomes. Thus, while assessing physical and sensory access to nature can help identify pragmatic ways of incorporating nature into daily life as part of the treatment plan, this assessment can also facilitate awareness and possible avenues for client empowerment and advocacy.

Protection (Nature Self-efficacy)

After I explore a client's connectedness with nature and their physical and sensory access to those spaces, I assess a client's pathways for experiencing EcoWellness. I use the term *pathway* because it enables us to consider any activity, nature-based skill, or way of being through the lens of nature self-efficacy, otherwise described as Protection, within the seven-factor EcoWellness framework. The general self-efficacy construct, rooted in Albert Bandura's (1993) social cognitive theory, broadly focuses on the role that human cognition plays in our underlying motivations and behaviors. It includes having the belief in one's own ability to achieve a desired outcome. Such beliefs are impacted by one's past experiences, observing others, and whether one sees a particular activity as being relevant to their cultural context or identities.

I've worked with families over the years who want to find ways to spend more time together as a family in nature, but they sometimes don't know where to start. This includes not only identifying the *where* in nature but also the *how*. For instance, devising a plan to have a family picnic, identifying what kinds of equipment may be needed to go on a short hike, or engaging with community resources or partners to partake in nature-based specific activities (e.g., biking, fishing, rock climbing, etc.). Clinicians might also help clients identify nature-based experiences they'd like to learn, and then explore avenues for learning those aptitudes. Then, over time, a client builds a sense of self-efficacy with such a skill, which in turn aids their access to a natural setting while also positively contributing to a sense of connection and safety with outdoor places.

Once again, this area of assessment depends on the individual client and their lived context. A client may have the desire to learn to mountain bike, but if they lack the economic resources or access to nearby trails, this desire can contribute to low nature self-efficacy on account of a goal that does not align with one's current reality. As we'll discuss in the coming chapters, this is one area where clinicians can join with clients to identify community resources by utilizing an advocacy framework to empower clients to take action that may be of benefit to both the client and their broader community.

Spirituality

The natural world facilitates awe and wonderment and sparks a deep fascination surrounding humankind's place in the broader landscape of existence. The land, the water, the sky, and the stars shimmer with riveting beauty and their mysteries draw us closer to both shared and idiosyncratic conceptions of our origins. Similarly, the power of nature humbles us. Experiencing the natural world can open our minds and our hearts; it possesses the ability to bring about new ideas and expand creative thinking. The Connection facet of the seven-factor EcoWellness model is a vital precursor to experiencing the Spirituality facet. We are much more likely to experience self-transcendence in places or spaces where we embody psychological safety, nurturance, and attachment. However, the spiritual domain of EcoWellness extends beyond the immediate emotional or cognitive connection one has with nature and results in feeling connected with something bigger than oneself and the immediate subjects of connection.

Sacred natural places and entities can be accessed even when we are not in their physical presence. They bring about feelings of unity and a sense of connectedness with all living and nonliving things. They elevate the self to feel part of the broader landscape, part of the more than human community or conceptions of a higher power. This sense of spiritual attunement often emerges when assessing a client's broader existential or spiritual self, though we need to be clear and intentional with what we ask. We very well could inquire, "Can you tell me about your spiritual or religious affiliation?" But in doing so, you'll likely be met with typical responses: "I'm Christian," "I'm agnostic," or "I was raised religious but now I'm an atheist." Instead, try asking, "What gives you life? What fulfills you? What brings you meaning and purpose in this life? When have you felt the most alive? When, if ever, have you experienced complete unity with the divine? When and where do you feel in greatest alignment with your truth?" Our spirituality is sacred. Thus, when we ask about a client's spiritual background with EcoWellness in mind, we do so with honor, creativity, and intentionality.

Community Connectedness

The Community Connectedness facet of EcoWellness is rooted within conceptions of collectivism, which is in stark contrast to our western individualistic culture. Many of our clients embody individualism within their approach to living, including minimal reliance on community for wellness and survival. Within this cultural schema, wellness-based activities often occur in solitude, in pairs, or in small groups. The same goes for dominant forms of nature-based recreation. Think of just about any major corporate outdoor company and the commercialization of their outdoor products. You'll often see one individual running, hiking, or canoeing. Thus, some clients heavily influenced by individualistic ideals may lack schema for community-based interactions within the natural world. They may even state preferences for being away from others and experiencing solitude. In this case, I find that psychoeducation within this realm, and the fact that nature can bring people closer together, is vital for many clients who report experiences of social disconnection.

In contrast, I've worked with many clients over the years who don't see the purpose or value of spending solo time in the natural world. Without the presence of family or community, what's the point? Nevertheless, in the United States and other developed countries, where individualistic nature-based recreation activities reign supreme, these clients can often feel marginalized or out of place when accessing natural environments. When I ask clients about their identity during the intake assessment interview, I listen closely for how they describe themselves. I ask myself, "Is the client defining their identity through their social network (i.e., family or community) or is the client defining the self through an individualistic framework?" Of course, this guiding question is helpful in addressing all areas of the client's life, and not just EcoWellness. Nonetheless, the more individualistic a client is in their responses, the more I find they emphasize experiences of solitude in nature—the more collectivistic in orientation, the more a client tends to highlight experiences of community in nature. Indeed, a client's attitude toward Community Connectedness provides potential insight into EcoWellness intervention areas within a client's broader treatment planning process.

Preservation (Environmental Agency)

Assessing the Preservation domain of EcoWellness is not dissimilar from assessing the Protection facet in that we look to identify ways in which clients can feel and experience a sense of self-efficacy in caring for aspects of the natural world. However, I find that it often takes greater finesse and wordsmithing to cater to a client's resources, lifestyle, and worldview. I pay attention to terminology that often gets politicized, and I'm cautious of how I use it with clients. For example, if I generally ask clients about climate change, or their concerns about global warming, I may very well receive emotional reactions from clients based on what they see or hear in their preferred news outlets. Clients tend to personify political affiliation in such moments, and my subsequent attempts to ask about their level of care for their neighborhood green spaces or their favorite places in nature are severely limited.

Katherine Hayhoe's (2021) *Saving Us: A Climate Scientist's Case for Hope and Healing in a Divided World* centers on finding solutions to tackling the climate crisis through authentic, vulnerable, and empathic dialogue that can foster shared understanding and community praxis. Clients will engage in praxis (i.e., dialogue and action) if they can experience self-efficacy—that what they are doing to address the climate crisis (and environmental justice issues more broadly) can make a difference in their immediate lives and community. This efficacy can have positive impacts on both individual client wellness and healing within the community. In my experience, just about every client cares about the nature that matters to them. They care about the places they live, their favorite pastimes in and around those places, nutritious foods, and their access to clean water. Thus, when assessing a client's environmental agency, we must speak to the values underlying our clients' interests with the natural world and cater our language to the environments and activities they hold close within their nature worldview.

By the time I informally assess the Preservation domain of EcoWellness, I likely already know their favorite outdoor places or spaces. I may have familiarity with their favorite nature-based activities or pastimes and their possible ancestral ties. I have a good sense of the importance of these spaces for social connections or traditions, and the value they hold regarding spiritual and/or religious significance. This knowledge enables me to explore a client's specific hopes or concerns about their favorite outdoor spaces without relying upon vague and potentially triggering terminology. We can identify the individual or collective actions they have taken to preserve the natural spaces they most value or the action(s) they might like to take as part of the treatment plan.

Tier 2 Summary

Tier 2 EcoWellness assessment is intricately linked with all aspects of the client's unique conception of self, their community, and their lived experiences. While the example questions in Appendix C provide a starting point, the informal questions you ask clients regarding the EcoWellness facets should be specific to their worldview, life experiences, and positionality. If we ask the same questions with each client, we likely aren't going to get the answers we need, and the client likely isn't sharing the true depths of their EcoWellness. Thus, assessing EcoWellness requires courage, vulnerability, and creativity. Let's now turn our attention to Tier 3 EcoWellness assessment, which includes the formal administration and scoring of the EI-15.

Tier 3 EcoWellness Assessment

The administration of the EI-15 may be appropriate when a client identifies EcoWellness as a specific goal in counseling. Additionally, some clients may benefit from, or prefer, a more structured approach to the assessment process. Completing an assessment, reviewing the results, and engaging in a pragmatic discussion about how EcoWellness can be meaningfully integrated into the treatment plan can offer valuable clarity and direction.

Since developing the EI-15, I no longer administer the EI-61 in my own clinical practice. The EI-61 is limited in its structural stability and administering and scoring a 61-item measure is time-consuming. As clinicians, we barely have enough time to engage in holistic intake assessment processes, and there are often additional screenings or assessments that may be required by your organization. Given its brevity, the EI-15 possesses significant utility for administration in clinical settings. Being that it is only 15 items, it's easy to administer and score during session, and it can be a helpful conversation tool. The results often point toward opportunities for enhancing areas of EcoWellness within the treatment plan.

The EI-15 can be administered and scored in about five minutes—sometimes even less—making it a convenient tool to introduce early in the counseling process, even during a session. If the assessment is readily available, clients can complete it on the spot. As with any assessment, my strongest recommendation is to ensure that clients fully understand the instructions and the response scale before proceeding. The EI-15 is designed to assess *trait* EcoWellness—that is, a client's general or enduring relationship without reference to a specific timeframe. However, clinicians may choose to adapt the interpretation to fit their context. For instance, you may wish to explore a client's *state* EcoWellness—how they've been feeling over a particular period, such as the past week or month, or during a certain season. This flexibility can provide valuable insights tailored to the client's lived experience and your therapeutic goals.

The EI-15 and scoring guide can be found in Appendix B. I'll often read the directions aloud with the client, word for word, and then give the client an opportunity to ask questions. I let them know that it's okay to ask questions if there is an item on the inventory that is confusing, but I encourage them to go with their initial inclination in responding to any item. For some clients, it may be helpful to read the items aloud, based on their familiarity with written English. After they complete the inventory, you can quickly score it using the same linear transformation we discussed in Chapter 5. Scores on the EI-15 range between 25 and 100, with higher scores indicating greater EcoWellness. While you can identify a global EcoWellness score across the subscales, the intended use of the inventory is to identify and interpret the three subscales.

After the inventory is scored, the clinician talks through the results with the client. There are no guidelines for interpretation, insofar as there are not score cut-offs for high, medium, or low EcoWellness. Thus, the meaning of the scores comes down to the client's own interpretation with the support of the therapist. As the results are discussed, I like to explore any items that were either confusing or potentially irrelevant to the client. From there, we further explore subscales and items that have salience for the client. While access to nature is not explicitly measured by the EI-15, it often becomes a meaningful part of the conversation when interpreting the results. Let's explore how the EI-15 might be integrated into a counseling assessment through the following case example.

The case of Bennett

Imagine you are working with Bennett, a 23-year-old, economically resourced, cisgender man. He just moved to the area, taking a job as a full-time city planner. Bennett reached out to you because he has been feeling depressed the past year, triggered by the ending of a relationship with a romantic partner of three years. He's also getting acclimated to living in a new place. On the initial intake paperwork, Bennett reports that nature has been an important component in maintaining wellness throughout life, but that he currently has been unable to spend meaningful time in the outdoors. He also reports a feeling of existential dread. He reports lacking a clear purpose in life, and on account of different events in the world, including the climate crisis, he is experiencing a sense of hopelessness. Bennett reports being close with his family of origin and having a close-knit group of friends. However, he does not have friends or family living in the immediate area, and he feels isolated on the weekends, further contributing to symptoms of depression.

During the intake appointment, Bennett indicates that he hopes to address EcoWellness as part of counseling. He agrees to taking the EI-15 prior to his next counseling session. Bennett's scores are as follows: 60 (Social EcoWellness), 85 (Environmental EcoWellness), and 35 (Mental EcoWellness).

After scoring the assessment, you invite Bennett to share his initial reactions to the results and discuss whether any items were unclear or difficult to interpret. You invite him to explore his scores relative to his overall wellness and in identifying opportunity areas of EcoWellness to address within the treatment plan. You ask, "What are some of your initial reactions to your scores?"

Bennett responds, "No real surprises, it's about what I expected."

You then inquire, "Overall, were there any areas of EcoWellness or items that were confusing or that you would like to talk about before we discuss specific areas of EcoWellness?"

"No, I don't think so," he responds.

You then ask which area of EcoWellness he might like to talk about first.

"Let's go with Mental EcoWellness," Bennett responds glancing at the survey results. "I just don't feel like I have a good sense for the nature here, the trails, that kind of stuff. I don't know where to begin."

"Do any of the questions on Mental EcoWellness jump out at you?" you ask.

He responds, "Yeah, normally I'm able to settle in with nature, but I don't feel like I have place or space I can go where I feel connected. I've tried going on walks, but my thoughts seem to speed up rather than slow down. I just don't feel like I can find a place where I can be at peace."

"Ah, I see," you respond. "It sounds like it's important for you to have a special place in nature, maybe a space that is more private and where there aren't as many people around."

"Exactly," Bennett affirms. "I guess I'm just new to this place. I'd like to figure out where I can go after work or on the weekends for some me-time. But I also love spending time with others in nature, too. So, I feel a little mixed."

"I wonder if any questions in the area of Social EcoWellness jump out at you?" you probe.

Bennett takes a few moments to respond, reviewing the items. "Yeah, the question about deepening my relationships with others," he muses. "I feel like nature has always been a place where I connect with other people, but because I don't know anyone here, I don't really feel that sense of community."

"Okay, so it sounds like finding a place or some places for you-time is important, and so is finding some ways to connect with other people in the outdoors," you reflect. "Is that right?"

"I guess," Bennett responds. "But there's another layer around the environmental stuff. I just don't feel like I'm making a difference in this world right now. Climate change makes me feel empty, along with a lot of the other terrible things happening in the world. So, anything I do is just a drop in the bucket."

"So, there's another layer here with Environmental EcoWellness," you respond.

"Definitely," Bennett affirms. "I think I rated all those items high except for the one about having an environmental cause. I don't even know where to begin with that, and I'm not sure even if I did if it would make a difference."

You proceed to help Bennett identify ways in which he addressed environmental concerns in the past. He discusses experiences as a child where he took part in efforts to plant trees, and he discloses being part of a club in college that engaged in environmental advocacy. Together, you continue exploring how the three facets of EcoWellness pertain to his broader areas of wellness and identify potential ways in which he might like to incorporate EcoWellness into the treatment plan. Clearly, Bennett is feeling socially isolated living in a new place. He's struggling with stress management and having difficulty connecting with and benefiting from nearby natural spaces. Additionally, part of his depression seems connected to a sense of existential angst, feeling like he doesn't have a clear sense of purpose and that his actions might be inconsequential.

Case Summary

What else would you want to know about in assessing Bennett's EcoWellness? What aspects of Bennett's identity and positionality seem most salient to explore? Here are a few questions I'd be curious about:

- Can you share more about what nature is to you now and what nature has meant to you in your life?
- What are the forms of nature that you are most drawn to and why?
- Here you are living in a new place. I'm curious what aspects of the natural world intrigue you the least? What aspects of nature pique your interest?
- Do you currently feel physically and psychologically safe when accessing nature near your residence?
- Are there any nature sounds, landscapes, or aromas that represent calm and restoration? If so, what are they, and do you have any access to those forms of nature currently while you are in your apartment?
- I'm curious to learn about some of the more impactful nature experiences in your life while growing up, positive or negative. Can you share some of those with me?
- What are some of your favorite nature activities or hobbies? Have you learned whether any of those opportunities exist in the area? Are there any new nature activities you might be interested in learning more about?
- In what ways have you cared for nature in the past that may be relevant to you now?

- When and where have you felt most clearly aligned with your life purpose? In what ways has nature played a role in that, if at all?
- Can you recall a time when you felt small and big at the same time while in nature? What contributed to this feeling?
- Would you able to elaborate on your preferred balance between solo nature activities and activities with others?

These are just a few ideas based on the limited information we have about Bennett. Certainly, the more you know about him, the more you would adjust questions like these. While we only formally assessed the three EcoWellness factors underlying the EI-15, exploring Bennett's access to nature, connection with nature, and spirituality all have possible relevance. Thus, when administering the EI-15, I find it important to keep in mind the original tenets underlying the seven-factor framework. These greatly assist in helping us develop a treatment plan that expands access and connection with nature to positively impact the three factors of EcoWellness.

Assessing EcoWellness With Adolescents and Children

To this point, I've discussed the tiered approach to EcoWellness assessment with adults in mind. Now, let's examine several special considerations for practitioners working with adolescents and children. While I'm narrowing this conversation to working with minors, please note that modifications to EcoWellness assessment can be relevant when working with clients of any age.

Modifications to Tier 1 and Tier 2 EcoWellness Assessment

Many adolescents are fully capable of engaging in dialogue surrounding their EcoWellness and how it ties into their holistic wellness. This includes taking the EI-15. Additionally, they often can clearly tell you how they would like EcoWellness incorporated into treatment. That said, adolescents often need us to modify the language we use to ensure they can comprehend the questions we ask. Some youth will have a prior set of experiences (i.e., schema) where they spent time in and around natural settings. Other youth may not have such experiences. In such cases, I like to generally ask, "What is the primary way you spend time with friends and family?" For some, it's spending time interacting on social media or gaming, while for others, it's spending time at a skate park. Either way, I like to get a sense of how much time they spend "outdoors." The term *outdoors* often resonates more, particularly for youth in urban settings with fewer opportunities for immersion in remote natural areas. Additionally, as we previously discussed, it's important to get specific. For example, "When you walk to school, are there trees, flowers, or bodies of water you've noticed?" Here we are simply exploring windows into their lived experience without causing too much confusion.

A primary draw I originally had to working with children and adolescents is the creativity that often accompanies working with this population. As part of this process, I'm always looking to learn about their interests and emerging passions. Embracing a beginner's mind and shedding any layers around being an expert is of critical importance. My goal is to enter the world of my client and see it as they do. In doing so, there are multiple ways we can assess a youth's EcoWellness without using too many words.

I incorporate the creative arts and aspects of play therapy when assessing Tier 1 and Tier 2 EcoWellness with both adolescents and children. The expressive arts can include an array of different practices such as art therapy (e.g., drawing, taking pictures, or sculpting nature), the performing arts (e.g., acting out nature), literary arts (e.g., books or stories about nature), music (e.g., nature sounds or music reminding the clients of nature experiences), creative writing (e.g., poetry or creative fiction or nonfiction), and indoor gardening (e.g., watering or nurturing an indoor plant). While play therapy can be a distinct approach from the expressive arts, its application can be quite useful when assessing EcoWellness. For example, I often use the sand tray or invite clients to use objects or toys to show their favorite nature activities, hobbies, or places. There's really no limit to how you can infuse the creative arts and play therapy into EcoWellness assessment. Here are some simple prompts you can use or adapt:

- Can you draw me a picture of a time you were outdoors with your family?
- I wonder if there is a song that reminds you of your favorite place in the outdoors. It may be a song you remember hearing or singing when you were there, or something different.

- You shared that you and your friends spend quite a bit of time hanging out in the promenade. You also said that you like taking pictures with your phone. Have you taken any photos there that you might be willing to share?
- Using the sand, would you be willing to show me your favorite thing that you do outside? You can use any of these figurines in creating whatever you like.
- You mentioned that you like to write. Have you ever written anything about the outdoors or nature, and would you be willing to share this with me at some point?
- I have a few plants here in the office that need some watering. Have you ever watered a plant before?
- Using any of these objects (i.e., toys), could you show me what it looks like when you spend time at the park with your family?

There is no one prescribed way in applying the creative arts and play therapy in Tier 1 and 2 EcoWellness assessment. Rather, I invite you and your clients to let your imaginations run wild as you creatively assess their experiences and connections with the natural world. Tier 3 assessment provides some additional structure.

Modifications to Tier 3 Assessment

Even though the EI-61 and EI-15 have not been researched with youth, I've administered them with success with adolescents ages 14 and above. Thus, depending on your client's English proficiency and reading level, administering and discussing the results of the EI-15 may have relevance with some adolescent clients. Regardless, when administering the EI-15 with younger adolescents, it may be helpful to be present when the client is completing the survey to address any questions or confusions they may have.

For young children, clinicians might consider adapting and administering the EI-15 with the child's parent or guardian. While parents may not have all the answers, they likely have a sense for their child's overarching EcoWellness. The adult(s) can complete the inventory based on their family system or how they think their child might complete the inventory themselves. However, to date, I haven't found as much benefit administering the EI-61 or EI-15 with parents. They often need to fill in the gaps of knowledge when they don't fully grasp their child's experience of EcoWellness. Thus, I prefer Tier 1 and Tier 2 strategies if a child or adolescent is unable to complete the EI-15 themselves.

While we have yet to empirically adapt the EcoWellness Inventory for use with children, this is something you might consider doing based on the characteristics of the population(s) you serve. If you are the researcher type, you may say that this wouldn't be a valid approach to adapting a survey. Indeed, if we used the EI-15 for diagnostic purposes that led to a formal diagnosis about the individual, I would agree. But remember, the primary utility of the EI-15 is in its ability to initiate dialogue and to help inform treatment planning processes. So, in my book (or in this book, anyway), adapting the EI-15 for use with children in your setting is permissible, so long you are not using it for diagnostic or research purposes. The interpretation of results should be client-centered and only one part of the treatment planning process.

Appendix D is a version of the EI-15 you might consider using with children. It uses a simplified three-point Likert scale with smiley, neutral, and sad face emojis. Depending on reading level, I recommend that you read aloud the different items and help clarify them, when needed. When possible, administer the scale in the presence of a parent or guardian in case there are items that they can help clarify based on the child's family or environmental context. For example, Item #6 on the Environmental EcoWellness subscale states, "My family uses energy from the sun, wind, or water when we can." If the child does not understand this statement, and their family happens to drive a hybrid or electric vehicle, a parent or guardian can provide the child with this information so they can better comprehend the question. To reiterate, if you do decide to use the child form of the inventory, please understand that this version has not been empirically validated and is not intended for diagnostic or research purposes.

Conclusion

The three-tiered approach to EcoWellness assessment can aid clinicians when appraising the human–nature connection across settings and across client populations. As a critical component to human holistic wellness, EcoWellness deserves at least one honorable mention during your intake assessment processes and procedures with all clients. While some clients may not identify with EcoWellness or indicate it as being relevant to them, many clients will. The more that clients identify EcoWellness having relevance in Tier 1, the more likely we are to address EcoWellness using Tier 2 informal assessment. The degree to which a clinician incorporates formal Tier 3 assessment into their practice depends on the setting, the available resources, and the client's particular interests in addressing EcoWellness in treatment. It is of primary importance that we as clinicians shift our language based on the unique needs and positionality of our clients while maintaining authenticity. I've found this to be particularly true when working with both adolescents and children. Being able to translate the underlying constructs of EcoWellness into a client's vernacular can help ensure that the universal aspects of EcoWellness are not lost in the clinical jargon we tend to overuse as clinicians.

Chapter 6 Reflection Questions

Self-awareness:

1. Discuss how your cultural and professional values influence your preferences for assessing EcoWellness in counseling.
2. Consider a client who has expressed adverse experiences with nature. How would you use your understanding of their life experience and the EcoWellness ethos to guide your approach to assessing their connection with the more than human world?

Knowledge:

3. What are the primary components of Tier 1 EcoWellness assessment, and how do they help in understanding a client's general relationship with the natural world?
4. What are key considerations when adapting tiered EcoWellness assessment with children and/or adolescents?
5. How can ongoing assessment be structured to adapt to the evolving therapeutic needs and EcoWellness-based interactions of clients?

Application:

6. Describe how you might implement the three-tiered EcoWellness assessment in your practice setting(s). What challenges might you anticipate?

7. How can Tier 3 EcoWellness assessment be utilized to create a more focused and effective treatment plan? Provide an example scenario.

8. Consider a hypothetical scenario where a client is hesitant to engage in outdoor activities due to past adversity. How might you apply the tiered assessment process to safely reintroduce the outdoors into the client's life?

Notes

1 In Chapter 7, we'll apply a trauma-informed lens onto EcoWellness counseling. We'll consider prior adverse experiences in or with the natural world and current presenting factors that shape the ways in which the clinician incorporates EcoWellness into the treatment planning process. For now, I want to mention the importance of identifying adverse nature experiences during Tier 1 assessment as doing so will impact how you explore EcoWellness in the subsequent tiers.

2 The time and place for utilizing the three-factor model is in Tier 3 assessment, which we'll soon discuss.

References

Bandura, A. (1993). Perceived self-efficacy in cognitive development and functioning. *Educational Psychologist, 28*(2), 117–148. https://doi.org/10.1207/s15326985ep2802_3

Hayhoe, K. (2021). *Saving us: A climate scientist's case for hope and healing in a divided world.* Simon and Schuster.

7

TRAUMA-INFORMED ECOWELLNESS
COUNSELING

In the previous chapter, we explored and positioned EcoWellness as a pathway for assessing the human–nature connection within the context of a client's broader holistic wellness. A tiered approach to EcoWellness assessment enables helping professionals to incorporate the natural world into traditional treatment planning processes with both intentionality and client safety as top priorities. In this chapter, we review core principles underlying a trauma-informed approach for infusing EcoWellness into treatment planning.

Trauma-informed Care

In 2014, Bessel van der Kolk popularized the trauma-informed movement in the helping professions with the publishing of his book *The Body Keeps the Score*. He advanced an unorthodox model of mental illness juxtaposing the disease model that pervades our western medical and mental health systems. Chronic stress and complex developmental trauma—experiences wherein an individual was subject to consistently overwhelming threats to their survival at different points of development—contribute to the manifestation of mental illness symptomology. Such responses are rooted in our evolutionary history and favor the survivability of the organism (i.e., client). The symptoms underlying what we label as mental health disorders (e.g., major depression, PTSD,

DOI: 10.4324/9781315697437-11

bipolar disorder, etc.) are viewed as neurodevelopmental adaptations to coping with and predicting future threats. Our bodies brilliantly respond to past and present adversity to prevent future harm from occurring through the development of patterned nervous system responses to perceived threats within our environment. These survival mechanisms include a variety of consequent behaviors such as fight, flight, freeze, withdraw, and seeking social safety.

The autonomic nervous system, inclusive of the sympathetic (SNS) and parasympathetic nervous systems (PNS), is centrally involved in the body's stress response. The PNS is largely responsible for experiencing calm and safety in the absence of threat (i.e., rest, and digest). In contrast, the SNS is responsible for our fight-or-flight responses. When we consider the cascading effects of stress in the body, the brainstem is one of the first areas of the brain to detect a threatening stimulus, which leads to further signaling in the hypothalamus and subsequent release of stress hormones. The amygdala, which is part of the limbic system, performs a central role in detecting threatening stimuli in the environment, which triggers emotional responses and further helps to activate the SNS in response to danger or perceived threat. The prefrontal cortex (particularly, the ventromedial prefrontal cortex), which is considered critical in executive functioning, helps to downregulate the stress response. That is, activation of the prefrontal cortex enables us to effectively interpret potentially stressful stimuli, make reasoned decisions, and promote behaviors that enact calm or relaxation.

According to Stephen Porge's (2009) polyvagal theory, the vagus nerve, which originates in the brainstem and extends throughout our body's major organs, plays a primary role in the functioning of the PNS. The vagus nerve includes two branches, the dorsal vagal complex (DVC) and the ventral vagal complex (VVC). The VVC is theorized to have a predominant influence on feelings of safety and social engagement. For example, if we detect a threat, we might seek shelter or safety with others nearby. By contrast, the DVC is conceptualized as being responsible for shutting down the nervous system (i.e., immobilization and dissociation) when a perceived threat is overwhelming and seeking social safety is not possible.

A key assumption of the trauma-informed perspective is that our knee-jerk responses to triggering events bypass our thinking brains (i.e., prefrontal cortex). When a threatening stimulus is detected within the environment, our autonomic nervous system responds in whatever ways that have previously been successful in helping an individual survive. Thus, our patterned survival responses aren't typically conscious until we stop and pay attention to them. Once we begin to develop somatic aware- ness, we can train our nervous systems to respond in different ways in situations where trauma responses are no longer adaptive or helpful. Thus, one of the most prominent goals of the trauma-informed approach is to help our clients become more in tune with their bodies' natural responses to coping with adversity and trauma and develop ways to help their nerv- ous systems function more optimally.

The window of tolerance (WoT; Siegel, 1999; Ogden et al., 2006) is an essential concept referenced within the trauma-informed literature and helps illustrate the relationship between the two branches of the autonomic nervous system within the context of polyvagal theory. It is a metaphor for the optimal zone of arousal that enables an individual to effectively regulate emotions, learn, and navigate stressors within their environment. The WoT includes high arousal and low arousal states (see Figure 7.1). At the window's center, we can effectively manage our emo- tions and physiological responses to stress. We have the capacity to access states of calm and focus via adaptive coping strategies that enable us to activate a sense of safety in our bodies. When stressors in our day-to-day experience surpass an individual's ability to cope, clients can experience either hyperarousal (e.g., panic-like symptoms, hypervigilance, anxiety, fear, anger) or hypoarousal (e.g., numbness, depression, emotional shut- down, or dissociation). Through the application of this metaphor, clini- cians help clients develop skills to expand their WoT so they can learn to function more optimally across settings. Clients with a tendency toward hypoarousal may benefit from counseling interventions that help them upregulate into their window; clients who tend to experience hypera- rousal may benefit from interventions helping them downregulate into their optimal window of arousal. Psychoeducation about the body's stress response, mindfulness activities, somatic grounding strategies, emotional

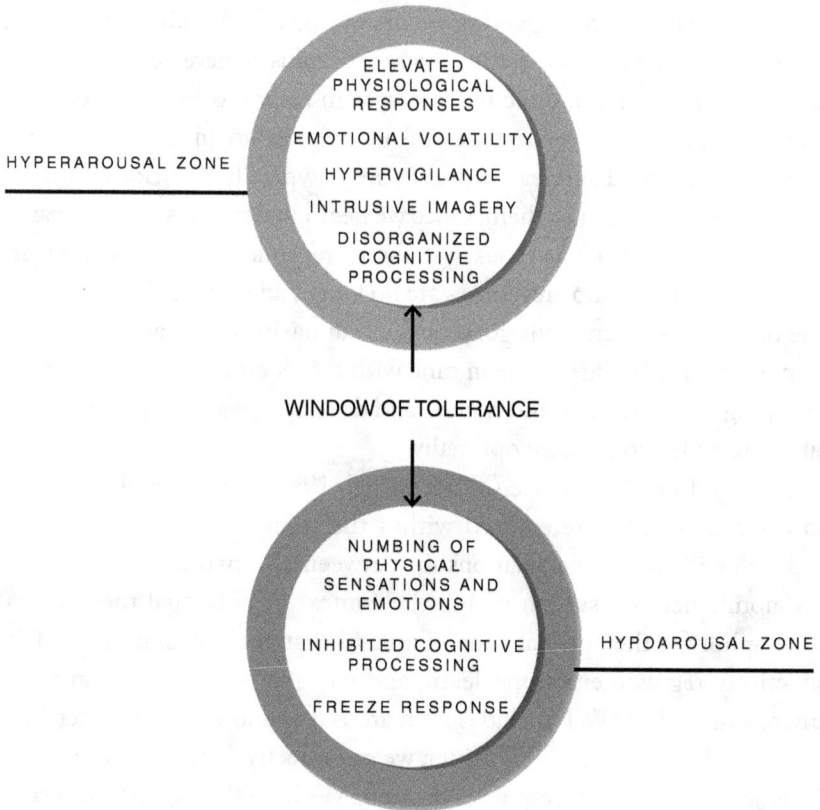

Figure 7.1 Window of Tolerance
Note: Adapted from Ogden et al., 2006

distress tolerance training, and trauma processing are all interventions that can help clients better access their WoT across time.

The therapeutic environment can have significant impacts on the client's WoT during therapy sessions, which, in turn, can affect both client retention and the effectiveness of counseling. One of the hallmarks of traditional indoor therapy is its promise to deliver a crucible of physical and psychological safety. The office provides physical containment: a closed door encased by four interior walls and confined within at least four additional exterior walls. The indoor therapy vessel minimizes the unpredictable and the uncertain. As we consider an EcoWellness approach, one that includes the possibility of counseling meetings outdoors, the potential for unpredictability within the environment increases.

Phasing the Outdoors Into EcoWellness Treatment Planning

When clients come to see us, some will have a lived history and prior schema for therapy; others will conjure a guess based on other potentially related life experiences. A trauma-informed lens would suggest that there is no one-size-fits-all container of talk therapy. As we'll discuss, meeting outdoors could be destabilizing, pushing a client out of their WoT. But the opposite could also be true: meeting indoors can be triggering to the nervous system. Consider the high attrition rates clinicians often face in community-based agency settings and what our medical systems might represent to many of our marginalized clients, including clients of color and LGBTQ+ communities. And then consider that meeting inside the four walls of a private room alone with a person of power (i.e., the licensed clinician) could be triggering to some clients based on their past traumas or present lived experiences. Thus, if we only take into consideration the environment as a standalone factor, it is possible that either an indoor or outdoor environment could be destabilizing and potentially detrimental to the therapeutic process.

The incorporation of outdoor-based sessions should be a phased endeavor (see Figure 7.2), based in the guiding EcoWellness ethical principles, tiered EcoWellness assessment processes, the client's goals and preferences, and the client's stress and trauma responses (i.e., WoT). Moreover, the degree to which the outdoors is incorporated into counseling depends upon the level of rapport and trust within the counseling relationship, client factors such as psychological stability, and the clinician's own developing assessment of safety within the helping relationship.

Trustworthiness and therapeutic rapport go a long way in determining whether the client, the counseling relationship, and the therapist feel secure and safe to withstand incorporating outdoor meetings into the counseling process. I usually find it difficult to fully appraise our collective readiness to go outdoors until I've met with the client at least two times in an indoor setting. In these first several sessions, it is paramount to develop a shared sense of and commitment to safety. If a client is

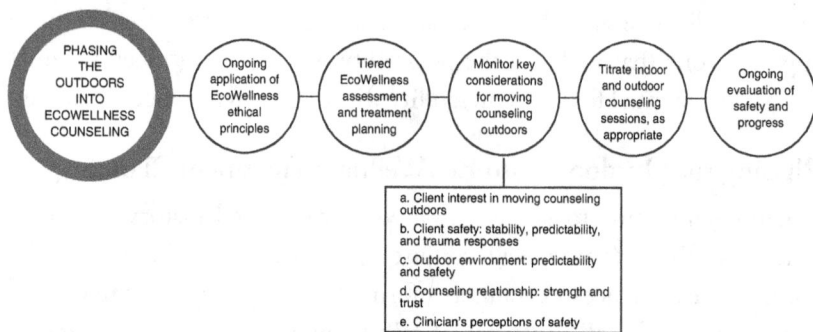

Figure 7.2 Phasing the Outdoors Into EcoWellness Counseling
Note: Copyright Ryan F. Reese, 2024

unable to initially commit to safety if hoping to meet outdoors, we'll find appropriate ways to incorporate EcoWellness within the indoor setting until they can. During the initial stage of counseling, I work with the client to develop a mutual and honest understanding of whether the client's nervous system can tolerate meeting in an agreed upon outdoor environment without the client experiencing overwhelming stress or re-traumatization. This is where the WoT metaphor can be a helpful barometer to determine whether counseling occurs indoors, outdoors, or whatever combination is decided upon by client and clinician.

As part of this process, clinicians apply clinical judgment in evaluating the client's overall psychological stability and predictability. This includes consideration of symptom severity, the client's potential risk to self or others, and developmental factors such as age. Typically, the more severe a client's presenting mental health symptoms (e.g., if a client is amid a manic episode, experiencing psychotic symptoms, or facing a bout of major depression), the greater the caution I employ when incorporating direct, outdoor nature access into the treatment plan. This includes both EcoWellness-based homework that might occur between sessions or meeting with clients outdoors during counseling sessions. With clients who may be experiencing suicidality, I further explore their concern for ideation or intention that may be triggered when accessing an outdoor setting. For example, when discussing a client's potential interest in spending time outdoors, I might ask, "Do you feel safe with yourself outdoors?" or "Are there any places in nature where you would feel unsafe with yourself or anyone else?" I once worked with a client who wanted to spend time in nature as part of their self-care practices. They presented with some suicidal ideation and previously reported having a plan to jump off a bridge near a natural area just outside of town. Through dialogue, the client came to their own determination that they would refrain from going to this place and instead frequented nearby nature that felt less triggering for them. In essence, the less psychologically stable the client, the less complicated the nature included in the treatment plan. Ongoing monitoring and adjustment to the treatment plan may be needed based on the client's progress, their shifting life circumstances, and the progression of the counseling relationship.

Moreover, as much as possible, I like to be able to anticipate whether a client's behavior will be predictable in an outdoor session. Specifically, when I work with younger clients or clients who have limited capacity for self-regulation, I assess whether they can commit to following safety guidelines. As with client stability, the less predictable the client, the more predictable the environment needed during counseling, particularly in the early stages of building trust and rapport in the helping relationship. When meeting with younger clients outdoors, I typically meet in parks versus on trails because there tend to be fewer hazards. I avoid steep hills, cliffs, and fast-moving bodies of water when working with clients who have difficulty following mutually agreed upon guidelines for safety. Ultimately, if I'm stressing too much about a client's physical safety during session, I'm less in touch with clients and their needs because my own nervous system can be more easily activated.

It is essential for the clinician to consider their own WoT when pondering the ways in which they phase the outdoors into EcoWellness counseling. The reality is that your own experience of emotional and physical safety will shift with each client and depending on the setting. This is completely normal. The important thing here is to be able to identify patterned responses within yourself, including which settings and client-presenting issues or characteristics may be more triggering for you. Personally, when it comes to meeting environment, I've found that accessing safety within my own WoT has greater stability when indoors. I have a great deal of comfort meeting clients in my office on account of there being a high level of predictability and a limited number of variables that are likely to shift in the immediate environment. By contrast, there are numerous variables that can rapidly change when meeting outdoors.

Likewise, we must be honest with ourselves about the client character-istics and presentations (e.g., specific diagnoses or presenting problems) that can be potentially triggering to our own nervous systems when meet-ing outdoors versus indoors. It is possible that you may feel physically or psychologically unsafe to meet with a client outdoors based on client characteristics and how such factors interact with your own lived history, life experiences, and positionality. Self-care and personal therapy become paramount to ensure we maintain awareness of and work through our own life adversities, biases, and assumptions. Additional areas of coun-tertransference to monitor might include a client's particular presenting challenges or the topics they discuss with you in therapy. While you may feel comfortable talking with clients about a particular issue in an indoor setting, exploring that same topic can have a different psychological or emotional charge when meeting outdoors. The indoor or outdoor meet-ing environment can change the tenor of the counseling relationship for both the client and the counselor, and at times, you may need to request meeting indoors. While the direct communication of a particular coun-tertransference issue(s) may not always be shared with the client, you can give clients a heads up that, at times, you may prefer to meet indoors, just as the client can.

Within a trauma-informed EcoWellness approach to counseling, the clinician and client partner together to work toward identifying poten-tially destabilizing EcoWellness-based experiences and mutually agree upon which EcoWellness interventions or meeting contexts seem most appropriate in addressing the client's stated goals for counseling. A pro-active approach to EcoWellness treatment planning will help ensure that a client feels prepared to navigate both favorable and potentially unpre-dictable experiences that may emerge, particularly when meeting outside the office. As we discussed in Chapter 2, regardless of the level of prepa-ration, the client must be informed that unpredictable events can emerge when meeting outdoors. Thus, while we can be as cautious as possible to titrate EcoWellness-based experiences to match the needs and treatment goals of the client, it is still possible that they may encounter a triggering event when engaging the outdoors in or out of session. If it is determined that a client may not initially be ready to meet outdoors, or at any point in the counseling relationship, it's important to talk about it. In such cases, meeting outdoors can become part of a goal to work toward in the therapeutic process, if appropriate. Thus, meeting indoors or outdoors is never an all-or-nothing venture, but instead, part of an ongoing and highly communicative process where together the therapeutic relationship phases the more than human world into counseling.

The Case of Bernice

Bernice was a 22-year-old Persian-American, cisgender woman who came to counseling as a coinciding curricular requirement for admittance into a college transition academic program. She reached out to me because she was interested in a nature-based counseling approach and preferred outdoor meetings. Bernice described being diagnosed with attention-deficit hyperactivity disorder (ADHD) in her teens and took Adderall to address symptomology affecting her ability to concentrate in school. Bernice also experienced anxiety in social settings and disclosed low self-concept. She initially reported wanting to attend therapy to improve overall self-esteem and to boost her confidence in school.

Bernice was forthcoming throughout the intake process. She shared about her family background, including her mother and father's experiences when they immigrated to the United States. She portrayed a great deal of pride in reflecting upon the social and institutional barriers that her parents overcame to become successful business owners. She was the youngest of four siblings, and she disclosed feeling like the least successful. "They've all graduated college and began their careers, and I've barely started community college," she lamented. She felt pressure to "figure things out," and she believed that the college transition program was her last chance to prove to her parents that she could be successful in college.

I generally inquired about recent or past adverse experiences in Bernice's life. She reported one negative experience "when I was in high school," though declined to share any details about what had happened. I asked how much the experience generally affected her now and she shrugged her shoulders. "Maybe a little bit, but it's something I feel like I don't need to talk about."

While I got the sense there was much more under the surface, I recognized that pushing her further for particulars would likely dampen the trust within our developing professional relationship. I trusted she would share if and when she felt ready and safe to do so. Bernice denied any past or present suicidal or homicidal ideation and she indicated she lacked any specific concerns for meeting outdoors. She couldn't recall any adverse experiences in nature and didn't disclose any medical concerns for meeting outside.

We explored Bernice's connection with the natural world using Tier 1 and Tier 2 EcoWellness assessment. She defined herself as a nature lover and couldn't recall experiencing any adversities in or with the natural environment. She loved the woods and recalled positive experiences going camping with friends growing up. Her favorite places included being by the water. Bernice shared ways in which she felt close to her cultural heritage in nature; she felt in sync with the natural world, asserting that she had a spiritual kinship with plants and wild animals. She excitedly reconstructed the thrill of going mountain biking for the first time. "I'm not very good at it," she stated. "But it was a blast." She noted that there was a park near her apartment but stated a hesitation to go there on her own. "It's right across the street," she indicated. "Super close with some beautiful trees. But I just don't know how I feel about going there on my own, even during the day." Given her love for the outdoors, this hesitance to be in solitude with nearby nature stood out to me.

We decided to meet indoors at least one more time before taking therapy outdoors. At the beginning of our second meeting, I prompted Bernice to consider how she might want to incorporate EcoWellness into her treatment plan. "I don't really know. Maybe just going for walks during our appointments."

I intuited there was something there she didn't want to address in the moment, which I acknowledged. "Bernice, I'm appreciative of you sharing so much last week about your life and your love of nature. I get the sense that there may be something we haven't touched on yet that is of importance for you coming to counseling."

Bernice nodded, staring out the window. Her demeanor shifted and the energy in the room flattened. She looked at me, tears welling in her eyes. "Something bad happened in high school." Bernice sobbed. "It's why I'm afraid to be alone. It's why I don't trust myself." Bernice went on to report the generalities of a traumatic experience that brought about enduring physical and mental harm. "It wrecked my confidence. I couldn't eat, and

I developed an eating disorder. I feel like that's gotten a lot better, but I still don't trust others or myself, and I still don't feel safe."

We began discussing safety in the immediate counseling relationship and what developing trust over time might look like. She disclosed additional details about her experience and that she now has a fear of being alone with men. "That's part of why I wanted to see you," she stated. "I thought maybe seeing you could heal some of the trauma by working with a guy, and the nature part made you feel more approachable."

I asked, "As we get going, do you think you would feel safer indoors with me or outdoors with me?"

"I really want to say outdoors, but I guess I'm not really sure," she responded.

I went on to describe the outdoor locations where I typically met with clients and let her know that we could do anything ranging from going on a hike, sitting by the creek or at a park bench. We could be near people in the community, or we could be more distant from people, depending on her preferences. Together, we agreed that meeting indoors was likely the best way for her to feel physically and emotionally safe in the early stages of the counseling relationship. Bernice wanted to work toward outdoor sessions, and the treatment plan began to take shape: "I want to be able to go on a hike by myself, and I want to feel safe in my body."

I asked Bernice what would need to happen or change for her to feel safe in solitude on a trail. "I need to heal from my trauma," she quickly replied. After further discussion we agreed to work toward trauma processing. First, in preparation, we would develop additional coping skills to help expand Bernice's distress tolerance so she could function more optimally in her everyday life. Second, Bernice agreed that she would like to work toward trusting herself and her own decisions. She was tired of second-guessing herself so much. Our third objective included trauma processing using eye movement desensitization and reprocessing (EMDR). I asked Bernice about the kinds of things she would be able to do if counseling was successful. "I could go to the park across the street by myself, and I would try mountain biking again. I would feel less anxious about school and finish an academic term."

After making the decision to work indoors, we first revisited Bernice's coping mechanisms and wellness resources. We explored a phased approach to EcoWellness, including incorporating sensory access to nature at home and group experiences with nature in her social life. We engaged in trauma processing using EMDR, which helped reduce the distress of prior memories and increased a sense of safety within the counseling relationship. We identified that when the memories of her prior trauma were triggered, a dissociative response was activated. Such a reaction may have initially helped her survive and cope with the trauma she endured, but the present-day trauma response was no longer adaptive; she was ready to address her body's automatic response to her memories and find ways to help her nervous system experience safety in situations that were triggering. Following several months of EMDR, these dissociative tendencies began to decrease, and Bernice felt ready to try meeting outdoors. Together, we identified appropriate outdoor venues and spaces for meeting. I made sure to always stay within Bernice's visual field and minimized walking behind her to help her feel more at ease. I ensured that our meeting spaces were open where the client could see all around us. During our first session, I frequently checked in with Bernice about her overall sense of safety and where she felt like she was at within her WoT.

In our work together, Bernice experienced significant change. She achieved greater trust in herself and her judgment. She developed additional coping resources and ended up going mountain biking again. Additionally, she began hiking by herself and attended a four-year university that following fall. While EcoWellness was addressed with Bernice from the outset, it took us several months of meeting before taking counseling outdoors. Our work on resourcing and trauma processing led to greater trust in the client's own intuition as well as developing an expanded WoT when working within the counseling relationship. This progress also led to her being able to access diverse nature-based environments for her own self-care, which translated into greater experiences of self-esteem and self-efficacy.

Case Summary

The case of Bernice demonstrates the critical importance of holistic assessment processes when treatment planning with clients wanting to address EcoWellness in counseling. While Bernice did not report any nature-based traumas or concerns during the intake, her prior trauma as a teen affected her approach to engaging the outdoors as a wellness resource. Additionally, our ability to meet in the outdoor context as she preferred was initially affected. Conceptualized through the WoT, Bernice was able to meet with me in an indoor context while staying within her WoT. However, if we had met outdoors early in the counseling relationship, she might have experienced significant distress counter to her therapeutics goals. Thus, it's critical to be methodical and communicative with clients when contemplating taking counseling outside the office. We worked together over time to build psychological safety and trust in the counseling relationship. We also addressed the client's past trauma using a trauma processing model before taking counseling outdoors. We were then able to phase meeting outdoors into counseling by attending a park in a community-based setting.

EcoWellness adds an additional layer of complexity within trauma-informed care. While the natural world can be incredibly healing and restorative, incorporating EcoWellness into a treatment plan requires a great deal of caution and intentionality, particularly when considering the appropriateness of phasing the outdoors into treatment.

Conclusion

In this chapter, I articulated a trauma-informed approach to infusing the human–nature connection within counseling. Clinicians should prioritize physical and psychological safety within the counseling relationship and engage in dialogue with clients that explores their potential triggers for participating in EcoWellness-based interventions. Together, clinicians can work with clients to assess and expand the client's WoT so they can learn to regulate the nervous system more effectively in and out of counseling, as well as collaboratively tailoring interventions that help clients maintain an optimal zone of arousal. In doing so, the inclusion of the outdoors can be phased into the counseling process in ways that honor the client's prior history and their capacity for navigating potential unpredictability in the outdoor-based environment. Clinicians must also consider their own WoT as their threshold for stress may present differently based on the therapeutic environment and the clients with whom they are working.

Ultimately, it is up to the clinician to evaluate and monitor a client's stability and commitment to safety when contemplating going outdoors, and gauge whether the counseling relationship is ready to meet in an outdoor context. For some clients, meeting outdoors too early in the counseling relationship can be destabilizing. On the contrary, some clients will feel physically safer and more emotionally secure when meetings take place outside the office. By adopting a trauma-informed lens within an EcoWellness approach, clinicians can position themselves to prioritize safety when phasing EcoWellness-based interventions into counseling and psychotherapy. This process, based in collaboration and mutual trust in the counseling relationship, will position clients to expand self-awareness, emotional regulation, and achieve their unique goals for therapy.

Chapter 7 Reflection Questions

Self-awareness:

1. Reflect on the case study of Bernice. How did the trauma-informed approach help her navigate her counseling journey? How might you apply similar principles in your own counseling practice?
2. Consider your own responses to stress and trauma. How might this awareness affect your ability to provide trauma-informed EcoWellness counseling?

Knowledge:

3. Discuss the importance of the "window of tolerance" in the context of EcoWellness. How can counselors use this concept to tailor their interventions more effectively?
4. Describe how understanding a client's autonomic nervous system responses can guide the choice of EcoWellness interventions.
5. What are some potential challenges of integrating outdoor therapy sessions for clients with a history of trauma, and how can these be mitigated?

Application:

6. Discuss how trauma-informed care principles can influence the assessment and integration of EcoWellness practices in therapy. How might these principles alter your approach to nature-based interventions?

7. How can counselors ensure that they are ethically and effectively using the EcoWellness framework in a trauma-informed manner?

8. Develop a strategy for ethically incorporating EcoWellness interventions for a client with a trauma history, ensuring the approach is both safe and therapeutic.

References

Ogden, P., Minton, K., & Pain, C. (2006). *Trauma and the body: A sensorimotor approach to psychotherapy.* W. W. Norton & Company.

Porges, S. W. (2009). The polyvagal theory: New insights into adaptive reactions of the autonomic nervous system. *Cleveland Clinic Journal of Medicine, 76*(Suppl 2), S86. https://doi.org/10.3949/ccjm.76.s2.17

Siegel, D. J. (1999). *The developing mind: Toward a neurobiology of interpersonal experience.* Guilford Press.

van der Kolk, B. A. (2014). *The body keeps the score: Brain, mind, and body in the healing of trauma.* Penguin Books.

8

THE SPHERED APPROACH TO ECOWELLNESS INTERVENTION MAPPING

Imagine for a moment that you engaged in EcoWellness assessment with three different clients, each with varying interests for addressing the human–nature connection in counseling. Client A specifically sought you out because you specialize in incorporating EcoWellness into counseling. They completed the EI-15 and want to prioritize increasing areas of EcoWellness as part of the treatment plan. Client B has some interest in addressing EcoWellness in counseling, and you informally assessed EcoWellness using Tier 2 assessment. Their primary goal in counseling is to work through past trauma or grief using a traditional counseling modality, but they are interested in incorporating elements of EcoWellness in the treatment plan. Client C sought you out because they heard you sometimes meet with clients outdoors, and they would rather meet in an outdoor context because they believe it would be more comfortable for them.

How a clinician applies the EcoWellness framework within counseling will undoubtedly vary by client. Lia Naor and Ofra Mayseless (2021) interviewed 26 nature-based practitioners (e.g., wilderness therapists, clinical psychologists, and psychotherapists) from five countries and conducted six field observations across counseling settings to better understand the possible therapeutic benefits of the nature-based therapies. These clinician-participants viewed the natural environment as

DOI: 10.4324/9781315697437-12

a growth-oriented metaphor (representing change, renewal, and aliveness) that fostered wholeness and self-acceptance. The practitioners described nature as a pathway that enabled clients to overcome challenges, such as those naturally occurring in the natural environment (e.g., navigating difficult weather during a wilderness experience) or adventure-based activities occurring in the natural setting. The clinicians also suggested that nature served as an active co-facilitator of the therapeutic process wherein the natural world contributes to change. Lastly, the helping professionals enrolled in the study suggested that awe-based experiences with nature and the facilitation of wonder in the natural world expanded egocentric views of the self, thus contributing to enhanced perceptions of interconnectedness and belongingness within the natural world.

This research points to several potential implications for addressing EcoWellness within traditional counseling settings. Given that the natural world positively impacts human holistic wellness, clients might directly benefit from outdoor settings that serve as a container or backdrop in counseling. Moreover, clinicians can partner with the natural world as a co-facilitator in the counseling process, wherein they apply intentionality when interacting with natural settings. In this chapter, I introduce a sphered approach to EcoWellness intervention mapping: EcoWellness as an adjunctive backdrop to therapy, EcoWellness as a complementary approach, and EcoWellness as a core intervention strategy. A sphered approach to EcoWellness is based on the client's broader goals for therapy and the agreed upon method to incorporating nature into therapeutic processes. Before exploring these spheres and illustrating them through case example, let's first examine EcoWellness-based strategies that may be thoughtfully incorporated across spheres.

EcoWellness-based Counseling Strategies

We reviewed several ecotherapeutic modalities in Chapter 1. Certainly, these approaches can be incorporated when addressing EcoWellness in therapy. Other nature-based approaches or paradigms might also be infused. In such cases, I once again invite us to consider our own scope of practice and fully engage clients in the ongoing informed consent process. While the ecotherapies can be helpful tools when merged with counseling and psychotherapy, I find that most often I work with clients to identify client-centered methods for bolstering EcoWellness.

The seven-factor EcoWellness framework lies at the heart of crafting client-centered EcoWellness strategies. Nature access, whether that be through direct or sensory means, can have positive effects on the nervous system. Facilitating therapeutic experiences wherein clients can generate nature self-efficacy, experience self-transcendence, and enhance a sense of environmental agency can help clients achieve greater EcoWellness, and subsequently, therapeutic outcomes. Across these facets of EcoWellness, facilitating mindfulness plays a pivotal role in both connecting with nature, and possibly maximizing the holistic wellness benefits of the natural world.

The Mindfulness Foundation

The purposeful act of tuning into the present moment and doing so without judgment is a core component of benefiting from contact with nature. This attentive process enables us to fully see, feel, hear, touch, and experience nature. Indeed, research demonstrates that mindfulness contributes to greater conceptions of connectedness with the more than human world, and this connectedness can serve as an intermediary to experiencing well-being (Huynh & Torquati, 2019). In my work with clients over the years, I've found that mindfulness is one of the most critical factors for clients to benefit from an EcoWellness approach. Through expanding curiosity and employing a beginner's mind, the natural world possesses beauty, ineffability, metaphor, and timelessness. The mindful pathway better enables clients to access self-compassion, gratitude, patience, openness, creativity, and togetherness—which can all serve to disrupt unhelpful thought and behavioral patterns over time. Contrast this with a preoccupied mind and heart; when our minds fixate on the past or worries about the future, it's easy to overlook nature's mystique. When we embody ourselves in the present, we can see the many colors of the more than human world and be touched by its grandeur; we can fully access its inherent value and the lessons that wait for us there.

Many clients will benefit from learning components of mindfulness as a precursor or concurrent process to infusing EcoWellness into the treatment plan. Mindfulness training programs such as mindfulness-based stress reduction (MBSR; Kabat-Zinn, 1990) provide a structured approach to learning and practicing mindfulness. If such programming is inaccessible or if individual applications of MBSR cannot be readily incorporated into counseling, mindfulness apps such as Insight Timer, Headspace, or Calm provide user-friendly approaches to learning and practicing mindfulness both during and out of session. By expanding a client's ability to be mindful, they can more fully benefit from the indoor or outdoor EcoWellness strategies incorporated into therapy.

Strategies for Fostering Sensory and Physical Access to Nature

With a foundation of mindfulness, clients can begin to experience their nature access with greater purposefulness. As explicated in Chapter 7, I encourage clinicians to phase nature into counseling before taking counseling outdoors. For example, clinicians can be strategic with how they arrange their office environment and what natural elements they include to facilitate mindful presence. This includes nature views, sounds, images, or objects that help reduce stress and bring the client's attention into the here and now.

For clinicians fortunate enough to have a window view of nature, I recommend structuring the seating configuration so that your client can see what's out there. The view might include a tree, some shrubs, or another building, but having the opportunity to experience sunshine, the clouds, or birds flying by can bring about a sense of calm, relaxation, and mindfulness. Even better is when the clinician and the client can share this view together, thus enabling the therapeutic dyad to mutually witness any events occurring outside (e.g., a hail or snowstorm, seeing a bird land on a branch, etc.).

Regardless of whether a window view is possible, adding live, indoor plants is another way to bring nature indoors. This could include having clients seed and nurture their own plants over time. Landscape photography or murals are another possibility. I've had less success in incorporating aromatherapy as individual clients will favor some scents and dislike others. It can also be difficult to fully eradicate some scents between sessions, and fragrances can contribute to allergic reactions.

Moreover, the presence of nature sounds (e.g., ocean waves, birds chirping, waterfall, and stream sounds) can facilitate calm and reduce client psychophysiological stress during session. I like to invite clients to consider whether they would prefer having nature sounds, and if so, they can select whatever they like. The presence of nature objects can also provide a sense of tactile grounding or possible direction for a therapy session. Psychologist Dr. Patricia Hasbach (2016) uses a basket of nature objects for clients to choose from in starting the counseling session. Clients identify an object that resonates with their mood or serves as a metaphor for what the client may be experiencing that week, which operates as a springboard for the session.

Beyond the immediate indoor environment, clients can benefit from guided imagery experiences wherein the clinician utilizes a mindfulness lens to guide clients through their senses within nature-based visualization. While clinicians can craft their own scripts and narratives, collaborative and personalized visualizations are the most impactful and culturally sustaining. These imaginings might be used for stress reduction purposes or helping clients develop additional distress tolerance skills as part of a trauma processing modality (e.g., prolonged exposure therapy or EMDR).

Incorporation of the creative arts is an additional strategy that can be utilized to address sensory access to nature. Clients engage in drawing pictures, poetry, nature writing, amongst other activities. This is where both you as the therapist and the client can employ quite a bit of creativity. In my work with youth over the years, I've observed clients benefiting from simple prompts:

"Can you draw a picture that shows the nature where you live?"
"Please draw a picture of you doing your favorite activity outside."
"Can you draw you and your family at the park?"
"You mentioned that you go outside when you feel upset. Can you draw a picture of that?"

By keeping the prompts simple and general, clients can respond to them in whatever ways that resonate for them in that moment. Their creations are then used to further discuss whatever is most salient to them about the picture or words, particularly as it relates to the client's treatment plan. My goal is to bring the client's senses alive, asking what they see, hear, touch, smell, and taste when reflecting on their work. I, too, attempt to immerse myself in whatever sensory information they disclose, thus enabling us to have a shared experience. In a similar way, the sand tray can be used as another canvas for our clients. Some of the same prompts can be used, but instead of using colored crayons or markers to construct their natural world, they use figurines in the sand.

As with incorporating elements of nature and nature connection within indoor counseling, some clients benefit from and prefer meeting in the outdoors. Within walk and talk therapy, the outdoor setting serves as the backdrop for the counseling experience. Movement and physical exercise in the outdoors, combined with nature stimuli and meeting in a different context with the clinician, may help open dialogue and creativity within the counseling process. This approach to therapy is gaining traction as an alternative to meeting indoors. In her book, *Walk and Talk Therapy: A Clinician's Guide to Incorporating Movement and Nature into Your Practice*, Jennifer Udler (2023) suggests that walk and talk therapy can provide a calming presence and opportunity for infusing natural metaphors into the client's experience. She also emphasizes rhythmic movement as a pathway for synchronizing the mind and body and providing a shared and deepened journey with her clients. For some clients, the primary motivation for meeting outdoors is to make the counseling environment more comfortable and less angst-provoking. In such cases, purposeful interaction with the natural world might be minimized. In contrast, other clients may want to both walk in and engage with the natural setting. Such sessions might include the incorporation of nature metaphor, mindful observation, or practices such as sitting meditation or mindful walking.

Facilitating indoor sensory access or outdoor physical access experiences in counseling can help bridge the client's direct experience of nature within their own living environments. Through dialogue, clinicians can better learn about the client's safe access to nearby nature or the lack thereof. They can work with the client or the client's family to identify outdoor spaces, transportation, and particular activities the client might engage in outside of session. As we'll later discuss, if the client lacks safe access to the outdoors, this is where clinicians can engage the client in forms of environmental agency, wherein they reflect together and/or as part of the community to identify forms of advocacy that promote safe and restorative nature access.

Facilitating Nature Connectedness

Some of the same strategies used for addressing sensory and physical access can also be utilized for enhancing connection with nature. This might include guided visualizations of a client's favorite or sacred places in nature. It might also encompass ancestral visualizations wherein clients imagine connecting with the natural world and cultural practices previously enacted by members of their historical community. Nature journaling is one of my favorite homework strategies to assign clients. Clients visit a space where they may or may not have prior familiarity. Within this space, clients observe their surroundings and write down their observations of self and the more than human world around them. I encourage clients to employ creativity with their writing, maybe taking a shot at poetry or songwriting, and maybe drawing or taking a picture of a wild animal inhabiting the spaces they are visiting.

When facilitating connection, I also invite clients to reflect upon their early memories or experiences with the natural world, including their interactions with important others in their life. If accessible, clients might venture to these places of earlier connection. This reflective process or the ritual of visiting sacred places can contribute to a healing process for many clients, particularly for clients seeking to feel more connected with family members or other loved ones who have passed on.

Moreover, much of my work with clients around nature connectedness has included facilitating a sense of place attachment. This has been particularly relevant when working with clients who have just moved to a new area with unfamiliar nearby natural landscapes. We identify places that elicit positive affective, cognitive, and spiritual affiliations, as well as identifying possible activities that may serve as pathways for connection to the space. Examples include helping clients and families identify safe and accessible spaces to nature and learning possible activities that will help with engaging or honoring that space. Employing mindfulness can help clients maintain an open posture to exploring a new setting. Encouraging a beginner's mind and non-judgment can help clients expand their curiosity and openness in exploring novel natural settings that may differ from prior conceptions of nature.

Interventions for Enhancing Nature Self-efficacy

Experiencing felt-sense confidence in exploring nature can help facilitate a sense of connection with natural landscapes. In prior survey research we (Reese & Lewis, 2019) explored relationships between the original 61-item EcoWellness Inventory and the Indivisible Self Model of Wellness. The Protection factor (i.e., nature self-efficacy) was one of the primary facets of EcoWellness that drove the predictive model between holistic wellness and EcoWellness, suggesting that facilitating opportunities for clients to build personal effectiveness in their relationship with nature might help contribute to holistic wellness outcomes. Helping clients identify and learn about culturally sustaining and accessible nature-based activities via experiential learning can positively contribute to general self-efficacy and self-esteem, which can serve as intermediate objectives in supporting clients to achieve their primary goals for therapy. For example, helping families identify the kinds of equipment they might need for a day of fishing at a local pond, and when possible, connecting families with community resources to access the necessary gear when there are financial constraints.

Potential applications for building client self-efficacy might also include nature-based child-centered play therapy (NBCCPT; Swank & Shin, 2015) and adventure-based counseling (ABC; Brown et al., 2023). Both approaches incorporate nature-based activity into counseling processes. NBCCPT provides a nondirective and client-led framework empowering clients to explore the natural environment, and ABC practitioners prescribe kinesthetic nature-based experiences. The counseling relationship within NBCCPT serves as a foundation and facilitates connection with the natural world. Through the incorporation of natural elements into therapy, clients freely explore nature, and the clinician recognizes and reflects the client's feelings while also enabling the client to solve their own problems in the immediate environment. In this way, the clinician follows the client's lead, and boundaries and limits are set as needed throughout the therapeutic relationship.

ABC incorporates nature-based activities into either group or individual counseling contexts. Common to ABC are hands-on or kinesthetic experiences that incorporate problem-solving or building skill around a particular activity. This approach takes advantage of the cognitive dissonance that can emerge when clients are navigating and working toward the mastery of a new skill. In such instances, client negative core beliefs and ways of coping and communicating are experienced in the here and now. The prescribed activity can include problem-solving games, trust activities, nature walks or hikes, or wilderness-based programming (Tucker & Norton, 2013). Prior to the experience, clients are first briefed about the activity and the expectations for participation. Following participation, they then engage in a reflective process wherein clients consider what happened, the significance of that activity relative to their treatment goals, and how they might then transfer or apply this learning to their lives more broadly (Brown et al., 2023).

Strategies for Facilitating Self-transcendence

Inclusion of the natural world into counseling can help clients see beyond themselves and how they fit into the broader landscape of the more than human community. Just by stepping outdoors, we are inviting opportunities for the client to experience self-transcendence, including feeling more connected with others. This sense of Social EcoWellness is intuitive for many clients, particularly for clients coming from community-oriented (i.e., collectivistic) backgrounds. However, I find that for many westerners it can take some time to open up to the idea of connecting with others in natural spaces. Thus, strategies for addressing Social EcoWellness might include identifying opportunities for social connection in outdoor contexts, particularly when clients report feeling isolated.

Moreover, clients benefit from eco-based strategies that tap into their spiritual and cultural traditions. In my experience, this has been particularly relevant when working with clients surrounding loss and grief. For example, clients going through the loss of a loved one will often report places that have deep spiritual meaning. However, it can be emotionally too overwhelming to visit these places or spaces initially, and clients can often benefit from a titrated approach to revisiting these spaces first in their minds, and later, physically accessing these spaces. Similarly, the loss of cultural sites and traditions is another critical factor when working with clients and communities who have endured the loss of cultural landscapes, sacred spaces, and practices. Working with clients to identify culturally sustaining practices and collaborating with spiritual or faith leaders, when indicated, will help ensure that clinicians are engaging in culturally sustaining services that may help clients work through grief and address experiences of intergenerational trauma. In a similar vein, I am seeing an increase in clients reporting the loss of favorite or sacred places in the natural world on account of forest fires, floods, and other natural disasters spurred by climate change.

Solastalgia is another factor to address relative to self-transcendence. Solastalgia is the emotional distress, grief, and possible trauma produced by environmental climate change and degradation. The loss or anticipated loss of spaces, species, and landscapes contributes to an adverse experience of self-transcendence. That is, when the more than human world is harmfully impacted and damaged and the individual client sees themselves as being part of that whole, the client can experience a perceived lack of control and a sense of loss pertaining to their broadened self-identity. Here I've found it important to approach clients from an existential or integrative lens that addresses the client's meaning-making system and helps them identify tangible actions they can take, however big or small, in caring for the world around them.

Bolstering Environmental Agency Through Praxis

Environmental EcoWellness, having the ability to positively impact and care for the natural world, is another important element to view through a client's cultural lens and other aspects of positionality. For some clients, being able to recycle, compost, and pick up litter can provide a sense of control and self-efficacy. Additionally, tending to a garden, a plant, or engaging in community environmental organizations can be healing for some clients struggling with solastalgia. But what happens if a community doesn't have a recycling program, the client doesn't view environmental climate change as a real phenomenon, or if the client does not have the resources or capacity to engage in a community-based organization?

Here again I remind us that EcoWellness is client-driven and client-defined. We must partner with clients and their communities to identify meaningful actions that can benefit the client and the ecological systems for which they are part. In alignment with *The Multicultural and Social Justice Counseling Competencies* (MSJCC; Ratts et al., 2016), clinicians can join with clients to engage in EcoWellness counseling and advocacy interventions contributing to critical consciousness and liberation. In my experience, working from a liberatory approach has been critical when addressing Environmental EcoWellness with clients. Paulo Freire was an education reformist in Brazil in the mid-to-late 20th century. His central thesis was that societal change can only be enacted through the shared acknowledgment and overcoming of institutionalized oppression. In *Pedagogy of the Oppressed* (1970), Freire suggested that examination of one's individual background and positionality, including one's own experiences of oppressing or being the oppressed, can contribute to critical consciousness-raising. Within this reflective and shared process, individuals can engage in authentic praxis, wherein we dialogue together about our shared reality and perspectives and take subsequent actions to address meaningful change.

Specifically, we can consider EcoWellness counseling as a co-constructed process wherein the clinician supports a client in liberating themselves from dominant narratives, including those about nature, nature connectedness, and environmental climate change. Without employing such a perspective, clinicians risk imposing their own framework and nature worldview onto clients. This includes the construct of EcoWellness itself and the administration of the EI-15. Items on this inventory, including the Environmental EcoWellness subfactor, should be viewed, modified, and discussed through the lens of the client. By utilizing open and inviting language and letting clients know that their experiences and definitions of "nature" or "environment" may be different but just as valid as your own, we can engage in authentic praxis wherein clients identify environmental issues and actions that are most salient to them.

EcoWellness-based Counseling Strategies: A Summary

There are no ready-made or cookie-cutter approaches to addressing EcoWellness in traditional settings. Rather, incorporation of this construct into counseling and psychotherapy means working closely with clients to identify the language and worldview they apply when considering the role of EcoWellness in their lives, including access to nature, connection, self-efficacy, self-transcendence, and environmental agency. Through joining together with our clients and employing a tiered approach to EcoWellness assessment, we work together with clients to employ appropriate and client-centered strategies into the EcoWellness counseling process.

The Sphered Approach to Incorporating EcoWellness Into Counseling

Now that we've overviewed possible EcoWellness-based counseling strategies, let's look toward their purposeful application within traditional clinical settings. I advocate that clinicians employ a sphered EcoWellness approach (see Figure 8.1) inclusive of adjunctive, complementary, and core interventions.

Sphere 1: EcoWellness as an Adjunctive Intervention

Client motivation for engaging the EcoWellness approach often includes a desire to lessen the anxiety or stress of meeting with a therapist

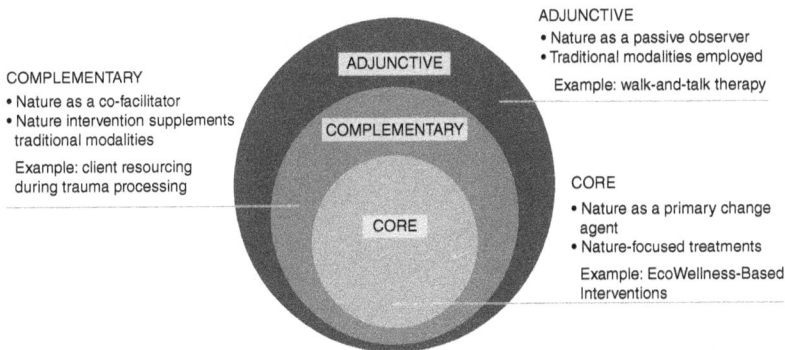

Figure 8.1 The Sphered Approach to EcoWellness Intervention Mapping

Note: Copyright Ryan F. Reese, 2024

inside the four walls. This might include a parent wanting their jittery elementary-aged child or nonverbal adolescent to meet outdoors to increase compliance for attending counseling, neurodivergent clients who feel more comfortable meeting outdoors to reduce perceived expectations for communicating in ways that adhere to social norms, or clients who generally feel stifled meeting in an indoor environment.

Within Sphere 1, EcoWellness intervention components passively support the counseling relationship and goals for therapy. Nature is conceptualized as a co-observer to the client's process, and interaction with nature is typically passive and nondirective. The primary benefit of an ancillary approach includes the presence of nature stimuli, with the assumption that incorporating nature into counseling might unconsciously help to reduce psychophysiological stress and promote attention restoration and rapport within the counseling relationship. Think back to Chapter 4, wherein we explored the holistic wellness benefits of nature. Exposure to nature can reduce stress, improve focus and concentration, and positively contribute to relational cohesion. Nature as a backdrop might include the incorporation of nature sounds during indoor counseling sessions, sharing a window view of nature with your client, or providing your client with a view of a tree or garden outside your office.

An adjunctive intervention might also include walk and talk therapy or sitting in an outdoor setting during sessions. In this way, counseling can occur without a single reference to nature, and the clinician relies primarily on their traditional theoretical modality or approach. In contrast to indoor counseling, where the clinician and the client are typically positioned toward one another in a seating arrangement, including frequent eye contact, nature stimuli absorb the senses. While both individuals within the therapy dyad will experience nature uniquely, there is also the shared experience, which can further contribute to a sense of connection within the counseling relationship.

Stephon was a mid-20s cisgender man presenting to counseling with intermarital conflict. He had also been recently evaluated for ADHD. He reported considerable challenges maintaining focus at his newly developed startup company and he described issues of distractibility when communicating with his spouse. Additionally, while the client was not diagnosed, the evaluating psychologist suggested that the client may have had undiagnosed autism spectrum disorder throughout his development, which contributed to challenges in the client's ability to form and maintain relationships with others. Our initial weekly appointments in the first month occurred indoors. These meetings were challenging for both Stephon and me. He averted eye contact and provided single-word responses. After one challenging session where it felt like the client barely uttered a word, I decided to broach the idea of outdoor counseling sessions.

"Stephon, how have our sessions been going for you thus far?" I inquired.

"Fine, I guess," he responded without any emotional tone in his voice.

I then gave my pitch: "I'm curious whether you might be open to trying something different. Like I shared a few weeks ago, I meet with many of my clients outdoors. Sometimes meeting outside the office can open things up a bit; conversation can flow a bit more naturally. I know you mentioned not having a strong interest in directly addressing your EcoWellness as part of our time together, but would you potentially be willing to give this a go?"

"I guess I would be willing to try that," he replied.

As I got to know Stephon during walk and talk therapy in the coming sessions, I discovered how difficult social interactions were for him. He had difficulty interpreting body language and he had a hard time accessing empathy when others disclosed challenges in their lives. Often, we would go upwards of 10 or 15 minutes without saying a word as we walked. Sometimes I would prompt a question, but often, I would follow his lead. Over time, he built confidence in initiating dialogue in our work together and this transferred into his relationship with his spouse. Meeting in this context enabled him to feel seen and heard; he felt accepted for his way of communicating in the world. And I think this acceptance went a long way in helping him expand his ability to communicate with others in his personal and professional life. Thus, while we didn't formally integrate any of the EcoWellness dimensions into his treatment plan, it was clear that a nature-based backdrop positively contributed to stress reduction, focus, and the ability to connect more deeply with others.

Sphere 2: EcoWellness as a Complementary Intervention

In Sphere 2, the clinician utilizes EcoWellness-based strategies to complement their traditional framework or methodology. As within Sphere 1, Sphere 2 might include utilizing nature as a backdrop for counseling, but there is also some level of intentional engagement with the natural world. In this way, I consider nature as a co-facilitator in the therapy experience. For example, while on a walk with a client, a counselor might ask them to identify an aspect of nature for which they experience a sense of connection. After the client identifies that entity, they then might be prompted to reflect on a metaphor for how that element connects with their broader life.

Goals might include stress reduction, expanding distress tolerance, aiding in trauma processing, psychedelic preparation and integration, and nature connection to titrate exposure therapy experiences. Such objectives might include elements of connectedness with nature and amplifying a sense of interconnectedness between the self and the broader world.

In the first publication introducing EcoWellness in the professional counseling literature (Reese & Myers, 2012), we described a client case wherein I worked with a nine-year-old boy at a nearby park. One session, I invited the client to identify an aspect of the natural world that reminded him of himself. He took his time in finding an isolated, dead tree. He emphasized the loneliness of the tree; it had no friends. After he shared, I then invited him to find an aspect of nature that he admired. It didn't take long. There was another nearby tree, but this one had many branches and leaves. He suggested that the tree's canopy provided shade for other neighboring plants and wildlife. He wanted to be more like this tree and share with others. Just as the leaves would gently fall from this tree during autumn, he, too, wanted to be able to find ways to drop his anger when he felt upset. These two trees represented a deep and rich metaphor that resonated for the client. Through the projection of his internal lived experience, for which he initially had few words to express, the client was able to identify with different aspects of nature and experienced transcendence in the form of yearning to be in community with others. Through the clearly visible metaphors of the distinctly different outcomes of these trees, he experienced a felt sense shift in his view toward himself and his relationships with others.

EcoWellness-based strategies or techniques might also be utilized to supplement traditional methods to treatment to address symptom reduction and stabilization. For example, within the trauma processing models such as EMDR, prolonged exposure therapy, or narrative exposure therapy, there tends to be an emphasis on client resourcing, wherein a client learns to expand their distress tolerance. Thus, a client might develop objectives for therapy that include accessing nature in or out of session for stress reduction purposes as a precursor and/or concurrent treatment for processing trauma in counseling. An additional example might include a client presenting to counseling with symptomology consistent with agoraphobia. Nature might be incorporated into the treatment plan initially to reduce stress, but over time, an exposure hierarchy might include outdoor meetings. These outdoor meetings might initially be in a park setting including relatively few others and natural features that bring about stress reduction, but over time, outdoor meetings would titrate additional exposures including perceived contacts with fellow community members.

Sphere 3: EcoWellness as a Core Intervention

Sphere 3 includes the application of EcoWellness strategies as the primary intervention within the treatment planning process. This might include facilitating client connectedness with nature, addressing client solastalgia, or facilitating client-led exploration of the natural environment (i.e., NBCCPT). One primary intervention strategy includes facilitating attachment to place. Interventions might comprise client exploration of their nearby access to nature and/or applying mindfulness-based skills in further exploring their connection via shinrin-yoku (i.e., forest bathing).

Addressing client solastalgia or client eco-grief includes helping the client work through grief and fear associated with climate change and/ or the loss of physical places or cultural practices within these places. Sarah was a 35-year-old cisgender woman who presented to counseling with significant eco-anxiety and generalized anxiety. We contracted to address her EcoWellness in counseling, which included increasing her time spent in and around her favorite places, nature journaling, and building upon mindfulness skills. Additionally, we identified tangible forms of advocacy that Sarah could take in addressing concerns in her community. She began volunteering for an environmental organization and was able to involve her children in some of the experiences. While her concerns for the future did not drastically shift in our work together, her anxiety reduced, and she reported feeling like she developed a clearer direction for actions she could take within her life to address climate change.

Some of my favorite work over the years has included the application of NBCCPT with children as the primary intervention in counseling. Clients are free to explore the natural environment and engage nature in ways that enable them to have direct effects and impacts on the environment. This might include the child constructing a play area, creating "homes" for critters, safely picking up garbage, and directing nature-based activities where I am the co-participant and co-learner. Over time, clients develop expertise and familiarity in navigating the outdoor environment. They also experience the ability to influence decision-making processes within the counseling relationship. The client develops a variety of skills over the duration of counseling, both in navigating and affecting the environment and in effectively communicating in the counseling relationship, which, in turn, contributes to broader experiences of general self-efficacy and self-esteem.

Conclusion

Potential strategies for addressing EcoWellness in counseling are nearly limitless and can be incorporated within a variety of clinical modalities. While the intervention components discussed in this chapter address the different facets of EcoWellness, such strategies are client-centered and reside within clinician scope of practice. The sphered approach to EcoWellness counseling provides an intentional approach for determining if, when, and how the natural world might be incorporated into counseling and psychotherapy. Clinicians work with clients to construct and tailor interventions that are trauma-informed, accessible, culturally sustaining, and relevant to the broader treatment plan.

Chapter 8 Reflection Questions

Self-awareness:

1. What facets of EcoWellness seem most relevant to address in your clinical setting(s) and why?
2. Reflect on the challenges that might arise when integrating EcoWellness into traditional counseling settings. How might these challenges differ across the three spheres?

Knowledge:

3. How can clinicians assess which EcoWellness sphere is most appropriate for a specific client based on their treatment goals and nature-related interests?
4. Discuss the potential therapeutic benefits of viewing nature as an active co-facilitator in the counseling process. Provide examples from your own practice or theoretical scenarios.
5. How can nature-based metaphors be used effectively within each of the three spheres to enhance client understanding and engagement?
6. What is critical consciousness and why is this concept relevant to EcoWellness counseling?

Application:

7. How can mindfulness and nature-based sensory experiences be integrated into EcoWellness strategies to enhance their effectiveness?
8. Provide a case study from your experience or construct a hypothetical scenario where EcoWellness was integrated into the counseling process within one of the spheres. Discuss the outcomes and lessons learned.

References

Brown, C. L., Christian, D. D., Reese, R. F., & Bellegarde, N. S. (2023). Using the AT-EcoWellness framework to increase the intentional use of nature in adventure therapy. *The Journal for Specialists in Group Work*, 48(3), 229–247. https://doi.org/10.1080/01933922.2023.2190780

Freire, P. (1970). *Pedagogy of the oppressed*. Seabury Press.

Hasbach, P. (2016). Prescribing nature: Techniques, challenges and ethical considerations. In *Ecotherapy: Theory, research and practice* (pp. 179–191). Palgrave Macmillan.

Huynh, T., & Torquati, J. C. (2019). Examining connection to nature and mindfulness at promoting psychological well-being. *Journal of Environmental Psychology*, 66, 101370. https://doi.org/10.1016/j.jenvp.2019.101370

Kabat-Zinn, J. (1990). *Full catastrophe living: Using the wisdom of your body and mind to face stress, pain, and illness*. Delacorte.

Naor, L., & Mayseless, O. (2021). Therapeutic factors in nature-based therapies: Unraveling the therapeutic benefits of integrating nature in psychotherapy. *Psychotherapy*, 58(4), 576. https://doi.org/10.1037/pst0000396

Ratts, M. J., Singh, A. A., Nassar-McMillan, S., Butler, S. K., & McCullough, J. R. (2016). Multicultural and social justice counseling competencies: Guidelines for the counseling profession. *Journal of Multicultural Counseling and Development*, 44(1), 28–48. https://doi.org/10.1002/jmcd.12035

Reese, R. F., & Lewis, T. F. (2019). Greening counseling: Examining multivariate relationships between EcoWellness and holistic wellness. *Journal of Humanistic Counseling*, 58(1), 53–67. https://doi.org/10.1002/johc

Reese, R. F., & Myers, J. E. (2012). EcoWellness: The missing factor in holistic wellness models. *Journal of Counseling and Development*, 90(4), 400–406. https://doi.org/10.1002/j.1556-6676.2012.00050.x

Swank, J. M., & Shin, S. M. (2015). Nature-based child-centered play therapy: An innovative counseling approach. *International Journal of Play Therapy*, 24(3), 151. https://doi.org/10.1037/a0039127

Tucker, A. R., & Norton, C. L. (2013). The use of adventure therapy techniques by clinical social workers: Implications for practice and training. *Clinical Social Work Journal*, 41, 333–343. https://doi.org/10.1007/s10615-012-0411-4

Udler, J. (2023). *Walk and talk therapy: A clinician's guide to incorporating movement and nature into your practice*. PESI Publishing, Inc.

9
APPLYING ECOWELLNESS
IN GROUP WORK

Extending EcoWellness to group work can be downright magical, particularly when working with clients presenting with trepidation for engaging in traditional forms of individual or group therapy. While groups can initially be intimidating for some clients, one selling point of the approach is that the spotlight isn't always on the individual, as in the case of individual therapy. Even with limited participation, there can be considerable social learning opportunities within the group context, whereby clients observe and practice communication strategies for self-expression. From a trauma-informed lens, clients can participate in ways that honor their individuality while maintaining psychophysiological safety. Adding the natural environment to the mix helps to soften the ego's defenses, which contributes to expanded conceptions of the self to include others and their surroundings.

In this chapter, we consider logistics for infusing an EcoWellness approach into group counseling and psychotherapy. I share my own journey as a clinician in phasing the natural world into group contexts, which has led to the development of the Group EcoWellness Model of Change, a conceptual framework applied in group intervention planning. First, let's address special practice considerations for addressing EcoWellness in group contexts.

DOI: 10.4324/9781315697437-13

Special Considerations in Forming EcoWellness Groups

In many ways, planning, implementing, and evaluating EcoWellness-based groups are like any other kind of therapeutic group. In the early stages of planning, group facilitators clarify their objectives and approach, ensuring that they align with the population(s) being served. Clinicians typically bear in mind some level of direction for the group, which can be open-ended or narrower in focus. A broad focus might include helping clients improve mental health, wellness, or interpersonal skills. A narrow concentration could encompass symptom reduction of a particular diagnosis (e.g., depression), stress management, or facilitating factors pertinent to EcoWellness.

In Chapter 5, I positioned EcoWellness as a client-centered modality wherein clinicians assess and honor client nature worldview when incorporating the human–nature connection into the treatment plan. In groups, maintaining the client-directed spirit of EcoWellness can become more cumbersome. For one, there are multiple group members with varying conceptions of nature and with differing presenting challenges, intentions, and goals. Additionally, groups that include a curriculum involving the implementation of nature-based interventions or strategies may not always align with a client's orientation toward nature. Thus, the specific type of group applied should depend on your client population and the therapeutic objectives. Gerald Corey (2016) described four types of therapeutic groups, including group counseling, psychoeducation, group therapy, and task groups.

Within group counseling, facilitators harness interpersonal dynamics that emerge between group members across sessions to help facilitate client change. Meetings are group-centered without there necessarily being an overarching topic from session to session. Clients come to counseling with a particular goal in mind, and this goal is addressed by utilizing the immediacy of group member interactions to address a client's presenting challenges in the here and now. Facilitators utilize group leadership skills (i.e., summarizing statements, reflection of feeling, linking group member statements, identifying themes, etc.) that aid in individual group members feeling heard, understood, and challenged, while also facilitating group cohesion that fosters individual self-awareness and growth.

While group counseling is most often nondirective, psychoeducational groups are didactic, and facilitator led. Facilitators work from a specific and pre-established curriculum based on explicit objectives, and there typically includes a predetermined number of sessions or units. Although clients likely have individual goals for attending and their personal motivations might be discussed, the pre-established curriculum objectives drive the topics and activities explored each session. Facilitators typically have less focus on here-and-now processing to ensure that the curricular components are accomplished. Additionally, while group member-to-member communication and participation is expected in group counseling, client self-disclosure in psychoeducational groups may be less emphasized. Instruction, skills demonstration, and feedback are key leadership skills used by facilitators in psychoeducational groups.

Group therapy and task groups can include elements of both here-and-now processing and didactic delivery. Group therapy tends to focus on treating the symptoms underlying a particular diagnosis, and thus, group members often will self-select or meet criteria for a particular diagnosis when enrolling. A task group includes facilitation wherein there is a specific purpose for the group other than therapy. This might include facilitating group clinical supervision or consultation work.

The type of group employed should fit with the population being served, the therapeutic intent of the group, and the available resources. For example, I typically would not recommend implementing an open-ended group counseling paradigm with children. I've done that before; the lack of structure can be a mismatch with a child's self-regulation skills, which can lead to some impressive chaos. Similarly, a purely psychoeducational approach would be a misfit with a support group for adults navigating grief, where individuals likely need space to self-disclose and explore group member shared experiences.

When infusing EcoWellness in group work, I tend to blend psychoeducation with elements of group counseling. I aim to foster experiences in groups where clients feel supported with the acquisition of new knowledge and skills and heard through relationship building and group process. Critical to this feel is the size and composition of groups, which depend upon the type of group employed, the presenting client issues, whether meetings are occurring outdoors, the presence and type of nature-based activities, and the number of facilitators available. In essence, the greater the physical or psychological risk and the more technical the experiential components of the curriculum, the higher the group member-to-facilitator ratio should be. Groups with a greater focus on psychoeducation can often accommodate a larger number of clients given that this approach can be instruction heavy. An approach emphasizing interpersonal communication and processing (i.e., group counseling), however, typically includes fewer participants given that these groups require a great deal of care and attention to group dynamics. Depending on the developmental level and the group structure, it is not uncommon to co-facilitate a group of 8 to 12 participants. When solo facilitating, I prefer working with four to six individuals, again depending on the client population and the type of group employed.

The careful screening and selection of group members should include Tier 2 and Tier 3 EcoWellness assessment strategies. Prior adverse and pleasant experiences with nature should be addressed. If the group will include outdoor meetings, the facilitators should explore whether clients have any specific concerns for engaging in the outdoor group environment. When the EcoWellness factors are emphasized in the group curriculum, facilitators might consider administration of the EcoWellness Inventory Short Form (EI-15), as this may help clients clarify possible goals for their group experience. Screening should also include formal elements of the informed consent process.

During informed consent, facilitators should clarify the ethical and legal considerations inherent to groups (i.e., the inability to guarantee confidentiality in a group setting) in addition to the ethical considerations pertinent to EcoWellness counseling (e.g., highlighting any above and beyond potential risks or benefits when meeting outdoors). The same ethical principles detailed in Chapter 2 apply within the group context, though the ethical concerns are made more complicated by there being more than one client. Facilitators must think through the anticipated impact of each group member's presence, and how their attendance might affect the overall dynamic, including perceptions of psychological and physical safety. Clinicians should work toward identifying outdoor meeting locations that are physically accessible with the varying abilities and disabilities of group members in mind. As part of this process, the facilitators should divulge any meeting locations with clients so they can make an informed decision on whether they would want to proceed in being part of the group. Similarly, the nature worldview or orientation of the group should be fully disclosed so prospective group members can make an informed decision regarding whether the group feels like a good fit for them.

In my experience as a professor and supervisor, it's not uncommon for new graduates and even seasoned clinicians to lack adequate group training, experience, and expertise. As discussed throughout this book, EcoWellness adds complexity to the counseling relationship, and this can be further amplified when addressing the more than human world in group approaches to counseling and psychotherapy. Thus, it is imperative that clinicians develop foundational group competence prior to incorporating EcoWellness into the group approaches.

Phased Group EcoWellness Strategies

For several years I facilitated weekly groups with a local nonprofit organization in Central Oregon that provided both housing and curriculum to help adults with histories of substance abuse, severe and persistent mental illness, and complex trauma. The leadership of the organization was interested in my work on EcoWellness because many of the residents were quite wary of traditional medical and mental health services on account of prior adverse experiences within those systems. Additionally, the organization prioritized nature-based outings (i.e., hikes, picnics, rock climbing, and fishing) in their programming.

Early in our collaboration, the facility asked me if I could come talk about EcoWellness and possible strategies for promoting mental health. So, I came and gave a presentation on the seven-factor EcoWellness framework. I shared about the wellness benefits of nature and nature connection, and we explored potential pathways for maximizing experiences with nature, such as mindfulness. The room full of residents, about 20 or so, didn't have a lot to say in response to the lecture. Silence. Curious, I asked if anyone might want to share about a special or impactful experience they may have had in the outdoors. The room came alive. Hands raised, and one by one, residents began opening up about their individual connections with the more than human world. The EcoWellness facets reverberated throughout their sharing. Early and fond memories with loved ones, prior times wherein residents felt alive and connected with something much larger than themselves, experiences where residents had mastered an outdoor skill or hobby. Many of these experiences had a shared element of ineffability. The residents couldn't quite put their finger on why or how these experiences had been so impactful. I could feel a sense of shared warmth entering the room—community abounded.

I began coming back each week. The psychoeducation groups were predominantly centered on the EcoWellness facets while also merging concepts of mindfulness. Each week I facilitated a guided nature visualization. Importantly, residents were encouraged to participate in whatever ways they wanted. As an open group, they could stand, they could sit, they could leave. Following the visualization, we spent most of our remaining time reflecting on what emerged within the meditation. While intentionality for the group centered on psychoeducation and skills practice, it became clear that the residents benefited most from conversing and interacting with one another. Time and time again, program staff enthusiastically asked me to come back. Residents who seldom engaged across most programming at the nonprofit would come alive during my visits.

I returned on a near-weekly basis to facilitate these groups across many months. It didn't matter whether the guided visualization was the same each week, or whether it was different. It didn't matter whether residents had already reflected on their EcoWellness. Each week we all benefited from sharing about our nature stories. EcoWellness served as the primary pathway for clients to explore and talk about issues they otherwise kept to themselves in an open and community setting. Clients discussed the loss of loved ones, adverse life experiences, living unhoused in the woods or the desert, and drug use in nature. Sharing was individually and collectively empowering, and yet it was so simple. The simplicity of EcoWellness, the simplicity of our connectedness with the natural world. I was certainly intentional and trauma-informed in how I approached facilitating these group meetings, but it was in the sharing of stories around EcoWellness that brought everyone together.

I remember when I was invited to facilitate my first outdoor-based experience with this organization. We were going to the river on a picnic. I, along with a member of the staff, met with all residents interested in engaging in a nature-based therapeutic experience. We discussed the pragmatics for the outing, what people could expect for timeline and activities. We talked about the potential risks and benefits of meeting in the outdoor space. I highlighted some of the trauma-informed considerations, such as possible interactions with community members, potential encounters with wildlife, and limitations surrounding privacy and confidentiality. We also discussed what to bring and what not to bring for the three-hour experience.

We arrived at the nearby park early afternoon. Most residents had not been to this place previously, and the organization and I identified an area prior to meeting that seemed conducive for both resident privacy as well as engaging the attendees with the nearby natural environment. Trees surrounded us, and we could hear the gentle movement of the river as the water tumbled downstream. Residents got out their sandwiches, chips, and Gatorade and we connected in informal conversations.

After eating lunch, we gathered in a circle. As an initial check-in, I prompted the residents to share what kinds of emotions they were experiencing entering the space and into the group. Most residents shared excitement, some shared nervousness, while others disclosed being preoccupied by other happenings in life. I then informed them that today's prompt would be simple. I invited the group to individually venture out into the park and find an element or space within the natural setting where they felt a sense of connection. Once they identified this spot, they would then navigate through their different senses: smell, sound, touch, and sight. When they returned to the circle 15 minutes later, I solicited initial reactions. Some participants wanted to share, and some participants did not want to share, while others required gentle nudging and encouragement to disclose what they had encountered in the natural space.

As with meeting indoors, once residents began sharing, the conversation floodgates opened. There was so much to say. Residents who had barely uttered a word indoors had much more to divulge in the outdoor space. Indeed, nature seemed to foster community cohesion. Participants could gaze off into the trees while they shared, which reduced anxiety and added a sense of openness not otherwise experienced when meeting indoors. The container that held us in the space, nature, served as the primary change agent. Many residents emphasized that they felt more effective in their ability to articulate themselves with their fellow group members. Group members also felt heard.

Following this outing, I continued to join the organization on outdoor treks. Some outings included more formal group experiences wherein I had a clear facilitator role while others were less formal. The informal experiences had me feeling ethically shaky. I didn't seem to have a clear scope of practice as a facilitator, and I got the sense that group members also felt uncertain with my presence. For example, I joined the group on a variety of outings where participants would fish. Was I there to teach them to fish? Was I there to facilitate a therapeutic process? Both?

Given my prior experiences fly-fishing and the organization's interests in getting their residents outdoors, there seemed to be an opportunity to develop a curriculum rooted within an intentional conceptual framework centered on nature-based activity and mindfulness. Thus, I developed a therapeutic program based in a conceptual framework that merges EcoWellness, mindfulness, and fly-fishing.

The Group EcoWellness Model of Change

In developing a conceptual framework for facilitating groups in nature, I reflected a great deal on the potential therapeutic factors that I observed in my prior facilitation experiences. Clearly, the social cohesion fostered within the group was one of the more impactful elements. Nature amplified social cohesion and individual self-disclosure. A foundation of mindfulness seemed to have a considerable connection with the residents' abilities to engage with nature and benefit from the overall experience. However, I felt less clear on how I might conceptualize nature-based activities in a thoughtful or intentional manner.

In my prior years as a fly-fishing guide in Alaska, there always seemed to be considerable cognitive dissonance that guests would encounter when first learning to fly-cast. Even experienced casters would become disgruntled, at times, when incorporating a novel technique. Indeed, fly-casting can be stressful, it can feel like all eyes are on you. The stress can feel overwhelming and frustrating. Respiratory and heart rate increase. Our minds can begin to critique us in ways that are both conscious and unconscious. However, when my fly-fishing guests could take a deep breath and work through their initial negative self-appraisal, they were better able to access a mindful approach to learning foundational fly-casting skills. The less self-judgment and the more patient one was, the more open, the more curious, and the more inviting they were to receiving feedback.

The Group EcoWellness Model of Change (GEMC; Reese & Gosling, 2020) is a conceptual framework for incorporating EcoWellness into outdoor group settings. Figure 9.1 outlines the GEMC, inclusive of potential intervention elements, the conceptualized mechanisms of change, and anticipated short-term and long-term outcomes. The theoretical mechanisms of the group are rooted in social cognitive theory, the nature theories examined in Chapter 4, mindfulness, and overcoming cognitive dissonance.

The foundation of GEMC includes facilitating individual and shared emotional security within the group setting. Relationship building is vital to group members' feeling safe to interact within the group and learn novel nature-based skills with one another. The outdoors serve as a stress-reducing environment for meetings. In Chapter 4, we overviewed the variety of ways that nature may contribute to human holistic wellness. Being in or with nature provides enhanced focus and reduced psychophysiological stress. Exposure to natural settings can also soften the ego, wherein group participants might experience enhanced interconnectedness with fellow group participants and the natural world. The presence of nature contributes to experiences of mindfulness. Relatedly, incorporating mindfulness skills practice into nature-based groups helps clients work toward experiencing themselves and their fellow group participants with greater curiosity and compassion. Concepts such as the beginner's mind can be integral in helping clients approach novel nature-based activities with curiosity and wonder. As we discussed early in this text, mindfulness can facilitate a pathway to noticing our immediate surroundings and enabling greater EcoWellness.

Social cognitive theory (SCT; Bandura, 1977) and cognitive dissonance theory provide the basis for the acquisition of skills underlying a novel nature-based activity. According to SCT, clients learn most effectively through observing and then by doing. Over time, both group leaders and members with diverse skill levels demonstrate and acquire abilities

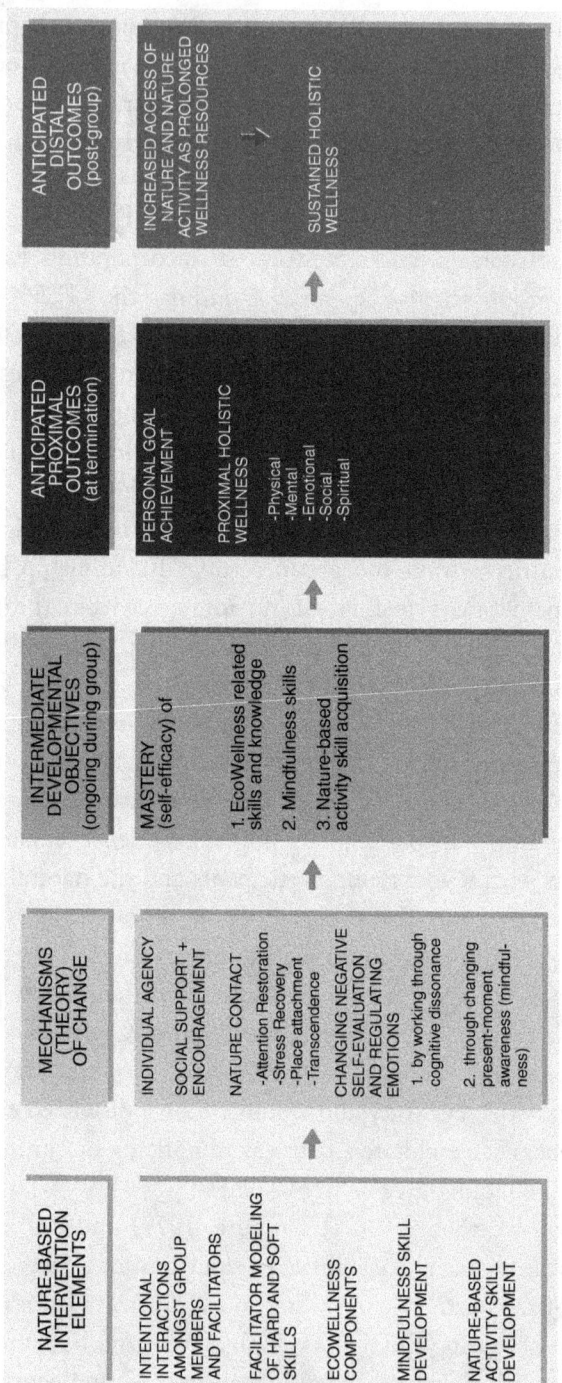

Figure 9.1 The Group EcoWellness Model of Change

Note: Copyright Ryan F. Reese, 2019

that foster the progressive development of clients' skills surrounding the nature-based activity. Facilitators honor client self-determination and encourage clients to participate in ways that align with their own internal motivation and goals. When clients experience distress in learning new skills, I conceptualize them as pushing up against their window of tolerance, wherein the goal of gaining mastery over a skill comes from a motivation to reduce cognitive dissonance and improve self-efficacy. As clients learn a new activity, it is imperative that they receive space, encouragement, and support from facilitators and group members in navigating the stress that emerges. Collectively, the underlying theoretical components of the GEMC aim to position a client's nervous system to expand self-awareness, reduce stress, and work through cognitive distortions. Clients are invited to explore the nature-based activity in ways that foster curiosity and expand openness to both internal and external feedback. Optimally, clients embody greater self-efficacy around their communication skills and in developing mastery over a particular nature-based skill, not to mention the potential holistic wellness benefits of engaging the outdoors.

Fishing for Wellness

As I was developing the GEMC conceptual framework, I concurrently built the Fishing for Wellness program (FFW; Reese et al., 2022). FFW is a six-to-eight-week curriculum embedded in principles of group counseling and psychoeducation. Intervention components include the EcoWellness factors, the seven mindfulness pillars (beginner's mind, non-judgment, trust, patience, acceptance, non-striving, and letting go; Kabat-Zinn, 1990), and foundational principles of fly-casting. The overarching goal of the group is to promote EcoWellness and facilitate participant self-efficacy and self-esteem through fostering feelings of social connectedness, mindfulness, nature connectedness, and developing fly-casting skills.

While there is significant facilitated interaction amongst group members, there is also considerable focus on the didactic presentation of mindfulness, EcoWellness, and fly-fishing instruction. Each week, clients learn one mindfulness pillar and engage in a coinciding mindfulness exercise (e.g., guided meditation, silent nature walk, five senses exercise, etc.).

Mindfulness is framed to group members as an approach for enhancing client observations of nature while supporting the restructuring of clients' automatic negative thoughts in the here and now, particularly in learning the new skill of fly-casting. Each week, clients also learn one facet of the seven-factor EcoWellness framework. Group members learn about the construct and some of the ways in which the natural world can impact holistic wellness. They identify personalized ways of increasing different areas of EcoWellness. Importantly, clients engage in shared self-reflection and storytelling, wherein comradery is built through disclosing pleasant and adverse experiences with the natural world.

With mindfulness and EcoWellness as the foundation, clients acquire introductory skills pertinent to fly-casting. Each week, participants learn one element of fly-casting and engage in skills practice with the ongoing invitation of noticing their present-moment judgments and psychophysiological stress. Following the fly-casting exercises each week, participants come back to the group to share about their internal and shared processes around fly-casting. During activities, participants are encouraged to cast in ways comfortable to them and adapt skills to their body, mind, and spirit. Skills practice typically occurs on a large and open grassy area. Learning foundational skills of fly-casting provides group members with immediate feedback, even without a facilitator sharing external perspective. The fly rod and fly line serve as an extension of the mind and the body. As the mind becomes synced with the body, so, too, does the fly casting. In this way, learning to catch fish is not emphasized, and it is not until later in the curriculum that participants take their fly-casting skills to the water. FFW sessions are typically two hours in length, with the last session including a half-day venture to the river.

We conducted a qualitative study wherein we explored the therapeutic factors of FFW (Reese et al., 2022). Two to three months following the group's termination, participants reported that some of the most valuable experiences encompassed building relationships with one another and their facilitators, including providing and receiving mentorship around fly-casting. Clients also reported benefiting from having the autonomy to participate in the ways that they desired. Group members discussed the beauty of meeting in nature and experiencing a coinciding reduction in stress during the group sessions. Participants further reported some of the most impactful experiences including the nature-based experiential activities that merged mindfulness and fly-casting. These experiences contributed to greater self-kindness and compassion. The mindfulness concepts of beginner's mind and acceptance persisted for many group participants in the months following the group. Post-termination, clients also reported feeling more strongly connected with nature and spending more time in the natural world than prior to the group. This included individuals who reported prior adversities in nature, such as houselessness or adverse experiences with addiction.

Learnings and Considerations

I've had many learnings over the years while facilitating EcoWellness-based groups. I think my first insight is akin to any other modality in counseling. It's critical for us as clinicians to get out of the way of the client's process. Certainly, having an underlying conceptual framework to guide nature-based activities can help clinicians be intentional when incorporating experiential activities into individual and group counseling processes. However, the nature-based activity is not the destination, it's simply the pathway for clients to accomplish their goals.

We need not be overly complicated in the interventions that we facilitate surrounding EcoWellness. It is the client's own lived experiences that are most important. Prompting client EcoWellness tends to tap into a client's presenting problem or challenge them in ways that are not accessed through talk therapy alone. Engaging the natural world inspires a creative and ego-melting process whereby clients are often more open. We seem better positioned to directly access our stress response, emotions, and automatic thoughts with nonjudgment in the here and now, which can help clients flourish when in the care of safe and trauma-informed group settings.

Next, I've learned that it can take considerable time and patience to develop relationships, particularly with clients with complex, developmental trauma backgrounds. Each time I facilitate a group, I connect with people indoors first. This is no different than my approach to individual counseling. Meeting in the outdoors can contribute to unexpected vulnerability, and vulnerability before trust can often result in disconnection and feelings of isolation. In my work with residents at the nonprofit agency, we took a phased approach to meeting with clients outdoors. Granted, I believe trust was developed much more quickly on account of the EcoWellness approach. We didn't immediately dive into the clients' presenting challenges or problems in life. Rather, we explored together one another's nature stories, some of which were joyful and some of which had much sorrow.

Likewise, I keep coming back to this idea of EcoWellness being client-centered. At all times clients should have full autonomy for their participation. A ground rule has always been that we cannot coerce or shame fellow group members into participating in any activity. We can encourage and provide challenge, but a foundational group norm is that clients have the freedom to engage in whatever ways that honor one's own window of tolerance. With this autonomy, clients continue to show up.

Group facilitators will face pragmatic challenges incorporating such an approach within traditional settings. As we'll further discuss in the coming chapter, the reality for many client communities that we serve is that we don't have the natural settings or access to economic resources to engage in nature-based activities to enable clients to thrive in some of the ways that I've described. Additionally, clinicians won't always possess nature-based expertise. In such instances, I encourage group facilitators to partner with trusted professionals within the outdoor industry to facilitate instruction and technical skill development. Otherwise, group facilitators must think through and consider whether they will have the competence and the capacity to facilitate both the therapeutic elements of the group as well as the learning of the nature-based skills.

Lastly, maintaining client physical and psychological safety can be more challenging when facilitating groups in the outdoors. It is imperative to develop clear boundaries and expectations for client behavior as well as knowing where your clients are at all times. This makes screening all that much more important. Clients must commit to physical and psychological safety, both for themselves and for their fellow group participants and facilitators. Depending on the factors discussed, it can be vital for group facilitators to partner with another licensed professional when orchestrating groups. Co-leadership can help promote physical and psychological safety, safeguard the evolving therapeutic relationships, and help group members work through intrapersonal challenges when practicing and acquiring nature-based skills.

Conclusion

Facilitating EcoWellness-based groups can be deeply impactful. When applied, the GEMC can complement or serve as the primary conceptual framework when facilitating groups. Further intentionality will likely be based on the facilitator's theoretical approach, the client population, the immediate context and resources, and the degree to which EcoWellness will be utilized as a adjunctive, complementary, or core intervention strategy. I invite readers to assert their own creativity and theoretical perspective when incorporating EcoWellness in group work. I could anticipate K–5 elementary school counselors partnering with teachers to engage students in a didactic large group guidance unit on EcoWellness that complements a curriculum on environmental education. I can imagine a group therapy approach wherein facilitators help clients address and reduce symptoms of social anxiety through shared connection with one another and the natural spaces that hold the container. Certainly, we are often only limited by our imagination and creativity. But as we'll examine in Chapter 10, systemic and professional barriers can also limit the degree to which we infuse EcoWellness into traditional counseling and psychotherapy settings.

Chapter 9 Reflection Questions

Self-awareness:

1. Reflect on a time when you observed or facilitated a group where nature played a key role. What were some of the outcomes for participants? If you have not observed or facilitated a group where nature was present, what are some of the possible outcomes you might anticipate within your practice setting(s)?

2. How can therapists ensure that all group members' nature worldviews are respected and integrated into the group counseling or therapy process?

Knowledge:

3. How might nature enhance the effectiveness of group therapy sessions, according to the Group EcoWellness Model of Change?
4. What are some key ethical and pragmatic considerations when forming EcoWellness-focused groups, and how do these considerations impact the therapeutic process?
5. Discuss how the natural environment can act as a co-facilitator in group therapy sessions. What are some benefits and challenges of this approach?
6. How does the EcoWellness framework challenge traditional approaches to group therapy? Discuss its potential to shift group dynamics and therapeutic outcomes.

Application:

7. Consider the ethical implications of conducting group counseling or therapy sessions in outdoor settings. What parameters can be put in place to maintain confidentiality and ensure safety?
8. In what ways can group therapists utilize the principles of EcoWellness to address social and environmental justice issues within group work?

References

Bandura, A. (1977). Self-efficacy: Toward a unifying theory of behavioral change. *Psychological Review, 84*(2), 191–215. https://doi.org/10.1037/0033-295X.84.2.191

Corey, G. (2016). *Theory & practice of group counseling* (9th ed.). Cengage Learning.

Kabat-Zinn, J. (1990). *Full catastrophe living: Using the wisdom of your body and mind to face stress, pain and illness.* Delacorte.

Reese, R. F., DeMeyer, M., Hoag, A., Glass, L., Madigan, C., & Avent Harris, J. (2022). A CQR study of the fishing for wellness nature-based group intervention for adults facing adversity. *The Journal for Specialists in Group Work, 47*(2), 90–109. https://doi.org/10.1080/01933922.2022.2058663

Reese, R. F., & Gosling, M. (2020). The group EcoWellness model of change: A conceptual framework for facilitating groups in nature. *The Journal for Specialists in Group Work, 45*(4), 331–352. https://doi.org/10.1080/01933922.2020.1799465

10
ECOWELLNESS ADVOCACY

To this point, we've discussed the application of EcoWellness within individual and group counseling contexts. In this final chapter we consider how an EcoWellness philosophy might be applied in community settings to inspire individual client empowerment and cultivate community action. We explore client, institutional, and professional advocacy through the lens of the American Counseling Association (ACA) *Advocacy Competencies* (Toporek & Daniels, 2018). We'll first address advocacy issues pertinent to a clinician's direct work with clients in the therapy context, particularly when serving marginalized individuals facing environmental or climate injustices. We'll then turn our attention toward institutional advocacy by addressing barriers and possible solutions for incorporating the more than human world into traditional counseling and psychotherapy contexts. Lastly, I will highlight professional advocacy issues within the helping professions and identify opportunities for addressing the human–nature connection in entry-level counseling programs accredited by The Council for Accreditation of Counseling and Related Educational Programs (CACREP).

Environmental and Climate Justice

The ACA (2014) defined social justice as "the promotion of equity for all people and groups to end oppression and injustice affecting clients,

students, counselors, families, communities, schools, workplaces, govern-
ments, and other social and institutional systems" (ACA, 2014, p. 21). *The Multicultural and Social Justice Counseling Competencies* (MSJCC; Ratts et al., 2016), highlighted previously in Chapters 3 and 8, identify four areas that foster socially just counseling practices. These include counse-lor self-awareness, client worldview, nurturing the counseling relation-ship, and utilizing counseling and advocacy interventions that empower critical consciousness and liberation. The MSJCC are particularly sali-ent when working with clients affected by climate and environmental injustice(s).

As discussed in Chapter 6, when informally assessing client EcoW-ellness during the intake process, we appraise a client's prior and pres-ent relationship with the natural world, including both adverse and wellness-fostering experiences. Tier 2 assessment includes a much more personalized exploration of client EcoWellness, based on factors of the client's lived history, positionality, and current life context. When clients live in geographic locations containing known environmental hazards, toxins, or weather-related disasters, I inquire more specifically about the possible ways the client's life or community has been impacted by such threats or experiences. During these conversations I keep an ear out for specific values, passions, and nature-based activities that the client engages with in solitude, with family, or with friends. As with any client, if they identify an aspect of EcoWellness as an integral component of their presenting challenges or goals, we may move into Tier 3 assessment.

Environmental justice has been conceptualized as "the fair treat-ment and meaningful involvement of all people regardless of race, color, national origin, or income, concerning the development, implementa-tion, and enforcement of environmental laws, regulations, and policies" (United States Environmental Protection Agency, 2022). A related concept, climate justice, asserts that climate change unequally impacts marginalized and vulnerable populations (e.g., children and the elderly). In Chapter 3, I asserted that colonization and white supremacy ideals dominate conceptions of nature in the United States and other devel-oped countries. Not only has dominant culture defined what nature is and what it is not, but the effects of colonization have further controlled who does and who does not have safe and restorative access to the natural world, including safe drinking water, fresh and nutritious foods, and outdoor spaces for recreation and cultural practices. A report published by the Trust for Public Land (2021) found that 100 million people in the United States, including 28 million children, lack access to a park within a ten-minute walk from where they live. White majority neighborhoods averaged more park acreage per person than BIPOC communities, further highlighting racial disparities.

Environmental injustices are firmly entrenched within historical systems of oppression and further perpetuated by policymakers and corporations. Communities of color and impoverished neighborhoods are more likely to live near environmental hazards and be more susceptible to the compounding effects of climate change (Intergovernmental Panel on Climate Change, 2023). These communities historically have lacked the necessary monetary means and resources to push back against companies placing industrial facilities that pump sledge and chemical byproducts into the immediate environment. As such, hazardous plants exist on the outskirts or in the middle of many marginalized communities. As we know, such inequities further intensify adverse health outcomes (Simmons, 2020).

This reality simply cannot be overlooked, as many client communities we serve have and will continue to be disproportionately impacted by environmental hazards and climate catastrophes. As our annual average temperatures continue to rise, catastrophic weather events are predicted to increase with frequency and intensity. Food and water supplies will decline, and their associated prices will increase. Clients with economic, familial, and community resources will be better prepared to navigate our worsening climate. They may be more likely to have transportation to leave their homes in the case of forecasted hurricanes, possess the economic resources to move away from locations adversely impacted by rising sea levels or wildfires, and purchase high-priced nutritious foods and water.

Socioeconomically privileged communities seemingly sheltered from environmental inequities are also impacted. In my work with clients with predominantly privileged identities, I often encounter an overwhelming feeling of helplessness when addressing Environmental EcoWellness. These clients are not naïve to what is happening in the world around them, but, rather, don't know where to start in addressing climate and environmental injustice. Individuals are not to blame. Our clients aren't lazy or ignorant. Our capitalist systems prioritize profit above all else and have conditioned westerners to be materialistic and often apathetic, placing individual wants and creature comforts above the broader community's needs. Yet we are reliant upon these same systems to fulfill our most basic needs. Most of us are helpless to understand where our food comes from, where our clothes were made, and what industrial chemicals sloughed off into the environment as a result. Thus, as we discussed in Chapter 8, clients across both privileged and marginalized identities can benefit from a counseling approach that fosters critical consciousness and meaningful praxis when addressing Environmental EcoWellness.

The ACA Advocacy Competencies

The ACA *Advocacy Competencies* (see Figure 10.1) provide us with possible direction for critical consciousness raising and advocating with and

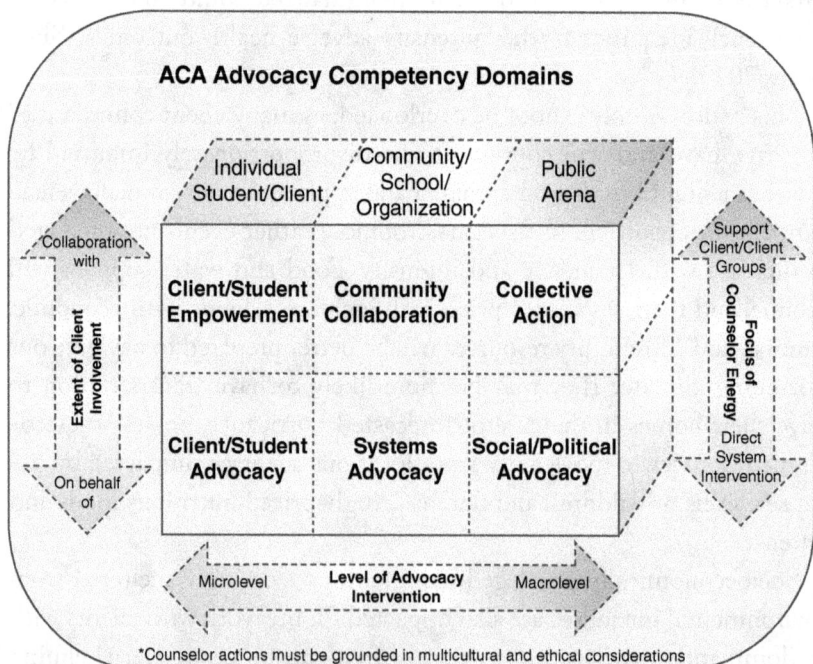

Figure 10.1 American Counseling Association Advocacy Competencies

Note: Original model by Lewis, Arnold, House & Toporek (2003) updated by Toporek & Daniels (2018)

on behalf of our clients. This framework can be applied when working with both clients directly facing climate and environmental injustice as well as clients keen to ally with those communities most affected. The competencies underscore foundational skills, knowledge, and behaviors that professional counselors and licensed therapists can apply when helping clients identify and address systemic barriers. The competencies are organized across two primary domains: extent of client involvement in advocacy and level of advocacy intervention. When serving individual clients, the clinician determines whether advocacy efforts are pursued in collaboration with the client and/or on behalf of the client. The level of intervention includes the client level, the institutional (e.g., school, agency, or community) level, or the public arena, which includes larger efforts to address societal or policy-related injustices.

The intersection of these two dimensions translates into six advocacy domains. Empowerment includes collaborating with clients to enable them to take individual action on a particular issue. Client advocacy embraces acting on behalf of a client to address a specific issue affecting them or their community. Community collaboration involves partnering with the community or groups to address collective concerns. Systems advocacy encompasses the clinician acting on behalf of the community to address barriers affecting stakeholders. Collective action includes collaborating with group or community members to address inequities by informing policy makers and the public about factors adversely affecting the client's community. Social or political advocacy comprises engaging in advocacy efforts on behalf of the client or community, which might include testifying at hearings, writing elected leaders, or raising awareness of issues in public venues.

Client and Community Advocacy

Addressing issues pertinent to environmental and climate justice is one of the primary ways that licensed clinicians can employ advocacy actions when addressing EcoWellness with clients. This might include advocating for equitable access to green spaces, wherein the therapist applies the advocacy competencies to empower the client to identify safe and nearby green spaces to address wellness. The clinician can also act on behalf of the client and the broader community by working with community groups and stakeholders to explore options for developing public green spaces such as community gardens or parks. Similarly, the clinician might engage in grant writing or partner with agencies to identify funding for nature-based activities requiring monetary investment (e.g., gardening, fly-fishing, biking, hiking). Often, however, environmental justice comes in the form of addressing environmental hazards affecting the community.

Imagine working with Mary, a 25-year-old cisgender woman presenting to therapy with symptoms of anxiety and depression. Mary lives in a low-income urban neighborhood located near an industrial park that includes an oil refinery and a chemical plant. She is a teacher at the neighborhood elementary school. In the past year, there have been several significant rain events atypical of the area that resulted in flash flooding. These occurrences contributed to several known instances of pollutants seeping into the community's water supply, though it had been downplayed and reportedly resolved. In that same timespan, she noticed what seemed to be more-than-usual smoke emitting from the oil refinery.

During intake, Mary reports experiencing significant distress about the pollution's possible health effects on her students. She reports, "I feel like I'm going crazy. I swear more of these kids are getting asthma and more seem to be getting sick at random points throughout the year than in the past few years."

Mary also discloses increases in her own experiences of respiratory and digestive illnesses in the past year. She suspects a lack of environmental policies and regulations are in place to protect the community's health and well-being, or, at the least, minimal enforcement of existing regulations. She references an opinion piece published in the newspaper a few months back wherein a university professor argued that the city was lax in requiring the local industrial plants to maintain appropriate oversight, which potentially led to unrestricted amounts of air pollution and contaminants entering the local environment and water supply. The academic alluded that her neighborhood was one of the most directly impacted. Mary declares feeling helpless and at a loss for what to do. She experiences a sense of apathy and hopelessness, identifying that the community has few resources to address these concerns directly.

In working with Mary, it would be essential for the clinician to recognize the intersection between her presenting mental health concerns
and the environmental injustices she is reporting. In employing an
EcoWellness perspective, the therapist can help Mary identify areas
of strength within her own EcoWellness while also further clarifying
her specific concerns regarding Environmental EcoWellness. While
she reports some concern for herself, the source of her anxiety and
depression seems most rooted in the environmental hazards disproportionally affecting the children in her community and her perceived
inability to protect them. While specific traditional psychotherapeutic
interventions (e.g., cognitive behavioral therapy, stress reduction) might
be utilized to help reduce some of the immediate symptoms Mary is
experiencing, it will be important to help Mary address the source of
her distress and possible pathways for taking action that results in an
experience of efficacy and community action. This might include both
client empowerment strategies and addressing other areas of the ACA
Advocacy Competencies.

First, Mary may or may not understand the historical roots of systemic oppression and its relationship to environmental injustice. While
she describes feeling "crazy," it will be important to affirm and validate Mary's experience and her underlying emotions. The clinician can
offer psychoeducation about the links between environmental health
and wellness. Through applying a liberation perspective, the therapist
might help Mary further explore the sources of her presenting anxiety and depression. Certainly, the environmental and climate-caused
hazards are one part of the story, but there may be other areas in her
life affecting the presenting symptoms (e.g., recent or past trauma,
relational conflict, grief, etc.). Should Mary identify the environmentally based issues as playing a critical role in affecting her symptoms,
we can help empower Mary to identify tangible actions she can take
in her community to address the issues. Through dialogue, the clinician can explore skills and resources that may be essential to effecting
systemic change. This process might include role play and titrating in
vivo experiences that contribute to Mary building confidence in herself over time. This could comprise helping Mary clarify her strengths
and find her voice and identifying prior times wherein Mary advocated

for herself or others. Avenues for communicating Mary's concerns with community stakeholders could be explored, such as talking with the school, the city council, or with teachers or families. The clinician might also explore the presence of local environmental or climate groups so Mary might partner with them to identify possible pathways for political advocacy.

Outside of the counseling relationship, the clinician might consider offering EcoWellness workshops or resources within the community on coping strategies for addressing environmental injustice and topics such as eco-anxiety. During such workshops, the clinician can provide psychoeducation about the oppressive roots of environmental injustice and the environmental (and climate exacerbated) issues affecting the immediate community. As with Mary, the clinician can provide resources and generate ideas with attendees for practical advocacy actions they could take within their community in demanding accountability from the industrial plants and policymakers.

Next, the clinician could partner with local, state, or national organizations to further generate awareness about the environmental and climate issues affecting Mary's local community. Licensed counselors and therapists have considerable skill in facilitating dialogue. They can offer to facilitate meetings, forums, and other community events wherein agencies and stakeholders join in collective action to address the environmental concerns.

Lastly, the clinician can engage in advocacy on a policy level, whether that be at the school, in the local community, or at the state level to help strengthen environmental regulations (or the enforcement of existing environmental regulations). Actions might include writing letters or emails to local and state government officials, leading or participating in community organizing initiatives, or joining groups that lobby environmental and climate justice initiatives.

The application of the ACA *Advocacy Competencies* assumes and acknowledges that the source of Mary's mental health struggles is not organic to her. Rather, the presenting issues are externalized, and the client identifies internal and external strengths and resources to provide her with self-determination, self-efficacy, and the ability to make concrete change. Doing so potentially contributes to both mental health and increases in community environmental health. As part of this process, clinicians can leverage their privilege as mental health providers and apply their diverse skillsets to effect systemic change outside of the immediate counseling relationship to address broader sociopolitical issues affecting the client and their community.

Institutional Advocacy

Licensed counselors and therapists face a variety of institutional barriers in addressing the human–nature connection in traditional counseling and psychotherapy settings. Taking clients outdoors might be perceived as too risky by the agency, the system, or the individual clinician. The liability issues may be deemed too burdensome, and thus, the door is preemptively shut on incorporating EcoWellness into counseling. In my experience, there are several ways that clinicians can proactively address stakeholder concerns.

First, I recommend becoming familiar with and being able to speak to the multidisciplinary literature linking natural environments with human holistic wellness. As we explored in Chapter 4, an extensive literature base exists linking the natural world with human health and wellness. Further, the EcoWellness framework provides clinicians with a clear, intentional, and culturally sustaining framework for addressing the more than human world in licensed therapy settings. They can make it clear to organizational leaders that taking clients outdoors would only occur if the potential benefits for doing so outweigh the risks. Should clinicians desire to move counseling beyond the office, it would behoove them to develop a clear proposal for what that might look like, including risk management strategies that address the ethical issues identified in Chapter 2.

Additional preparatory work can be done by consulting with an attorney in the clinician's state or region to clarify specific legal concerns, and drafting language that might be used on agency informed consent documents when engaging clients in an EcoWellness approach. Regarding insurance, most professional liability policies in the United States will cover licensed therapy wherever counseling sessions occur, indoors or outdoors, so long as a therapist is operating within their scope of practice. However, general liability policies (i.e., policies that cover physical injury) may or may not cover the licensed therapist if meeting at an outdoor location different from the physical address listed on the policy. Thus, additional liability coverage may be needed.

One additional challenge includes billing insurance. Billing insurance for mental health therapy typically requires a location of service (i.e., physical address) that matches the address(es) associated with the organization and provider's National Provider Identifier number (NPI). In my experience, insurance companies often lack flexibility in covering locations not associated with the NPI (e.g., a park or trail). So, this is something to be aware of prior to talking with the clinician's organizational leadership or when thinking through their strategy for billing insurance within a private practice setting.

Moreover, clinicians may need to address structural issues pertaining to the organization's office environment, location, and nearby access to the outdoors. I'm an advocate for finding ways to incorporate sensory forms of EcoWellness into indoor settings. These can sometimes be simple actions such as orienting the seating structure around a window view, incorporating nature sounds, or hanging natural murals or photos on the wall. At other times, this can be more of a monetary investment, such as installing windows. If planning to meet with clients outdoors, clinicians should identify the specific locations for outdoor sessions. They should also think through whether clients would meet the clinician where the outdoor sessions will be held or if they together will meet at the office and then venture outdoors. Being able to speak to the safety of the actual location and its accessibility to clients are also key considerations to clarify.

With this information in hand, licensed therapists can propose a cogent pathway for incorporating EcoWellness specific to their organization and population(s) served. While there will inevitably be challenges that the organization must address (e.g., the mentioned insurance issues), outlining the potential benefits, drafting a clear and detailed risk management plan, and clarifying the vision for EcoWellness counseling will assist decision-makers in the organization to better understand and support the proposed initiative.

Institutional advocacy efforts addressing EcoWellness can also manifest in the form of consultation, workshops, and trainings, particularly after the clinician has developed significant experience, skills, and expertise in this area. As we've discussed, there are a variety of misconceptions about EcoWellness as it often gets lumped into being considered an exclusively outdoor-based approach. Consulting services might include working with organizations to develop EcoWellness risk management practices specific to their institutional structure, setting, and population(s) served. They can also help organizations identify forward-thinking ways of incorporating sensory EcoWellness into indoor therapy sessions, such as the arrangement of office furniture, maximizing window views and outdoor landscaping, décor, and lighting. Further, as the climate crisis continues to adversely affect our communities and client populations, there will be increasing opportunities to join with organizations to provide EcoWellness-related trainings and workshops that specifically address community members' mental health, wellness, and advocacy.

Professional Advocacy

In Chapter 1, we surveyed some of the ecotherapeutic and nature-based counseling approaches, including their underlying theory and research evidence. While some approaches possess solid empirical grounding (e.g., equine-facilitated therapy), the ecotherapy research is broadly plagued with methodological challenges and often conducted in professions outside counseling and psychotherapy. Thus, an expanded research base is needed to better understand the possible benefits and risks of applying nature-based approaches withing licensed settings. While EcoWellness counseling is not a specific set of interventions, per se, research should be conducted to better understand the possible benefits or limitations when employing the framework with clients. Specifically, qualitative paradigms might be utilized to elucidate the perceived benefits of addressing client EcoWellness as part of holistic wellness. Mixed methods research can be conducted with clients who have engaged in Tier 3 EcoWellness assessment to clarify the degree to which addressing specific components of EcoWellness in counseling positively contributes to counseling outcomes.

Despite an overall lack of research supporting the direct application of the ecotherapies in licensed counseling and psychotherapy, a host of ecotherapeutic and nature-based counseling certificate programs exist across the United States. At present, these nature-based programs are not recognized by external counseling or psychotherapy accrediting bodies (except, in some instances, those awarding continuing education credits). As such, preparation standards do not exist. I don't share this information to discourage clinicians or trainees from enrolling in these programs—particularly certificate programs rooted in the licensed professions (e.g., the Center for Nature Informed Therapy). Rather, it's one factor to consider when exploring options. Although such programs are available, they are currently pursued by a relatively limited number of clinicians—highlighting an opportunity for broader engagement. Recall the study I cited in Chapter 2 wherein Jacqueline Swank and I (2021) explored a national sample of helping professionals' (professional counselors, social workers, and psychologists) attitudes toward and practices for engaging in nature-based counseling. We found that just 18% of clinicians reported having prior training in nature-based counseling. In a separate published study, we (Reese et al., 2023) found similar results when surveying licensed helping professionals about their prior training and current practices for addressing climate change in counseling and psychotherapy. Just 5% of the sample reported having received prior training for addressing climate change in their work and less than 10% of the sample reported having access to resources to address climate change in counseling. Meanwhile, 45% of the sample reported feeling incompetent to address climate change in their clinical practice.

It is imperative that clinical training programs take action to address the more than human connection across their core curriculums. The CACREP (2023) standards lie at the foundation of accredited professional counseling programs in the United States. They encompass eight core areas: Professional Orientation and Ethical Practice, Social and Cultural Identities and Experiences, Lifespan Development,

Career Development, Counseling Practice and Relationships, Group Counseling and Group Work, Assessment and Diagnostic Processes, and Research and Program Evaluation. The research, theory, assessment practices, practical interventions, ethical issues, and professional considerations discussed in this book could easily be addressed within each of the CACREP core areas. For example, the scope of practice and ethical considerations discussed in Chapter 2 could be explored when examining informed consent processes, confidentiality, and the application of innovative practices in therapy. A unit could focus specifically on the effects of the natural world on holistic wellness across the lifespan within a developmental course. Environmental and climate justice should be addressed in courses focusing on sociocultural issues. A career development course could include information about careers contributing to identifying tangible solutions to the climate crisis, including the roles licensed clinicians might play on interdisciplinary teams to address such issues.

Addressing EcoWellness in counselor preparation programs does not need to be complicated, overly burdensome, or something "extra." Certainly, a specialty course on EcoWellness counseling could serve students well, but I recognize this would be in addition to all the other curricular and licensure requirements in training programs, which are plentiful. However, as the climate crisis continues to burn through the door of humanity, clinical training programs must find ways to proactively infuse diverse perspectives and experiences that adequately prepare our next generation of clinicians to address client experiences with the natural world.

Furthermore, ongoing advocacy within our professional organizations is imperative to ensure that the more than human world is acknowledged in our professions' graduate training accreditation standards. While the Council on Social Work Education (CSWE, 2022) addresses environmental justice within their accreditation standards, none of the major accrediting bodies—CSWE, the American Psychological Association (APA), or CACREP—currently address climate change within their professional training benchmarks. The APA was the first of the licensed helping professions to address global climate change within its organization (Swim et al., 2009), and they continue to lead the way amongst the licensed helping professions in developing initiatives to address climate change in the field. The ACA (2018), however, was late to the table. Led by Drs. Judy Daniels and Debbie Sturm, I was part of the ACA climate change task force in 2018 that developed a resource document wherein we outlined strategies for addressing climate change in counseling and advocacy efforts (Sturm et al., 2020). The ACA leadership can further position our profession as a leader among the helping professions by launching prevention and wellness-based initiatives that support its members in addressing climate change and environmental justice within professional counseling practice.

I am increasingly hopeful about the counselor education field's efforts to address climate change in the preparation of master's level and doctoral students. Recently, I co-chaired a task force within the Association for Counselor Education and Supervision (ACES) that developed the *Climate Change and Environmental Justice Competencies for Counselor Education* (Sturm et al., 2025). In a significant milestone, the ACES Governing Council unanimously approved these competencies in April 2025. This approval offers hope that the counselor education field will not only take climate and environmental justice seriously but also advocate for integrating these critical issues into our ethical mandate of advancing social justice within our profession. Additionally, an interest network has been spearheaded within the organization, predominantly including a new generation of counselor educators and doctoral students, focusing on climate change research and coalescing ideas for addressing climate change across the CACREP curriculum.

Obviously, additional professional advocacy is needed, and strength comes in numbers. I encourage you to step up, get involved, and use your voice within your profession. It can take a long time for change to come about within our systems, even ours, which is theoretically grounded on principles of social justice and advocacy. In my experience, there is plenty of opportunity to serve on committees and task forces, and to join lobbying efforts and editorial review boards within our national organizations. One just needs to step up. Find a mentor or mentors you trust who can help guide you and provide encouragement.

Our licensed helping professions are waiting for you to show up and to speak up.

Conclusion

Our individual clients face vastly different realities and pathways to experiencing EcoWellness based on factors of positionality and lived context, rooted in systems of oppression. Many of the client populations we serve, particularly BIPOC communities, live within or nearby environmentally hazardous geographic zones where their air, drinking water, and food is contaminated with harmful pollutants. Issues of climate change can exacerbate these environmental injustices.

We as licensed professionals must be vigilant to the sociocultural issues affecting our clients and identifying when employing an advocacy lens may be indicated. While a liberatory and critical consciousness-raising philosophy lies at the core of an advocacy approach, it can be applied in tandem with other treatment modalities that focus on the individual, including EcoWellness. Applying principles of EcoWellness counseling alongside the ACA *Advocacy Competencies* can help to empower *all* clients to take actions within their individual lives and communities to address environmental and climate injustice. Through their application, clients can engage in critical consciousness without blame or judgment, which is so vitally important in an era of sociopolitical divisiveness. In doing so, clinicians can help clients identify forms of dialogue that prioritize empathy, shared values, and individual and collective actions.

Moreover, additional advocacy is needed across institutional and professional contexts to educate stakeholders about the importance of the natural world on human health and wellness. Licensed clinicians can address institutional concerns by familiarizing themselves with the multidisciplinary nature–wellness research, developing clear proposals for EcoWellness risk management strategies, and identifying practical ways of integrating EcoWellness into therapy. Expanding the research literature on nature-based approaches, incorporating EcoWellness into counselor preparation programs, and engaging in ongoing professional advocacy are essential for our licensed helping professions as we move further into the 21st century.

Chapter 10 Reflection Questions

Self-awareness:

1. In what ways have you been affected by issues pertinent to environmental and/or climate justice in your own life, and how do these experiences affect your approach to EcoWellness advocacy?
2. Reflect on the concept of community collaboration within EcoWellness. How can you foster partnerships that enhance community EcoWellness within your setting(s)?

Knowledge:

3. Discuss the role of environmental justice in the context of professional counseling. How can clinicians ensure their EcoWellness-based practices are equitable and inclusive?
4. How do the *Multicultural and Social Justice Counseling Competencies* intersect with EcoWellness practices, particularly in addressing climate and environmental injustice?
5. Discuss the potential impacts of climate change on mental health and explore how counselors can prepare to meet these challenges within their practice.

Application:

6. How can counselors apply the ACA *Advocacy Competencies* to enhance EcoWellness practices in their professional settings?
7. What are some of the institutional and professional barriers to integrating EcoWellness in traditional counseling settings, and how might these be overcome?
8. Consider the implications of systemic advocacy in counseling and psychotherapy. How can clinicians influence policy to better integrate EcoWellness into healthcare and community settings?

References

American Counseling Association (ACA). (2014). *ACA code of ethics.* ACA.

American Counseling Association (ACA). (2018). *Climate change statement.* https://www. counseling.org/docs/default-source/resolutions/climate-change-statement-novem ber-2018.pdf?sfvrsn=a65c552c_2

Council for Accreditation of Counseling and Related Educational Programs (CACREP). (2023). *2024 CACREP standards.* https://www.cacrep.org/wp-content/ uploads/2023/06/2024-Standards-Combined-Version-6.27.23.pdf

Council on Social Work Education (CSWE). (2022). *Educational policy and accreditation standards for baccalaureate and master's social work programs.* https://www.cswe.org/ getmedia/bb5d8afe-7680-42dc-a332-a6e6103f4998/2022-EPAS.pdf

IPCC. (2023). Sections. In Core Writing Team, H. Lee, & J. Romero (Eds.), *Climate change 2023: Synthesis report. Contribution of working groups I, II and III to the sixth assessment report of the intergovernmental panel on climate change* (pp. 35–115). IPCC. https://doi.org/10.59327/IPCC/AR6-9789291691647

Ratts, M. J., Singh, A. A., Nassar-McMillan, S., Butler, S. K., & McCullough, J. R. (2016). Multicultural and social justice counseling competencies: Guidelines for the coun seling profession. *Journal of Multicultural Counseling and Development, 44*(1), 28–48. https://doi.org/10.1002/jmcd.12035

Reese, R. F., Swank, J. M., & Sturm, D. C. (2023). A national survey of helping pro fessionals on climate change and counseling. *The Journal of Humanistic Counseling, 62*(3), 201–215. https://doi.org/10.1002/johc.12211

Simmons, D. (2020). *What is 'climate justice?'* https://yaleclimateconnections.org/2020/07/ what-is-climate-justice/

Sturm, D. C., Daniels, J., Metz, A. L., Stauffer, M., Reese, R. F., Milner, R., & Torres-Rivera, E. (2020). *ACA task force: Fact sheet.* https://www.counseling.org/docs/default-source/center-resources/climate-change-fact-sheet.pdf?sfvrsn=83c7222c%5C_2

Sturm, D., Reese, R. F., Boyle, L., Coleman, M., Garrett, M., Griffith, J. A. H., & Peter son, G. H. (2025). *Climate change and environmental justice competencies for counselor education.* https://www.multibriefs.com/briefs/ACES/ACES_Climate.pdf

Swank, J. M., & Reese, R. F. (2022). Do counselors and other helping professionals use nature-based counseling? *Journal of Creativity in Mental Health, 17*(4), 443–455. https://doi.org/10.1080/15401383.2021.1911725

Swim, J., Clayton, S., Doherty, T., Gifford, R., Howard, G., Reser, J., Stern, P., & Weber, E. (2009). Psychology and global climate change: Addressing a multi-faceted phe nomenon and set of challenges. A report by the American Psychological Associ ation's task force on the interface between psychology and global climate change. *American Psychologist, 66,* 241–250. https://doi.org/10.1037/a0023220

Toporek, R. L., & Daniels, J. (2018). *American counseling association advocacy competencies: Updated.* https://www.counseling.org/docs/default-source/competencies/aca-advo cacy-competencies-updated-may-2020.pdf?sfvrsn=f410212c_4

The Trust for Public Land. (2021). *Parks and an equitable recovery.* https://www.tpl.org/ parks-and-an-equitable-recovery-parkscore-report

United States Environmental Protection Agency. (2022). *Environmental justice.* https:// www.epa.gov/environmentaljustice#:~:text=Environmental%20justice%20is%20 the%20fair,laws%2C%20regulations%2C%20and%20policies

APPENDICES

Appendix A. The EcoWellness Inventory (EI-61; ©Ryan F. Reese, 2013)

Appendix B. The EcoWellness Inventory Short Form (EI-15; ©Ryan F. Reese, 2022)

Appendix C. Tier 2 Informal EcoWellness Assessment Questions (©Ryan F. Reese, 2015)

Appendix D. The EcoWellness Inventory Short Form (EI-15)— Child Version (EI-15 Child Form; ©Ryan F. Reese, 2024)

APPENDICES

APPENDIX A

ECOWELLNESS
INVENTORY (EI-61)

Purpose

The purpose of this inventory is to assess the extent to which nature is incorporated in your life and contributes to your sense of wellness. Answer each item to the level that it is true for you. Answer all items and do not spend too much time on any one item.

In answering items, think of nature as you would define it in regard to your interactions with other living systems and non-human species. Nature here not only refers to wilderness settings and native animals, but also includes pets, parks, gardens, and indoor and outdoor plants.

Instructions

Please use the following rubric in responding to each statement:

(4) Strongly Agree   if it is true for you most of the time.
(3) Somewhat Agree   if it is true for you some of the time.
(2) Somewhat Disagree   if it is usually not true for you.
(1) Strongly Disagree   if it is never true for you.

1. Nature surrounds me in my daily life.
2. It is important for me to have nature in my daily life.
3. I have hobbies that include nature.
4. Even when in a car on the freeway, I am aware of the nature around me.
5. My access to nature makes me feel good.
6. I need to access nature to feel healthy.
7. I touch plants.
8. Physical touch with nature is important to me.
9. There are smells of trees and plants in and around my home.
10. I enjoy the smells of nature.
11. I am happy when I can smell nature.
12. Smells of nature are among life's greatest pleasures.
13. The place I spend most of my time includes a view of nature.
14. I have photos or pictures of nature within eyesight during the day.
15. It is important for me to be able to see nature from my home.
16. I need to see nature each day.
17. I have plants in my home.
18. I feel less stress when I see nature.
19. When I step outside I hear nature.
20. I like to hear the sounds of nature.
21. Listening to the sounds of nature is important to me.
22. It calms me to hear sounds of nature.
23. Nature brings about pleasant thoughts for me.
24. The anticipation of being in nature puts me in a good mood.
25. Important life events of mine happened while in nature.
26. The best times in my life occurred while I was in nature.
27. My relationship with nature makes me feel good.
28. I feel like I can be myself in nature.
29. I am happiest when in nature.
30. I have one or more favorite places in nature.
31. I grew up having at least one favorite place in nature.
32. I have a favorite spot in nature.

33. I include nature when describing myself to others.

34. I understand where my food comes from.

35. I use renewable energy when I am able.

36. I feel good about my carbon footprint.

37. I am concerned about climate change.

38. I remain calm when near animals that could harm me.

39. I am able to identify plants that can cause me harm.

40. I am open to trying nature activities that may be discomforting.

41. There are aspects of nature that can protect me.

42. I feel strongly about an environmental cause.

43. Having a positive impact on the health of the planet is important to me.

44. I do my part in preserving nature.

45. If I see litter on the ground I pick it up.

46. I make it a priority to recycle.

47. I am satisfied with my efforts to preserve nature.

48. I feel connected to something bigger than myself when I am in nature.

49. I gain clarity on my life's purpose when I am in nature.

50. The stresses in my life seem to go away when I am in nature.

51. I go to nature to find peace.

52. My thoughts slow down when I am in nature.

53. Walking in nature is a spiritual experience for me.

54. I experience a sense of privacy in nature.

55. I go to places in nature to get away.

56. I feel a sense of community with others when together in nature.

57. Experiences with others in nature deepen my relationships with them.

58. I feel connected to all of life when in nature.

59. When in nature I am more giving to others.

60. I feel compassionate towards others when they are with me in nature.

61. When I am in nature, I find myself thinking about others in my life.

Scoring Guide to the EcoWellness Inventory (EI-61)

You can calculate your EI scale and subscale scores by using a linear transformation. The minimum possible score is 25 and the maximum possible score is 100. The higher the score the higher one's perceived EcoWellness, as defined by the EI. Here is how you go about calculating scores:

Formula

$$\frac{\text{Sum Score of Scale or Subscale}}{\text{\# of Items on Scale or Subscale}} \times 25 = \text{Scale or Subscale Score}$$

EI Items by Scale/Subscale	Scale/Subscale Score
EcoWellness: Items 1–61	
Physical Access: Items 1–6	
Sensory Access: Items 7–22	
Connection: Items 23–33	
Protection: Items 34–41	
Preservation: Items 42–47	
Spirituality: Items 48–55	
Community Connectedness: Items 56–61	

APPENDIX B

ECOWELLNESS INVENTORY
SHORT FORM (EI-15)

Instructions

The purpose of this inventory is to assess the extent to which nature is incorporated in your life and contributes to your sense of wellness. In answering items, think of nature as you would define it in regard to your interactions with other living systems and non-human species. Nature here not only refers to wilderness settings and native animals, but also includes pets, parks, gardens, and indoor and outdoor plants.

Please indicate the extent to which each statement below reflects your experience with nature and its impact on your sense of wellness. Answer all items and do not spend too much time on any one item. Please use the following rubric in responding to each statement:

Strongly Agree (4)	if it is true for you most of the time.
Somewhat Agree (3)	if it is true for you some of the time.
Somewhat Disagree (2)	if it is usually not true for you.
Strongly Disagree (1)	if it is never true for you.

	Strongly Agree	Somewhat Agree	Somewhat Disagree	Strongly Disagree
Social EcoWellness				
1. I feel a sense of community with others when together in nature.	4	3	2	1
2. Experiences with others in nature deepen my relationships with them.	4	3	2	1
3. When in nature I am more giving to others.	4	3	2	1
4. I feel compassionate towards others when they are with me in nature.	4	3	2	1
5. When I am in nature, I find myself thinking about others in my life.	4	3	2	1
Environmental EcoWellness				
6. I use renewable energy when I am able.	4	3	2	1
7. I am concerned about climate change.	4	3	2	1
8. I feel strongly about an environmental cause.	4	3	2	1
9. Having a positive impact on the health of the planet is important to me.	4	3	2	1
10. I make it a priority to recycle.	4	3	2	1
Mental EcoWellness				
11. I feel connected to something bigger than myself when I am in nature.	4	3	2	1
12. The stresses in my life seem to go away when I am in nature.	4	3	2	1
13. I go to nature to find peace.	4	3	2	1
14. My thoughts slow down when I am in nature.	4	3	2	1
15. I experience a sense of privacy in nature.	4	3	2	1

Scoring Guide to the EcoWellness Inventory Short Form (EI-15)

You can calculate your EI-15 scale and subscale scores by using a linear transformation. The minimum possible score is 25 and the maximum possible score is 100. The higher the score the higher one's perceived EcoWellness. Here is how you go about calculating your score:

Formula

$$\frac{\text{Sum Score of Scale or Subscale}}{\text{\# of Items on Scale or Subscale}} \times 25 = \text{Scale or Subscale Score}$$

EI-15 Items by Scale/Subscale	Your Scale/Subscale Score
EcoWellness: Items 1–15	
Social EcoWellness: Items 1–5	
Environmental EcoWellness: Items 6–10	
Mental EcoWellness: Items 11–15	

APPENDIX C
TIER 2 INFORMAL ECOWELLNESS ASSESSMENT QUESTIONS

Connection:

1. Can you describe your emotional, cognitive, and ancestral connection with nature?
2. How do you define nature, and how do you see yourself in relation to the natural world?
3. Can you share any early recollections or experiences in nature that have shaped your current perceptions?
4. Do you feel a sense of connectedness to the natural world? If so, can you elaborate on that?
5. How do you view or interpret your ancestral connections with nature, if any?

Physical and Sensory Access:

1. How frequently do you access nature, and how do you perceive the quality of your access?
2. Can you describe the nature around you in your immediate environment, such as indoor plants, windows with a view, or nearby parks?
3. What sensory experiences of nature do you value the most, such as aromas, sounds, or visual elements?

4. Have you encountered any barriers in accessing nature, particularly regarding safety or transportation?

5. How do you experience the accessibility and safety of nearby nature spaces?

Protection (Nature Self-Efficacy):

1. Can you share any activities or nature-based skills you are interested in or have experience with?

2. How confident do you feel in your ability to engage in nature-based activities or skills?

3. Are there any specific goals related to nature activities that you would like to achieve during our time together in counseling?

4. Have you faced any challenges in pursuing nature-based activities, and how did you overcome them?

5. Can you describe any experiences where engaging in nature-based activities positively impacted your sense of self-effectiveness?

Spirituality:

1. What role does nature play in your spiritual or religious beliefs and practices?

2. Can you share any experiences where you felt a deep sense of connection or unity with nature?

3. In what ways have you observed the relationship between nature and spirituality in your life, if at all?

4. Have you encountered any challenges or conflicts in integrating nature-based spirituality into your belief system?

5. Can you describe any practices or rituals involving nature that hold personal significance for you?

Community Connectedness:

1. Do you typically experience nature in solitude or with others?

2. Can you describe any meaningful social interactions or community experiences you have had in natural settings?

3. Do you feel a sense of belonging or connection to a community through your engagement with nature?

4. Have you encountered any cultural or societal influences that shape your experiences of community in nature?
5. How do you perceive the value of community connections in enhancing your EcoWellness experiences?

Preservation (Environmental Agency):

1. In what ways have environmental concerns impacted your mental health and overall wellness, if at all?
2. What are your concerns or hopes regarding the preservation of natural spaces that are important to you?
3. Can you share any individual or collective actions you have taken (or might like to take) to preserve the natural environments you value?
4. How do you view your role in caring for the natural world around you?
5. Have you encountered any challenges or obstacles in advocating for environmental preservation in your community?

Appendix D

EcoWellness Inventory Short Form (EI-15)—Child Version

Instructions

We would like to learn how much you enjoy spending time in nature and how it makes you feel. Nature isn't just forests and animals—it's also your backyard, parks, and even plants inside your home.

Below are some statements about how nature makes you feel. We want you to tell us how much you agree with each one using faces. Here's what the faces mean:

(3) Circle the 😊 if you feel this way most of the time.

(2) Circle the 😐 if you're not sure or if it doesn't happen very often.

(1) Circle the 😞 if you don't feel this way very often.

For Each Question, Please Circle the Face that Shows How You Feel

Remember, there are no right or wrong answers, so just pick the one that feels closest to how you feel. Ready? Let's get started!

Social EcoWellness

1. I feel happy when I'm with friends or family outside.   ☺ 😐 ☹
2. Playing with others outdoors makes us better friends.   ☺ 😐 ☹
3. I like to share my toys outside.   ☺ 😐 ☹
4. I care about my friends' feelings when playing outside.   ☺ 😐 ☹
5. Being outside reminds me of my friends and family.   ☺ 😐 ☹

Environmental EcoWellness

6. My family uses energy from the sun, wind, or water when we can.   ☺ 😐 ☹
7. I sometimes worry about the weather and animals losing their homes. ☺ 😐 ☹
8. I care about keeping rivers and rivers clean.   ☺ 😐 ☹
9. It's important for me to keep the earth happy and healthy.   ☺ 😐 ☹
10. I put things like bottles and paper into special bins so they can be used again.   ☺ 😐 ☹

Mental EcoWellness

11. I feel like I'm part of nature when I'm outside.   ☺ 😐 ☹
12. When I play outside, I feel less worried about the sad things in my life. ☺ 😐 ☹
13. My body feels calm outside.   ☺ 😐 ☹
14. I feel like my mind relaxes when I'm in a park.   ☺ 😐 ☹
15. I have my own special place when I play outside.   ☺ 😐 ☹

Scoring Guide to the EcoWellness Inventory Short Form (EI-15)—Child Version

You can calculate the EI-15 Child Version subscale and scale scores by using a linear transformation. The minimum possible score is 25 and the maximum possible score is 100. The higher the score the higher the child's perceived EcoWellness. Here is how you go about calculating those scores:

Formulas

Subscale Score = (Sum Score of Subscale − 5) × 7.5 + 25

Total EcoWellness Score = (Sum Score of Scale − 15) × 2.5 + 25

EI-15 Child Items by Scale/Subscale	*Scale/Subscale Score*
Total EcoWellness: Items 1–15	
Social EcoWellness: Items 1–5	
Environmental EcoWellness: Items 6–10	
Mental EcoWellness: Items 11–15	

INDEX

Note: Page numbers in *italic* indicate a figure and page numbers in **bold** indicate a table on the corresponding page.

For Product Safety Concerns and Information please contact our EU
representative GPSR@taylorandfrancis.com
Taylor & Francis Verlag GmbH, Kaufingerstraße 24, 80331 München, Germany

www.ingramcontent.com/pod-product-compliance
Lightning Source LLC
Chambersburg PA
CBHW050644280326
41932CB00015B/2777

* 9 781138 902459 *